DIGITAL MEMORY AGENTS IN CANADA

EDITED BY MATTHEW CORMIER
AND AMANDA SPALLACCI

DIGITAL MEMORY AGENTS IN CANADA

PERFORMANCE,
REPRESENTATION,
AND CULTURE

UNIVERSITY
of **ALBERTA**
PRESS

Published by

University of Alberta Press
1-16 Rutherford Library South
11204 89 Avenue NW
Edmonton, Alberta, Canada T6G 2J4
amiskwaciwâskahikan | Treaty 6 | Métis Territory
ualbertapress.ca | uapress@ualberta.ca

Copyright © 2024
University of Alberta Press

Library and Archives Canada Cataloguing in Publication

Title: Digital memory agents in Canada : performance, representation, and culture / edited by Matthew Cormier and Amanda Spallacci.
Names: Cormier, Matthew, editor. | Spallacci, Amanda, editor.
Description: Includes bibliographical references.
Identifiers: Canadiana (print) 20240316959 | Canadiana (ebook) 20240316983 | ISBN 9781772127447 (softcover) | ISBN 9781772127867 (PDF) | ISBN 9781772127850 (EPUB)
Subjects: LCSH: Collective memory in mass media. | LCSH: Digital media—Social aspects—Canada. | LCSH: Mass media and culture—Canada. | LCSH: Internet and activism—Canada.
Classification: LCC P96.C652 C3 2024 | DDC 302.230971—dc23

First edition, first printing, 2024.
First printed and bound in Canada by Houghton Boston Printers, Saskatoon, Saskatchewan.
Copyediting and proofreading by Jenn Harris.

All rights reserved. No part of this publication may be reproduced, stored in a retrieval system, or transmitted in any form or by any means (electronic, mechanical, photocopying, recording, generative artificial intelligence [AI] training, or otherwise) without prior written consent. Contact University of Alberta Press for further details.

University of Alberta Press supports copyright. Copyright fuels creativity, encourages diverse voices, promotes free speech, and creates a vibrant culture. Thank you for buying an authorized edition of this book and for complying with the copyright laws by not reproducing, scanning, or distributing any part of it in any form without permission. You are supporting writers and allowing University of Alberta Press to continue to publish books for every reader.

University of Alberta Press is committed to protecting our natural environment. As part of our efforts, this book is printed on Enviro Paper: it contains 100% post-consumer recycled fibres and is acid- and chlorine-free.

This book has been published with the help of a grant from the Federation for the Humanities and Social Sciences, through the Awards to Scholarly Publications Program, using funds provided by the Social Sciences and Humanities Research Council of Canada.

University of Alberta Press gratefully acknowledges the support received for its publishing program from the Government of Canada, the Canada Council for the Arts, and the Government of Alberta through the Alberta Media Fund.

CONTENTS

vii **Introduction**
Matthew Cormier and Amanda Spallacci

1 **1 | Digital History Making during a Crisis**
A COVID-19 Archive

Jim Clifford, Erika Dyck, and Craig Harkema

27 **2 | From Counter-Memory to Legislative Reform**
Sexual Assault Activism on Social Media in Canada

Amanda Spallacci

51 **3 | "I Make *In Rem*—Against the World—
the Following Order"**
Survivor Agency and Refusal in the Independent
Assessment Process's Digital Memory

Caroline Hodes

75 **4 | Virtual Museum Tours**
Queer Nostalgic Pasts and Utopic Futures in
Canadian Nightlife Memories

Braidon Schaufert

101 **5 | Counter-Cartographies and Activist Archives**
Navigating Petrocultural Memory in Brian Holmes's
Petropolis

Jordan B. Kinder

125 **6 | Socially Mediatized Identities versus The Law of the Heart**
Posthuman Memory in Sophie Deraspe's *Antigone*

Russell J.A. Kilbourn

151 **7 | "You Are Not One Thing"**
Narrative and Memory in Zalika Reid-Benta's *Frying Plantain*

Uchechukwu Peter Umezurike

175 **8 | Toward a Literary Métis Homeland**
A Digital Analysis of Gregory Scofield's *Louis: The Heretic Poems* and Marilyn Dumont's *The Pemmican Eaters*

Matthew Tétreault and Stephen Webb

203 **9 | Beyond the Borders of the City and the Digital Space**
Queer (Un)belonging and Memory Work in Dionne Brand's *Thirsty*

Anna Kozak

225 **10 | Through the Digital Prism of Acadian Identity**
Aesthetics, Politics, and Counterculture

Matthew Cormier

251 **Contributors**

INTRODUCTION

MATTHEW CORMIER AND
AMANDA SPALLACCI

COMPUTERS RUN ON MEMORY. Whether in terms of RAM, the short-term memory that enables us to operate multiple programs simultaneously and in coordination with each other, or of a hard drive, the long-term memory that stores our files and software, the mechanism that is memory has always been and continues to be central to the configuration and logic of computation and, consequently, the digital possibilities that stem from it. Memory, after all, functions much the same way as computers do: even a simple, successfully executed "copy and paste" command is the result of a sequential, rhizomatic, and iterative process of *remembering*, the performance of a set list of tasks with the purpose of recalling previously stored information within a present, immediate context. As we also know from experience, even a task as computationally quotidian as this one demands a certain mediation that ensures the conformity of the precise "memory"—what was copied—to the contemporaneous circumstances under which it is pasted: a change in font, perhaps; an adjustment in grammar or syntax, in other cases. Although this particular comparison is, admittedly, an oversimplification, the fact remains that the conceptual design behind the increasingly complex and powerful computational processes that serve as the building blocks for the various digital spaces through which we currently learn and connect, mediate and create, experience and memorialize owes a significant debt to the apparatus of memory. Indeed, we evolve *through* these digital spaces, these virtual wormholes that have their *own* agency in the form of rational constructs that are programmed to intake massive amounts of data and to learn from human tendencies to alter their behaviours in response. These digital spaces are processual, functioning as dynamic, *living mediums* of transformation and transmission in their own right— in other words, they may reason and animate independent modes of remembering, modes that grow and change the more we interact with them.[1] Indeed, the digital era marks an irrevocable and ongoing shift in terms of how and where memory takes shape not only due to the fact that virtuality collapses space and medium, but also because this new vessel for memory possesses its own intelligence and agency.

Accordingly, the interdisciplinary field of memory studies responds to this shift, theorizing that, in transcending physical space and extending into this burgeoning virtual realm, memory becomes embedded in growing networks that have the potential to move beyond the political economies of place to account for more complex systems of ideas, social positions, and temporal processes.[2] Social media platforms such as Facebook, YouTube, and Twitter immediately come to mind as prime examples of such digital space–mediums, and rightly so: by virtue of their intuitive interfaces designed to facilitate and encourage representation and performativity, in addition to their capacity to reach millions of people online, each serves simultaneously as creative tool, archive, and means of communication. And while digital space–mediums such as social media—not to mention the countless news outlets, marketing and advertisement algorithms, and interactive resources of all kinds that propagate on the World Wide Web—are changing the ways in which we remember publicly, others allow for personal self-reflection and creative expression through digital mediation. Today, well-known and easily accessible software programs—including Microsoft Paint, Adobe Photoshop, and Apple GarageBand and iMovie—provide users with basic visual and audio editing tools to work on creative projects *offline*; others still, such as RStudio, Python, MySQL, and Microsoft BI, similarly allow users to privately initiate and workshop coding and data visualization projects. Yet versions of such private expressions of memory and representation often find their way online eventually, consensually or not, transcending their private digital space—mediums to evolve publicly. The porosity of the partition between the private and the public, especially, prompts us to consider the numerous and varied ways in which memory functions in the digital age, as well as the stakes involved. If these digital space—mediums suggest that memory is performative rather than reproductive, then they demand a reconsideration of memory's agency with the potency, diversity, intelligence, and longevity—in addition to, sometimes paradoxically, the brevity—that the digital age now offers.[3] At any given moment, the sheer volume of information in circulation online and in digital cached archives means that memories either proliferate or fade away depending, precisely, on their agency: once they are performed and represented, what agency might they take on in the cultural imaginary, virtual or otherwise?

PAST AND PRESENT, INDIVIDUAL AND COLLECTIVE: ACTS OF MEMORY TRANSFER

To complicate matters—or perhaps to make them all the more interesting—the rise of memory's digitization has been so meteoric that it has influenced and continues to influence generational acts of remembering as they overlap and coincide, particularly for those who performed memory differently *before* its emergence. In 1990, for instance, Jane, a recently tenured academic, flips through her planner while having her morning coffee, looking to cross off the talk that she is giving that afternoon as part of a panel for one of her department's speaker series. She finds and unfurls the folded-up flyer that she had tucked into the planner, which reminds her that, in addition to a colleague that she knows quite well, Jane is speaking alongside a recent hire whom she has not met yet. She feels guilty, having forgotten to inquire as to her new colleague's research areas, and resolves to show up early at the event in the hopes

Introduction   ix

of offering her an apology in exchange for a quick briefing about her work. Even worse, Jane now notices that hidden under the flyer was also a reminder that her consciousness-raising group had agreed to go out and distribute their feminist newsletter at the same time as her talk. Conceding the fact that she would have to miss this crucial activist work, Jane acknowledges the challenges of balancing activism and academia.

The years—though not *that* many years—go by, and in 2022, Jane is a senior academic in her department. As she rinses her empty coffee mug, the cool, even voice of a woman cuts off her favourite podcast to remind Jane of her itinerary that day. She is giving a departmental talk that afternoon and so she had spent part of the previous evening skimming her institutional library's digital collection for any new scholarship on her topic—and then Google, for good measure. Earlier that morning, while enjoying her coffee, she had revisited the website of the colleague with whom she has been paired in preparation for the brief discussion that is to follow their talks. Now, Jane tries to return to her podcast, but the daily influx of her students' emails is well underway; she briefly indulges in nostalgia for the days when she could not be contacted so conveniently. Her final itinerary reminder, coincidentally silenced by a student email, runs across the screen of her smartphone: she must remember to distribute her feminist collective's newsletter. Before leaving for campus, then, Jane takes a minute to share the newsletter through the collective's website, social media accounts, and email.

Even within the day-to-day details of Jane's life, from past to present, the necessity to remember is pervasive—pervasive perhaps because of the growing role of *others* in the incitation of the act. Memory is a highly intricate process that unites personal and collective acts of remembering: it may look to the past or the future to direct the present, it continuously shapes and influences identity, and it is always to some degree constitutive of representation. Digital technology, in turn, has added a radical dimension to memory by imbuing it with the agency that virtuality offers, but that is at the same time often more dependent than ever on external or social circumstances. Look at Jane: to some,

Jane might appear to engage in acts of memory on her own; after all, she actively thinks about the tasks that she must complete for the day and takes actions based on her remembering. Yet when Jane recalls why she made certain commitments and anticipates how her day will unfold, these acts of memory are triggered by the very external or social situations that sustain the acts to begin with. For instance, the planner represents Jane's social memories; she consults its pages, and it reminds her of her commitments and engagements. More invasively, however, and with more agency, the flurry of student emails activates her memory of a past era when students could not contact her with such immediacy. In these scenarios, Jane's memories are personal, but they are activated by social processes—an activation facilitated by digital technology. Yet this effect is multidirectional: previously, Jane's feminist collective had to physically distribute their newsletters to circulate their narrative, and because she had a commitment scheduled at the same time, she could not join them; now, however, she can distribute the newsletter across various digital platforms and reach more people without leaving her home and in a shorter amount of time. Undoubtedly, one of the most significant shifts in the mechanism of memory in the digital age is its ability to transcend physical place. Previously, Jane's students shared their queries, experiences, and narratives with Jane after class or during her office hours; now, with email communication, these students can zip through cyberspace to reach Jane at her home. Material objects and analogue technologies such as planners, books, flyers, newsletters, and alarm clocks have shifted to digital formats that have the capacity to produce and transmit an endless array of new and evolving acts of memory; these digital memory agents transcend physical space, transforming not only representations of memory themselves, but also the ways in which we remember who we are both individually and collectively.

Collective forms of memory have always shared a symbiotic relationship with representation. People have invariably passed on their stories through narrative, material, or spatial forms, sharing them with members of their communities and making collective memories possible. In doing so, they engage in what memory specialist and social anthropologist Paul Connerton calls "acts of transfer" (39).[4] Connerton's phrase captures the complex potentiality of memory: an "act" evokes a sense of purpose, of agency, and the notion of "transfer" in particular, of course, implies the presence of a targeted audience; in other words, acts of memory can persist through deliberate social processes that become or add to a collective (Hirsch and Smith 7). Prior to the creative multimedia and instantaneous mass communication made possible by digital technologies, representations of memory and their transmissions—"acts of transfer"—were limited, circumscribing research in the interdisciplinary field of memory studies that sought to trace them and expose the political economy of memories as they spread through and even establish distinct collectives.[5] As a result, much of the work involved in studying the political underpinnings of these representations relied on situating representations of memory and the networks in which they circulated in a culturally, socially, and politically specific geographic location. In the Canadian context, most of the scholarship on collective memories conceptualizes their representations through understandings of Canada as a geographical—*topographical*—place, one whose tethered imagery immediately recalls situated memories juxtaposed with colonial histories, and this inevitably leads to debates on nationalist issues.

Yet Canada remains a fascinating case study for work in memory studies because many deem it one of the most multicultural countries in the Western world—meaning that, in the context of collective memory, citizens are not necessarily connected through a common culture, religion, ideology, or even language, complicating a collective remembering.[6] Despite these differences, citizens are expected to reside under a common federal government, education system, health care system, criminal justice system, and so forth. One of the means by which Canada attempts to create a national sense of unity, however futile, is by promoting favourable stories of a distinctly "Canadian" heritage; memories of a peaceful, multicultural utopia past are evoked to unify people in the present under a singular national identity and sense of pride. These collective memories repeatedly appear and circulate across Canada and its institutions: Canadian literature, museums, archives, photographs, monuments, sports teams—even companies such as Tim Hortons rely and capitalize on mnemonic cues that are meant to remind citizens what it means to be Canadian.

The deployment of these representations of collective memories is worthy of consideration, and accordingly, memory studies scholars whose research is situated in Canada consider the political economies behind both representations of memories and acts of transfer networks that are tethered to Canada as a geographical location and national paradigm. Some of the questions driving these analyses ask whose interests and goals these representations serve and to what end, as well as whose positions of power these representations reinforce and which groups they alienate; others grapple with the very resources that creators use to develop and circulate these representations. Generally speaking, and perhaps as to be expected, most studies conclude that those in positions of power mediate narratives of history that serve their interests and goals, often performing these narratives under the guise of a collective national memory that inherently also works to erase and oppress counter-narratives from marginalized voices. Scholars tend to agree that Canada has no monolithic collective memory; instead, it encompasses a multiplicity of collective memories, some of which conflict at various intersections of sociohistorical power. The stakes in these studies, although highly important, chiefly involve *pre-digital* representations of memory and how they are tied to ideas of Canada as a national complex; perhaps more accurately, the memory work in question is grounded in particular understandings of place that often serve to interrogate a national collective memory.[7]

But now activists, artists, and scholars are initiating innovative, persistent, and effective new discourses that challenge national memories, and they use digital media and the internet to instantaneously circulate numerous counter-memories in resistant forms to wide audiences. Such acts of transfer using digital media furthermore expose and reveal the values—patriarchy, white supremacy, homophobia, settler colonialism, ableism, and capitalism—that these official narratives attempt to uphold. They also simultaneously enact and extend the agency and resistance of

Introduction xiii

marginalized people; they encourage the public to remember differently than in the frictionless, uninterruptable ways that previous national and historical representations of memories put forth. For a counter-memory to be accepted or recognized as collective memory, memory studies originator Maurice Halbwachs argues that the memory must "be functionally related to the achievement of the group goals of a community, and the content and structure of the memory have to exhibit meaningful relationships to these goals" (qtd. in Wang 306). So, while counter-memories attempt to infiltrate official narratives, they rarely replace them permanently; however, they *do* leave traces across digital platforms—traces that survive, gain renewed traction as they evolve, and continue to subvert, disrupt, and trouble with the fluidity and adaptability that the digital, virtual space—sometimes for better or for worse—ensures.

This volume thus grapples with questions, among others, of memory enaction, activism, and agency; digital and generative memory; the act of forgetting; and dynamic archiving, with ties to Canada, though not necessarily in the context of a *national* paradigm. Rather, the contributors to *Digital Memory Agents in Canada* are interested in understanding how memory performances and representations with different cultural and spatial relationships with Canada move across, through, beside, under, and above digital spaces—put otherwise, they want to move from discourses on the national place to a focus on the digital or virtual space, on how certain cultures, subjectivities, or positionalities use digital media to document or represent their memories. This volume is intersectional as well as interdisciplinary, investigating memorialization, documentation, and online activism during the COVID-19 pandemic and currently; aesthetic productions and counter-productions of identity in literature, film, and beyond; queer and feminist archiving and consciousness raising; and maps of Indigenous, Métis, and Black narratives of resistance.

DIGITAL MEMORY AGENTS IN ACTION

Collaborators Jim Clifford, Erika Dyck, and Craig Harkema open this collection by sharing the processes and challenges of their innovative memory work on the continuing effects of the COVID-19 pandemic in Saskatchewan. Relying on digital history, medical history, and digital heritage information systems, this interdisciplinary research team takes readers through the establishment of a digital community archive that enlists local cooperation to capture and memorialize the diversity of experiences and coping mechanisms that reflect the sacrifices as well as the resilience of their communities in Saskatchewan.

Calling memory to public action in the chapter that follows, Amanda Spallacci emphasizes its important work in social activism, particularly as it has applied to discussions of sexual assault in Canada. Spallacci demonstrates how social justice movements on social media can lead to significant changes in sexual assault legislation and considers how this form of activism can influence, alter, or challenge widely held misconceptions about sexual assault and survivors. More specifically, she examines the ways in which contemporary sexual assault activists in Canada use various social media platforms to publicize their activism to meet these ends.

Similarly focused in her chapter on the intersection of memory, digital mediums, and the public sphere, Caroline Hodes problematizes the fear of digital technology as a tool for policing and surveillance. While highlighting the criticisms suggesting that the rapid electronic processing and preserving of large amounts of information, whether through state records or social media accounts, will lead to an increase in state incursions into our everyday lives, she matches these criticisms with celebratory narratives claiming that such informational availability will not only democratize the archive but also usher in a transformational and revolutionary era of accountability. As a case study, Hodes investigates the proceedings that led up to and are informed by the Supreme Court of Canada's exceptional 2017 ruling in *Canada (Attorney General) v. Fontaine* to uphold a destruction order for thousands of residential school testimonies.

In his archival study, Braidon Schaufert opens the next chapter with an example from the American competitive reality television show *RuPaul's Drag Race* before asking how Canada remembers its queer nightlife spaces. He addresses this query by examining the material collected on drag queens and queer nightlife in digital archival projects like *The ArQuives* as well as Toronto's *Then & Now* series and *Edmonton City as Museum Project*. Working at the intersection of queer theory's approaches to nostalgia, utopia, and homonationalism, Schaufert challenges the archival impulse to produce a settled, white, heteronormative national image and reckons with drag's collusive potential.

Jordan B. Kinder's chapter follows suit by reading cultural critic Brian Holmes's interactive digital mapping project, *Petropolis*, as both a form of counter-cartography and an activist archive that memorializes, mediates, and performs resistance against Canadian extractivism. Kinder posits the disruptive cartography of *Petropolis*, with its focus on the flows of oil that originate in the Athabasca oil sands, as an extractive practice, charting the infrastructural underbelly of extractive capital and its colonizing impetus not for the reproduction of extractive capital, but against it. He engages contemporary critiques of Canadian extractivism from Indigenous theorists alongside work that addresses the relationship between cultural memory and land, probing the limits and possibilities of digital memory agents as activist media.

The volume next turns to a case study of digital memory agent representations in film with Russel J.A. Kilbourn's chapter, which engages the formal memory work in Sophie Deraspe's 2019 film adaptation of the same title as Sophocles' Greek tragedy, *Antigone*. Kilbourn suggests that the modern titular character's refusal to compromise her personal, family-centred values and capitulate to state law makes for a highly original model of multidirectional Canadian/Quebecois/North African/immigrant/youth/subcultural/diasporic memory. In particular, he studies this model of multidirectional memory as it is performed through the film's use of high-definition digital video technology in non-narrative montage sequences that combine elements of music video, narcissistic social media self-promotion, animation, and experimental art.

Uchechukwu Peter Umezurike's chapter shifts to literature, exploring author Zalika Reid-Benta's accounts of individual and cultural memories in her short fiction and online performances to illustrate the nexus between memory and narrative and the ways in which memory is (re)inscribed within the digital space. Umezurike asserts that Reid-Benta's positionality as a young Black Canadian author offers us a way to contemplate the representability of Black life in Canada, namely with respect to what he conceptualizes as "the circuitry of memory"—that is, how personal and collective experiences are narrativized and articulated digitally. Drawing on ideas by Paul Ricoeur and from memory and critical race studies, Umezurike examines Reid-Benta's collection of short stories, *Frying Plantains*, in relation to its online iterations through print and video interviews with the author to probe questions about diaspora, race, and heritage. He argues that Reid-Benta portrays Canada as a site for contesting the idealization of multiculturalism, or what Paul Barrett describes as "Blackening Canada," suggesting that Reid-Benta's narratives circulate and affirm Black subjectivities in cyberspace.

The subsequent chapter sees Matthew Tétreault and Stephen Webb explain and critically analyze the process of creating their *own* digital memory space–medium based on literary data. Interested in the circulation of historical Métis narratives, they deliberate the exceptional utility of poetry in re-storying the Métis homeland and complex Métis kinscapes while also providing these accounts with a virtual presence and renewed agency. Using digital tools and images, Tétreault and Webb map the places and persons referenced in Louis Riel's poetic oeuvre, Gregory Scofield's *Louis: The Heretic Poems*, and Marilyn Dumont's *The Pemmican Eaters*, revealing a dynamic narrative entanglement that can be studied from entirely new perspectives. In the comparative study that their virtual network fosters, the authors show how these contemporary works resume and re-story narratives of Métis resistance and identity.

Considering yet another intriguing relationship between literature, memory, and digital mediums, Anna Kozak's chapter reflects upon the experiences of living in the city of Toronto for the queer African-Caribbean diasporic subjects of Dionne Brand's poetry book

Thirsty, alongside its supplemental social media content. Kozak's theoretical framework borrows from Johanna Garvey's notion of queer (un)belonging to examine how Brand's poetry highlights the tension between assigned intersectional identities and the desire for more fluid or self-created identities in the wake of an act of police brutality on the streets of Toronto. The book assumes the non-linear form of collage, intertwining multiple voices together that underscore the spatial and temporal fragmentation and alienation that city inhabitants experience if they are queer, Black, and diasporic. Her chapter analyzes how Brand's text calls for a redefinition of diaspora to encompass queerness as a disruption to heteronormativity, and how this appeal extends into digital platforms such as YouTube and Twitter.

Matthew Cormier closes the collection with a study of the digital memory agents that are intrinsically linked to Acadian literature's tangled sociolinguistic history and minor cultural status as well as the ways in which such agents perform and inform Acadian culture. Herein, Cormier examines online platforms that intersect print culture and identity formation, from promotional material to book reviews to performance art, in an effort to demonstrate the power dynamics at work in trying to direct Acadian cultural memory in a minor context.

The vast majority of this volume was conceptualized and drafted while the COVID-19 pandemic kept most people in Canada in their homes, granted that they were fortunate enough to have one. The result was an unprecedented increase and diversification of digital memory-making, perhaps especially fuelled by the pandemic's intensification of social, cultural, and political division and discourse. While the United States was perhaps the nearby catalyst for such upheavals, Canada was no more immune to them than it was to the pervasive disease: the dangerous politicization of public health recommendations in this "post-truth" era, the passionate and widely attended Black Lives Matter protests in response to the murders of George Floyd, Breonna Taylor, and Ahmaud Arbery in the US, and Regis Korchinski-Pacquet in Toronto—right here in Canada— among numerous others, the deepening socioeconomic inequities, and the growing concerns regarding our deteriorating climate all contributed to the spike of memory-making in a year when most people were spending more time online than ever before.

With these developments forming the backdrop, we must remember that most memory studies scholarship argues that, as Marianne Hirsch and Valerie Smith note, cultural memory "can best be understood at the juncture where the individual and the social come together" (7). Yet even this framework could not anticipate the social isolation that the COVID-19 pandemic would produce in our communities and the new ways in which this juncture would evolve digitally. Before the pandemic, some memory studies research acknowledged the role of digital media in the many social, cultural, and material forces and practices that intersect to form memory; however, what does it mean that, for many people during the COVID-19 pandemic, most of their memory work shifted predominantly to cyberspace? How have the rising social, cultural, and political divisions during the pandemic been motivated by the fact that people are consuming massive amounts of digital content that is more accessible than ever before and, due to social media algorithms, often prone to confirming their biases? At the same time, while people stayed home, presumably slowed down their lifestyles, and consumed more media, how have the stories and memories that society has historically and presently tried to silence become more widely circulated, made accessible, and consumed, particularly by people who, under non-pandemic circumstances, may never have encountered this content? Is digital media both the problem and the solution? We hope that this volume begins an essential conversation about these memory practices that speak to contexts within Canada.

NOTES

1. See the highly informative volume *Social Movements, Cultural Memory and Digital Media*, edited by Samuel Merrill and colleagues, for further theoretical studies on the potentiality of memory online.
2. Michael Rothberg's work (2009) takes up the Holocaust as a powerful example to emphasize the link between memory and the politics of place, for instance, while scholars such as Liedeke Plate and Anneke Smelik (2013) argue that *performance* is the means by which they remain inseparable—to perform one is to perform the other.
3. Among a number of others, see Erll and Rigney (2009), Eakin (2008), Karin Tilmans et al. (2010), and Kilbourn and Ty (2013) for insightful work on the performativity of memory.
4. With the notion of "acts of transfer," Connerton participates in a long theoretical lineage ranging from Halbwachs (1925) and Bloch (1925) to Confino (2010) and Radstone and Schwarz (2010), for instance.
5. For more scholarship on political economy in memory studies, see Olick et al. (2011), Allen (2016), Belmonte and Rochlitz (2019), and Autry (2013).
6. According to the *World Population Review*, for example, "Canada is the only western country among the top 20 most diverse countries" (n.p.).
7. In particular, see the works of Julia Creet and Andreas Kitzmann (2011), Ruth W. Sandwell (2006), Daniel Francis (1997), Cynthia Sugars and Eleanor Ty (2015), and James Opp and John C. Walsh (2010).

WORKS CITED

Allen, Matthew J. "The Poverty of Memory: For Political Economy in Memory Studies." *Memory Studies*, vol. 9, no. 4, 2016, pp. 371–75.

Autry, Robyn. "The Political Economy of Memory: The Challenges of Representing National Conflict at 'Identity-Driven' Museums." *Theory and Society*, vol. 42., no. 1, 2013, pp. 57–80.

Belmonte, Alessandro, and Michael Rochlitz. "The Political Economy of Collective Memories: Evidence from Russian Politics." *Journal of Economic Behavior and Organization*, vol. 168, 2019, pp. 229–50.

Bloch, Marc. "Mémoire collective, tradition, et coutume: à propos d'un livre." *Revue de Synthesèse Historique*, no. 40, 1925.

Confino, Alan. "Memory and the History of Mentalities." *Cultural Memory Studies*, edited by Astrid Erll et al., De Gruyter, 2008, pp. 77–85.

Connerton, Paul. *How Societies Remember*. Cambridge University Press, 1989.

Creet, Julia, and Andreas Kitzmann. *Memory and Migration: Multidisciplinary Approaches to Memory Studies*. University of Toronto Press, 2011.

Eakin, Paul John. *Living Autobiographically: How We Create Identity in Narrative*. Cornell University Press, 2008.

Erll, Astrid, and Ann Rigney, eds. *Mediation, Remediation, and the Dynamics of Cultural Memory*. De Gruyter, 2009.

Francis, Daniel. *National Dreams: Myth, Memory, and Canadian History*. Arsenal Pulp Press, 1997.

Halbwachs, Maurice. *Les Cadres Sociaux de la Mémoire*. Presses Universitaires de France, 1925.

Hirsch, Marianne, and Valerie Smith. "Feminism and Cultural Memory: An Introduction." *Signs*, vol. 28, no. 1, 2002, pp. 1–19.

Kilbourn, Russell J.A., and Eleanor Ty, eds. *The Memory Effect: The Remediation of Memory in Literature and Film*. Wilfrid Laurier University Press, 2013.

Merrill et al., eds. *Social Movements, Cultural Memory and Digital Media: Mobilising Mediated Remembrance*. Palgrave Macmillan, 2020.

Neatby, Nicole, and Peter Hodgins, eds. *Settling and Unsettling Memories: Essays in Canadian Public History*. University of Toronto Press, 2012.

Olick, Jeffrey K. et al., eds. *The Collective Memory Reader*. Oxford University Press, 2011.

Opp, James, and John C. Walsh, eds. *Placing Memory and Remembering Place in Canada*. UBC Press, 2010.

Plate, Liedeke, and Anneke Smelik, eds. *Performing Memory in Art and Popular Culture*. Routledge, 2013.

Radstone, Susannah, and Bill Schwarz. *Memory: Histories, Theories, Debates*. Fordham University Press, 2010.

Rothberg, Michael. *Multidirectional Memory: Remembering the Holocaust in the Age of Decolonization*. Stanford University Press, 2009.

Sandwell, Ruth W., ed. *To the Past: History Education, Public Memory, and Citizenship in Canada*. University of Toronto Press, 2006.

Sugars, Cynthia, and Eleanor Ty, eds. *Canadian Literature and Cultural Memory*. Oxford University Press, 2014.

Tilmans, Karin et al., eds. *Performing the Past: Memory, History, and Identity in Modern Europe*. Amsterdam University Press, 2010.

Wang, Qi. "On the Cultural Constitution of Collective Memory." *Memory*, vol. 1, no. 3, 2008, pp. 305–17.

World Population Review. "Most Diverse Countries 2022," https://worldpopulationreview.com/country-rankings/most-diverse-countries. Accessed 28 December 2022.

1

DIGITAL HISTORY MAKING DURING A CRISIS

A COVID-19 ARCHIVE

JIM CLIFFORD,
ERIKA DYCK,
AND CRAIG HARKEMA

WHILE GLOBAL PANDEMICS are thankfully rare, they have historically been important forces that shape generations and often change our cultural and political priorities. COVID-19 is no exception to this trend. While its projected death toll is much smaller than the 1918 influenza pandemic, the totalizing effects of the COVID-19 pandemic are leaving permanent impressions on all of us living through this event, marking this moment in collective memory. COVID-19's impacts have been felt at global, regional, and hyperlocal levels, and this virus has claimed lives at alarming rates.

In this interdisciplinary chapter, we explore the logistics of remembering and memorializing the COVID-19 pandemic in Saskatchewan. We describe our experiences as researchers trying to capture this historic moment as it happened. Our team decided to invest in creating a public archive, along with an interactive website[1] hosting a

COVID-19 news library and a digital memorial, a project that came with its own challenges in terms of how we could possibly both memorialize and witness a crisis at the same time. We examine some of the reasons for, as well as different approaches to, commemorating COVID-19, beginning with an assessment of its significance as an episode of medical history. In particular, the growing demands on people as digital consumers during a pandemic have affected how we use and create digital resources as instructors, researchers, and communicators. We believe that these digital memories will be an important resource for future decision makers. While this pandemic has affected every part of the globe, in order to balance scope with detail we had to set some boundaries. In terms of scale, we restricted our project to the province of Saskatchewan so that we could concentrate on a political jurisdiction and group of communities subjected to similar policies, but with enough diversity to allow for comparisons on a smaller scale. Engaging in direct solicitation also privileged a project in which we could rely on personal contacts and connections. Our intention was never to produce a comprehensive analysis of COVID-19, but rather to facilitate the process of remembering this moment in one province.

We have also privileged materials that are not necessarily collected elsewhere. We knew that the Ministry of Health has a mandate to collect and archive information created by its office, for example, so we were less concerned with managing or overlapping with government records. We were primarily interested in how people living in Saskatchewan made sense of this pandemic moment.

Monitoring experiences over the course of three years has revealed a variety of anticipated and unanticipated responses. Successive waves and new strains, along with vaccines and associated mandates, were met with diverse policy initiatives across Canada, and people started taking matters into their own hands, responding with resistance to public health orders and a growing desire to "return to normal." Our research team grew as we partnered with more scholars and community organizations. Ultimately, we secured funding from the Social Sciences and Humanities Research Foundation (SSHRC) to enhance the archival and commemorative side of this project, and through a partnership with the Saskatchewan Population Health and Evaluation Research Unit we received Canadian Institutes of Health Research funding to do targeted research with Saskatchewan residents who experienced food and/or housing insecurity, or who sought support for mental health and/or addictions. We also received a small grant from Archives Unleashed, allowing us to train students and to enhance our digital archiving strategies. Combining quantitative analysis with qualitative data collection and digital humanities, our strategies for capturing information about the impact of COVID-19 in Saskatchewan have evolved alongside the pandemic.

COVID-19 COMES TO SASKATCHEWAN

During the first few days of March 2020, we observed COVID-19 ravage northern Italy and New York as we waited for it to arrive in Canada and make its way to Saskatchewan. Residents watched for daily updates on new infections, cases that required hospitalization, and ultimately death rates as we sheltered in place in our homes. The pandemic galvanized and divided communities and nations in ways that forged memories of these traumatic events, as they put society on pause and shut down the economy. We witnessed a battle between proponents of public health and those who focused on prioritizing the economy or personal freedom, as the infection rates and deaths increased in racialized and impoverished communities. Governments explored strategic bailouts, lockdowns, or plans to stay the course and prioritize an open economy. The pandemic forced us to consider some of the core values and priorities that guide our decision making with respect to both individual choices and those concerning larger structures of governance.

In this chapter, we describe our efforts to create a community-based archive in the midst of a pandemic as a way of tracking, collecting, and coping with the uncertainty created by living in this moment. In producing the archive, we explored some of the multifaceted stories and reflections that appeared in public along with the omnipresent statistics, public health models, and political rhetoric that circulated in the press and brought these tensions between individual choices and collective decision making into contrast. Our work revealed some of the inherent frictions produced in the dual acts of witnessing and memorializing in real time. We recognized that the social and political reactions to the unprecedented global panic and uncertainty were causing us to confront deep divisions in our society.

COVID-19 is the first global event of this scale since the widespread adoption of social media. A cross-section of society has engaged with social media platforms to debate public health policy as daily case counts and deaths have been posted online, creating a sense of urgency and eliciting real-time reactions, emotional responses, denial, and outpourings of grief and anger. Members of the public using social media have been in constant conversation with newspaper columnists, medical experts, and politicians. We too increasingly resorted to digital tools to sustain daily routines and to help us make sense of the consequences of this pandemic. Facebook and Twitter created new opportunities for citizens to express themselves, whether by holding leaders accountable or spreading baseless conspiracies. Social media posts have created an enticing archive of citizens' different perspectives as they have engaged with discourses related to the pandemic in real time. Historians have never had access to such a broad range of perspectives from a diverse set of people with differing roles and responsibilities in the public discourse. Unfortunately, these digital artifacts are hosted on proprietary platforms, making it difficult, but not impossible, to archive the everyday digital fragments that have shaped peoples' experiences of the pandemic, and the scale of public engagement in this conversation creates new challenges.

The challenge of archiving experiences with COVID-19 also extended beyond social media discussions. With many people working online from home using new tools such as Zoom, Teams, and Slack, we have no longer been generating a traditional paper trail that records our conversations, and even the archiving approaches developed to collect emails have missed a great deal of information about how people coped in this moment. The discussions between the authors of this paper about creating a COVID-19 archive, for instance, were divided between emails, text messages, Teams chats, phone calls, and Teams video calls. As researchers we have been creating digital fragments that have traversed numerous platforms, making it exceedingly difficult for future historians to track and analyze the processes that underpinned these moments and decisions. Historians and archivists have recognized the challenges produced by these information gaps, and they have consequently raised serious concerns that COVID-19 will be the "21st century's forgotten pandemic" (Jones, Milligan, and Sweeney n.p.).

FORGOTTEN PANDEMICS

Forgotten pandemics are not simply beyond the grasp of living memory but are rarefied public health moments that have been overshadowed by other events: in the case of influenza in 1918, for instance, the end of World War I dominated the historical narrative of that period. But beyond locating a pandemic in history, other motivations are involved in forgetting pandemics. The feeling of stasis produced by living in a lockdown generates a desire to move past this moment, to "get back to normal," and to put the pandemic behind us; therefore, coping involves features of forgetting. In combining this pressing desire to overcome a pandemic with the logistical reality that the records of personal lives, behaviours, and even political debates are largely recorded on fragmented digital sources, our collective capacity for remembering and learning from this event is significantly diminished.

Remembering—including analyzing and learning from—COVID-19 requires new approaches in order to capture and preserve the experience for future generations. Working with an interdisciplinary team using digital and medical history methods alongside digital heritage information systems, we aimed to do just that. Jim Clifford is a British historian of nineteenth-century London, its environment, and the related health of its residents. An expert in digital historical methods, Clifford immediately recognized the need to create a space for capturing COVID-19 responses. Craig Harkema leads a team that develops and delivers a wide range of digital scholarship services and investigates methods for interacting with and preserving digital cultural heritage. Erika Dyck is a medical historian who has focused on the ways in which health and social justice campaigns intersect. Together, we began by establishing an online community archive to encourage local cooperation in the form of voluntary submissions of photographs, letters, statements, videos, or any kind of digital record that shows how residents of Saskatchewan have experienced this moment. We also targeted submissions by seeking interviews with members of our community, whether business owners, researchers, or health workers, to capture reflections on how their lives or work changed during this period. It became clear early on, however, that building the infrastructure for capturing reflections was not enough to elicit submissions.

HISTORY OF MEDICINE MATTERS

The infrequent nature of a pandemic on the scale of COVID-19 makes it difficult for health professionals to learn from past experiences. Without comparable experiences in living memory, public health officials, political leaders, and the rest of the population have struggled to find the right balance between risk of exposure and the economic consequences of lockdowns. Searching for comparable public health moments in the past few decades appears futile: SARS had a much more limited impact and HIV/AIDS followed a very different transmission route that resulted in highly targeted public health advice. Pandemics like influenza, cholera, and typhoid fever offered better epidemiological comparisons, but these have required historical interpretation to make them relevant for the people leading us through this moment. Finding meaningful comparisons also raised questions about what was being compared: Death rates? Duration? Social unrest? Resistance? Comorbid factors?

It became clear that the pandemic was as much a political and cultural event as it was a medical one.

Historians of medicine and disease have participated in the public discourse on COVID-19, largely to remind us that historical lessons are important for both health and social coping strategies. The history of disease is a history of panic and social breakdown. Early modern historian Mary Fissell suggests that "pandemics come and go, [but] the way people respond to them barely changes" (n.p.). In her comparison of COVID-19 with an outbreak of the bubonic plague in 1665 London, England, Fissell argues that the twinned concerns about health and economy dominate the early stages of panic, exacerbating underlying inequalities that become more severe during these times of stress (n.p.). Rumours circulate, groups are blamed for spreading the disease, new and often unsafe remedies emerge; Fissell outlines a playbook for the salient features of a pandemic, underscoring the fact that despite humans overcoming these kinds of episodes in the past, we have a habit of forgetting history.

Diseases have always attracted historical inquiry, and the interpretation of these events has often illuminated major turning points in history. The plague of Athens, described by the arguable father of history, Thucydides, was memorialized as a significant event that led to considerable changes in the city-state, not the least of which was the death toll that affected the outcome of the Peloponnesian War. Additionally, Athenians, according to Thucydides, also began losing faith in their religious orders as the disease wreaked havoc in ways that could not be stopped or explained by contemporary authorities, including himself. In the 1960s and 1970s, historians began interrogating the relationship between disease and society in a wave of social history, or history from below. Using historical analysis, medical historians began tackling power imbalances by using epidemics as a lens for exposing systemic social inequalities. In the 1970s, for example, William MacNeill generated a powerful revisionist history of the so-called conquering of North America by focusing attention on the devastation brought by the spread of smallpox in Indigenous communities in North America (13). Medical and social historians have also reminded us that containing diseases or understanding pathogens is not always a clear product of science, but is inextricably related to public attitudes towards hygiene, authority, and religion. Charles Rosenberg, for instance, argued that the US cholera epidemic in the nineteenth century revealed as much about social attitudes towards filth and dirt as it did about the epidemiology of the disease itself (6). More recently and in the Canadian context, Esyllt Jones argued in her study of the 1918 influenza pandemic that this deadly outbreak fomented tensions in urban spaces like Winnipeg, where contending with influenza meant that working-class citizens had different options compared with middle-class homeowners. The 1919 general strike in Winnipeg erupted in the aftermath of a pandemic that had intensified class differences in the city. Historians have shown us that responses to epidemics are never isolated from their broader social and cultural contexts: their appearance reveals pre-existing inequalities, and responses to epidemics often reinforce systemic power structures, whether colonial, patriarchal, or economic forces of disenfranchisement.

Historical perspectives on disease outbreaks and their containment help to generate retrospective analyses of the impacts of disease, as well as the relative success or failure of public health strategies aimed at containment and reducing adverse health impacts. But the medical and scientific lessons are often less important than the social and political consequences that a historical analysis provides. In episodes of panic, people lose faith in institutions, governments, and conventional authorities. Collective and individual protection takes on an ideological dimension as pandemics tend to divide societies that are driven by fear and confusion. As historians, we are particularly keen to study how disease narratives, or information about disease causation and spread, fuel panic during an epidemic. These historical perspectives are necessarily generated by examining an outbreak in hindsight, allowing for critical distance that gives rise to perspectives that cannot be fully realized within the moment in question. These retrospective analyses are essential for measuring the social and cultural impact of diseases and can be instructive for producing models or examples about how past epidemics have played out. To do this well, historians need a broad record of how a diversity of people—which includes government leaders, doctors, and scientists but also mothers, children, teachers, and grocery clerks, among numerous others—experience a public health crisis.

Most public health officials and political leaders are not equipped to think with history as they confront the daily challenge of adapting their public policy response to the crisis. Alix Green, a historian who focuses on the importance of history for decision makers, explains that government officials work under tight time frames, and this makes the linear statistical model–driven paradigm of "predict, plan and provide" a lot more attractive than embracing the uncertainty that comes with historical thinking (177). She argues that the "historian's cognitive toolbox" can help decision makers significantly improve their process by including "careful analogical thinking; examination (placement) of issues, individuals or organisations in their synchronic and diachronic contexts; historicisation of perceived verities and established beliefs; use of disciplined imagination to construct narratives from evidence; a strategic mindset and an appreciation of the long view" (179).

Epidemiologists warned leaders about the high probability of multiple waves in the pandemic and the likelihood that new variants would immerge, but this basic knowledge of historical patterns did little to help politicians develop effective communication strategies or public policies to prepare for this inevitability. Would a better collective memory and widespread education of the 1918–1919 flu pandemic have helped? That event claimed over 50 million lives, and at the time its spread seemed to be hastened by unprecedented international travel as soldiers were demobilized and viral transmission routes seemed to follow the flow of people moving in and out of the conflict in Europe. Historians have written about the influenza pandemic and its multiple waves and variants, yet lessons from past pandemics rarely influence responses to new pandemics (Barry).

Does our collective disregard for events that occurred a century ago stem from a general ignorance of history or from a cultural arrogance that our tools for handling a crisis today are inherently more sophisticated or advanced than those available to people facing the flu in 1918? To compare international travel in 1918 with 2020 is a case in point: although international travel during World War I may have been unprecedented for its time, it now pales in comparison with the scale of mobility in the twenty-first century. Historical thinking involves contextualizing and necessarily gaining perspective on a particular circumstance. Situating an event or public policy issue "within the stream of history makes it part of a narrative, a story that extends in both directions, past and future" (Green 175). This approach of "giving something a past makes it historical. It humanizes and demythologizes what can appear to be timeless realities or ideas and, in doing so, breaks down determinism and opens up the possibility of different futures" (175); it gives leaders the tools to consider the importance of continuity, context, and contingency (179). This way of thinking is a powerful addition to the constant focus on statistics and forecasts developed from mathematical models created by epidemiologists and economists or the shifting scientific consensus on transmission. Thinking with history and related disciplines like medical anthropology can help leaders face the challenges of maintaining the trust of the public during an extended crisis, when conflicting disinformation creates as many challenges as the virus itself.

WE MUST REMEMBER

Living through COVID-19 makes it difficult to imagine forgetting this moment in history. The pandemic transformed our lives in a way that few of us living today have experienced. The pandemic was all-consuming for nearly two years in Saskatchewan, since the second week of March 2020, and it profoundly transformed our lives, jobs, the economy, sports, culture, and the performing arts. Those of us old enough to remember pre-COVID life are not likely to forget this pandemic in our lifetimes; for some of the younger generation they may never remember cultural habits and patterns of the pre-pandemic era. But will the pandemic be seen as historically significant a generation or two from now? The 1918 global influenza pandemic, having been crowded out by the end of the Communist revolutions and the Paris Peace Conference in 1919, was largely forgotten until scholars brought it into renewed focus during the first decades of the twenty-first century (see Barry; Crosby; Humphries; Jones). Similarly, COVID-19 will contend with the rise of authoritarian populists, Russia's war in Ukraine, and intensifying climate change, which future historians may emphasize as more significant than the pandemic.

Partly to combat this process of forgetting or diminishing, we developed a practice of memorialization by capturing a diversity of experiences and coping mechanisms that show the sacrifices as well as resilience of our communities. Recording expressions of what happened in the workforce and in personal lives helped to move beyond remembering the high-level political decisions and the rates of infection to produce a more accurate picture of the effects of the pandemic on the people living and working in our communities. We were keen to establish a space for individual reflection that allowed for qualitative assessments about coping, thriving, and even grieving. We did so by soliciting, collecting, and archiving digital fragments and records outside of government documentation: the responses, effects, or thoughts of everyday people experiencing this moment. Through web archiving, interviews for the public online archive, and other targeted digital initiatives, our team gathered data that was born digital and combined it with solicited contributions to create a digital memory of this historic event-in-the-making.

Histories of epidemics have readily revealed that in moments of global health crisis, balancing the rights of individuals over security for the collective requires perspective, or critical distance from crisis itself. Faced with new and often changing epidemiological evidence, though, public health officials are not always equipped to provide immediate advice that satisfies this balancing act, nor do they have the luxury of waiting for critical distance from the event. Shutting down the economy, for example, may be justified by following scientific advice about reducing the spread of the virus, but doing so would create financial disaster that would be felt unevenly across society. Harnessing economic data may result in different advice for how to manage the pandemic and protect businesses. Labour organizations could mount their own evidence to inform their perspectives on the safety and appropriate working conditions for front-line workers. These examples suggest that in the midst of a crisis, no amount of evidence is enough when informing policy decisions. But prioritizing evidence or modelling outcomes— techniques that can help to avoid ideological or reactionary responses— requires different perspectives and comparisons. During a pandemic, lives are immediately at risk and comparisons are not necessarily on hand; therefore, historical comparison and thinking are valuable tools for establishing critical distance in a pressurized moment of panic.

The COVID-19 pandemic has demonstrated the importance of public health policies and communication strategies in limiting the spread of the pathogen. Having the public adopt social behaviours such as vaccinating, distancing, hand washing, and wearing masks has been essential to minimizing the consequences of the current pandemic. This behaviour lends itself to more abstract concepts of disease management: for example, public understanding and embracing of concepts like "flattening the curve" has likely saved countless lives (Barro 2020). Extensive control measures that enforce behavioural practices require a high level of public compliance, and this compliance is a function of public trust, the quality and clarity of the information communicated, and the level of pandemic fatigue in the population. We believe Green's arguments that narratives are as important as statistical models in communicating risk and that maintaining public trust is necessary for establishing public health restrictions. There is a great deal we can learn from the diminishing effectiveness of public health communication during the second wave of COVID-19 as public health officials start planning for future pandemics. We thus need social scientists and historians to start working on this history in the near future, and doing so means preparing today by collecting a wide range of perspectives and artifacts across numerous COVID-19 archives.

Life during COVID-19 has also shared space with other cultural moments and even generated cultural expressions that underscore injustices that have been exacerbated by the pandemic. Protests focused on racial inequalities, police brutality, or white supremacy may not be directly related to COVID-19, but they have significantly influenced public discourse and memories of this period. While these events are not wholly distinct from a pandemic culture or mentalité, we resist the desire to forget the distinctive qualities of the pandemic period, which involves epidemiological information as much as it does cultural and personal reflections. The overwhelming amount of information about the pandemic at global, national, provincial, and local levels make it difficult to imagine how this moment could be forgotten. Surely, historians in the future will simply use Google to search through the near infinite archive of information posted online (Milligan 19–24); moreover, in addition to the open internet, academics can access databases with all of the scholarship published during and after the pandemic through university library collections, including grey literature and reports from endless studies measuring and predicting outcomes. The government records about public health responses, economic programs, and vaccine development will all be collected in national, provincial, and city archives. But these records do not capture the scale, scope, or diversity of everyday experiences for most people: the pain associated with not being able to publicly mourn for lives lost; the fierce debates over vaccines; the frustration of either closures or the lack thereof that disrupt our sense of safety and security; the fog of existence that inhibits our social contact, planning, and mental health. These more delicate, personal, and even intimate reactions to the pandemic are beyond the purview of conventional archival strategies but are critical to understanding how we have learned to cope in such times of extreme uncertainty.

THE REVOLUTION WILL NOT BE DIGITIZED

The pandemic shaped life well beyond what official policies might later reveal. We have confidence that the Provincial Archives of Saskatchewan as well as the Saskatoon and Regina City Archives will properly collect, preserve, and make accessible official documents about pandemic responses, infection rates, hospital beds required, and so on, but these facilities are not resourced to collect a lot of material outside their core focus or jurisdiction. Over time, other collections will be deposited that might include more personal information or reflections on the pandemic, but this work will take time and it will be piecemeal by nature. While *ProQuest*'s "Canadian Major Dailies" database includes Regina's *Leader-Post* and Saskatoon's *StarPhoenix* and will be an important source for any research project on the pandemic in Saskatchewan, it does not capture smaller media sources or independent media that may contain important local reactions. The CBC News website and the corporation's archive will also provide another rich collection of stories about all aspects of COVID-19 in Saskatchewan, with local stories dating back to late January 2020, but this content has already been taken down from the original public website (Quesnel). Despite all of the uncertainty swirling in the news media in 2020, these collections of stories should be safe even if the newspapers are sold or the CBC loses funding in the future.

Stories published online by local television stations, on news radio websites, or on small newspapers, however, are at a greater of risk of not being saved or retained in accessible formats. This unfortunate repercussion is an important reminder that other local perspectives on COVID-19 might be lost at any time as news media websites struggle with lower advertising revenue during the pandemic. The Wayback Machine, run by the Internet Archive, records copies of local newspapers, but this occurs sometimes as infrequently as once a month. *Eagle Feather News*, for instance, focuses on stories in First Nations and Métis communities but also relies on donations to sustain its content; its closure would mean the loss of an important perspective for future generations of researchers. We are thus using Archive-It, a web archiving service for libraries and archives built by the Internet Archive, to target and more frequently crawl specific websites in order to expand collection of these news sources.

Meanwhile, social media provides a new opportunity to record the perspectives of a wide variety of people in different social and political positions and across generations; capturing these digital conversations can reveal how members of the public interact with political and medical leaders. Yet social media also gives a platform for anti-mask or anti-vaccine activists to organize their semi-regular protests in Saskatoon and Regina or even nationally, as we have seen with the truckers' convoy to Ottawa. Social media also creates numerous challenges from an archiving perspective. While Twitter and Facebook are currently dominant companies in our culture and economies, there is no guarantee that they will continue to exist in the future: for example, Geocities was once a major development tool for people to build simple websites and share their ideas during the early years of the mass adoption of the internet, but it was later shut down when people moved onto different platforms, making the Wayback Machine the only way to find such lost content. Flickr, which was once the largest photo-sharing platform on the web, still exists, but it has been considerably downsized in recent years. Digital platforms change over time: just as the 1918 residents of Saskatchewan relied on radio broadcasts, church sermons, and newspapers to deliver news, our mechanisms for reporting and remembering have changed and will predictably continue to change in ways that are not immediately clear to us at present.

Twitter/X is an attractive social media platform for archiving, as the available tweets are explicitly public and it is a place where journalists, academics, doctors, politicians, and other members of the public maintain an ongoing conversation about COVID-19 in Saskatchewan. Moreover, Twitter/X makes its data accessible to academics and this project has a free licence to mine the Twitter/X database for content related to the pandemic in Saskatchewan. Medical experts like Drs. Kyle Anderson, Dennis Kendel, and Tamara Hinz have taken on prominent roles as critics of public health policy, while People's Party of Canada activists like Mark Friesen took up the fight against masks and other public health restrictions. Untethered from concerns like peer review, re-election, or public responsibility, some contributors to Twitter/X can engage in public debates that do not hold the same level of accountability and may also reveal more candid layers of emotional responses to COVID-19 than official records. These fragments nonetheless require critical analysis, since social media followers or retweets may not be an accurate measure of public engagement or support. For example, polarized perspectives attract followers and may generate "buzz" or hype not afforded to public commentators, who are compelled to provide responses that match a political script, or to journalists who are expected to provide informed perspectives. The untethered social media commentator thus produces historical evidence on a platform that may in fact distort the message's significance as a historical artifact.

Facebook's parent company, Meta, in contrast with Twitter/X, does not provide academic access to their data and they actively block the Internet Archive tools from working on their websites (Facebook and Instagram). We are working around these limits on a small scale, using a browser plugin that records WARC files of the content as a student navigates around Facebook pages. It is very time consuming and Facebook occasionally suspends our accounts, but we feel the historical importance of some of the content justifies the trouble. Premier Scott Moe used Facebook to communicate directly with the public in Saskatchewan through posts and videos. These regular posts on Facebook also became a version of the public sphere, with people coming together to debate the government's policy. The Webrecorder software from ArchiveWeb.Page allows us to capture these public discussions and add them to our Archive-It collection for long-term preservation. However, this is a very small part of the discussion of COVID-19 in Saskatchewan that took place on Facebook. Because many people only share with their network, large sections of Facebook content are effectively private. Facebook also allows private groups, some of which develop into forums for conspiracy theories, pseudoscience, and disinformation. These closed groups might have some of the most pertinent information for future social scientists and historians trying to understand public resistance to medical advice, but they are not open to archiving and aggressively police their membership to remove reporters or individuals who oppose their views. So while this information is very important, it is not ethical for the archives project to try and harvest it using the Webrecorder software.

The experience of COVID-19 demands a more coherent archival record, but the rapid move to online work exacerbates a decades-long struggle to develop effective archival techniques to preserve digital records. Archival records have always been incomplete and uneven. Only literate people leave a written record from their own perspective and archives were much better at preserving the records of the elite. Social historians have struggled for decades to piece together fragmentary records to better understand the experiences of ordinary people. The internet and social media create new opportunities to record a far wider sampling of human experience, but they also create a wide array of new challenges. General public expressions on social media and in comments on newspaper articles do not represent a random sample of the population. People with strong beliefs are more likely to leave a public record online and social media is plagued with trolls and bots that gravitate towards controversy and exaggerate extreme positions.[2] Twitter/X and Facebook are likewise dynamic social media platforms, unlike stable websites or blogs. Every user is served a unique and changing timeline of content produced by algorithms designed to keep users engaged. To make matters more difficult, these are global platforms and their scale and structure make it impossible to capture everything in an archive. We are left with challenging questions about how to record the public discourse about COVID-19 in an ethical manner that does not leave the record overpopulated by fringe actors.

ARCHIVING A MOMENT/CRISIS

Early in the pandemic, Harkema began to create a web archive using the Archive-It.org platform to schedule web crawls that have captured posts from key institutions in Saskatchewan, including the provincial and major municipal governments, the provincial Health Authority, school boards, and the University of Saskatchewan. He also worked with the university archivist, Tim Hutchinson, to capture the daily results for a Google News search for COVID and Saskatchewan. This approach, while somewhat imprecise, has been successful in tracking the announcements and news stories available to the public as the pandemic unfolded. Much of this material will remain online, stored by the provincial, municipal, and institutional archives in the aftermath of the pandemic, but web archiving has the benefit of preserving the original versions and serves as a backup for anything lost or deleted along the way (Milligan 62–105). For example, deleted posts from politicians or public figures that include important or inflammatory information are critical to accurately preserving the historical record.

A few weeks later, on 20 March, a group of researchers at the University of Saskatchewan began a conversation about expanding on Harkema's Archive-It project to create an open digital portal to collect people's thoughts on the pandemic. The plan was to create an online archive modelled on the September 11 Digital Archive that allowed Americans to contribute to and create a community archive to capture the diversity of experiences of the terrorist attacks. We thus quickly developed a website on which residents of Saskatchewan could upload their personal reflections, photos, artwork, stories, or comments on life during the pandemic.[3]

Our intention was to help witness this historic moment as it was happening, expanding the Archive-It collection and trying to record some of the public discourse about COVID-19. We aimed to preserve the real-time responses that revealed fears but also leadership and coping strategies presented by journalists, politicians, medical officials, educational leaders, and others as they made public statements about how to control infection rates or, at times, whether to control the spread at all. Our longer-term objective was to add reflections on life during COVID-19 from people living in the province to help future observers understand how ideas changed over time, but also to appreciate the diverse responses to the pandemic from different members of our community. People began donating materials, including photographs of playgrounds with barricades or warning tapes, reminding us that the play structures for our children were for a time perceived to be vectors for disease transmission; photographs of businesses and churches closed with messages encouraging people to stay safe. Some submissions were more hopeful, leaving traces of individual actions that foregrounded our collective sacrifices; images of masked statues of past heroines, reminding us of our connections to the past and the resilience of our communities. Our goal as researchers was not to analyze reactions, but simply to witness these responses and archive them for future analysis, perhaps also by a future generation of scholars or public health officials who might face a new crisis and appreciate the perspectives offered by looking back to think forward.

However, what began as a simple premise became complicated as we attempted to put it into practice. Before we could create an online portal for capturing any data or reflections, we were faced with ethical challenges. Is it ethical to record people's ideas and post them on a public website? Is it moral to ask physicians or front-line health workers to divert energy from their pandemic response to share insights with us for the purpose of an archive? Could people participate in this project anonymously? Our university's research ethics board is not designed to adjudicate this kind of activity: most often, it requires the destruction of research data after a period of time instead of preserving it in an open archive. Moreover, our goals were not conducive to a systematic approach of engaging oral history in the classic sense, but instead our desire to record people's perspectives seemed better suited to practices that one might find in an archive. Due to our interest in asking people to simply tell their stories, our project pushed the boundaries of archival collections strategies too. From the beginning, then, our objectives fell outside the typical protocols of academic work.

Delays in securing ethics approval, however, merely masked another set of obstacles, in that COVID-19 had displaced or dispersed university services in uneven ways. Sabbaticals disappeared as travel options ended and caring responsibilities took on new degrees of significance, especially as schools and public services closed and care homes locked down. University employees scattered to their homes with differing degrees of responsibility or capacity to continue their regular work. Layoffs ensued across many sectors of the economy, while other segments experienced increased demands for labour in conjunction with inconsistent opportunities for sustained support. For example, in order to create an online archive, we relied on the continued functionality of the library, archives staff, IT support services, and research ethics board members. In a moment when people were forced to react to an immediate sense of danger or disruption in their lives, our desire to witness this stress or catalogue reactions did not warrant prioritization.

It took us eight weeks of focused effort to launch the COVID-19 Archive. Despite the challenges in securing appropriate ethical protocols and the IT support to create a publicly accessible and user-friendly platform, our project had captured the attention of local and national news media. For several weeks we conducted media interviews, prepared videos, spoke on radio programs, and excitedly advertised this project as a service to the people of our province. By this time, we had framed the Archive as a way to witness this historic moment but realized that it was also becoming a public space for sharing coping strategies and learning from one another as we sunk into isolation and separated from our social routines, and many people hunkered down in their homes seeking interaction.

At this time, we felt that our memory-making objective was on track and we were optimistic about public participation. The flurry of media interests also seemed to indicate that for some people, participating in a memory-making project helped to create a sense of community at a time when many of us were living in isolation like never before in our lives. Our interviews and radio broadcasts were treated as public interest stories, even positive and encouraging local news, contrasted with the frenetic number-watching of COVID cases, lockdowns, and doomsday stories of economic collapse. Buoyed by the local interest in sharing stories through a virtual platform, we began expanding our mandate and seeking stories and photographs to illustrate this period of resilience.

We pooled our faculty resources and hired students whose employment prospects had been largely quashed in the wake of the pandemic. Eager research assistants shared ideas about potential interviewees: for example, with bike store owners who experienced a surge in customers looking to avoid buses, maintain fitness when the fitness centres closed, or simply as an excuse to safely move around outside as the snow melted and residents embraced the public health recommendations to socialize outside. Health care workers, doctors, nurses, and hospital cleaning staff became another coveted group that could inform people about how their daily routines had been affected amid the rising rates of infection, but they proved more difficult to interview than the local business owners. For several weeks we held regular meetings and enthusiastically made plans to record perspectives that we agreed would help future generations appreciate the diversity of experiences during this unprecedented moment; however, the responses were not what we had anticipated. Even as we convinced ethics committees, research assistants, and journalists about the significance of commemorating this part of the pandemic experience, community participants were not altogether eager to share their views. Many people were hesitant to share perspectives that they felt might change, or to disclose protocols or new strategies in a workplace that might be considered confidential, or, for many people, the crisis was too present to provide an opportunity to reflect or say something meaningful. Although our team felt that the objective was to witness, the notion of contributing to an archive had already characterized this process as a form of memorializing, and in summer 2020 people were still confronting COVID-19; most people did not seem ready to remember something that at that moment they were more intent on solving and forgetting. We were perhaps simply simultaneously a little too late to capture the initial enthusiasm to discuss the pandemic in Saskatchewan and too early to capture people reflecting on the pandemic in its aftermath.

By May 2020, the local lockdown had successfully prevented a serious first wave. Saskatchewan residents watched the virus hit northern Italy, New York, and Montreal, but the case count remained low and the province only experienced a handful of deaths. We were asking people to reflect on a pandemic that had yet to fully arrive to the province, even if it brought widespread disruption to our economy, schools, and social lives. Our media interviews resulted in a handful of community posts to the archive and the students recorded seven oral history interviews over the course of the summer, yet with those came many failed attempts to secure interviews. As we all began to come to terms with the reality that COVID-19 would continue to shape our lives through 2020 and into 2021, the leadership of the archive project realized that this project would take years instead of months. We thus began reorienting our thinking towards when people in Saskatchewan might be ready to contribute and how we could adapt and be ready.

The project team began with a simple website that allowed users to upload content (audio, text, and video files) with a free text field to comment on a digital object of significance and/or simply post, Twitter/X style, how they are currently feeling about the pandemic experience. While not as simple as contributing via an application on their phones, the process has been relatively straightforward from the outset, even if the required sign-in and a less elegant method for file upload likely contributes to lower submission numbers. Aside from a general statement about the sort of content we hoped to gather, there is little direction given in terms of a collection mandate; we did not want to limit possibilities.[4] We included prompts or examples in fields used to add content and believed early submissions would serve as examples for others to follow. Much could have been done to improve this process if the team had had the time and resources.

Two years later, with a generous injection of federal research funds to support this project, we are restarting the project under the new label of Remember Rebuild Saskatchewan. We are currently updating the website and hiring students to help solicit materials and interviews from community organizations. We are helping to gather documents from different front-line organizations, from Food Banks to the Nurses Union. As restrictions relax and front-line workers in some sectors shift from crisis to burnout, the need to collect impressions and experiences may be even more urgent. We learned from community organizations that many service providers had to pivot their activities to balance public health measures with the needs of their clients, whether providing food, shelter, or health services. Clients in long-term care facilities faced different sets of lockdowns than many of us who chose to comply or resist. Hospital beds were repurposed to serve the needs of the pandemic, leaving many in need on long wait lists or contemplating private options, putting more pressure on the public system to reform. We remain committed to capturing real-time responses and collecting the records of makeshift organizations and structures that emerged to respond to the pandemic and gaps in service coordination. We recognize that changes to our health care, economy, and service delivery will result from pandemic experiences, but our collective effort to move past the pandemic may minimize its influence on these changes down the road, contributing once more to a forgotten pandemic moment.

CONCLUSION

One of the strengths of our project has been the collaboration among scholars and community members and organizations. Despite a clear desire to move beyond the pandemic, communities have been deeply affected by the medical, political, and social realities altered by COVID-19, and many people want to harness the insights we have gained in order to invest in meaningful changes. There is no consensus on what a post-pandemic community should look like, and if anything, COVID-19 illustrated that there are deep divisions in the population when it comes to matters of public/private interests in health care as well as individual choices or freedom. The impact of COVID-19 may not ultimately be measured in death rates or vaccine victories, but future scholars may instead emphasize this period as one of growing or exacerbated social and political divisions. Our efforts to archive the pandemic provided clear evidence of the resilience of communities and, especially, the ingenuity and creativity of front-line service providers who shifted priorities within a crisis to reach many of the most vulnerable members of our communities. As the pandemic recedes, fading from emergency to memory, response teams have dispersed but this experience has also impoverished our public health system—through burnout, depleted trust, and a return to socioeconomic disparities that have been merely exacerbated. We hope that our archiving efforts and public-facing summaries, interviews, and library of news stories will provide evidence to support future emergency planning.

NOTES

1. See https://rememberrebuild.ca/.
2. Internet troll: someone who intentionally instigates arguments online (Wikipedia, https://en.wikipedia.org/wiki/Internet_troll. Accessed 3 May 2021). Bots: a software application that runs automated tasks (scripts) over the Internet (Wikipedia, https://en.wikipedia.org/wiki/Wikipedia:Bots. Accessed 3 March 2021). Bots have been used to increase acrimonious debates about COVID-19 on social media platforms (Uyheng and Carley).
3. The COVID-19 Community Archive: https://covid19archive.usask.ca/recent-contributions.
4. Homepage statement on COVID-19 Community Archive: https://covid19archive.usask.ca/

WORKS CITED

Barro, Robert J. "Non-pharmaceutical Interventions and Mortality in US Cities during the Great Influenza Pandemic, 1918–1919." *National Bureau of Economic Research*, 2020, https://www.nber.org/papers/w27049. Accessed 3 May 2021.

Barry, John. *The Great Influenza: The Story of the Deadliest Pandemic in History*. Viking Press, 2004.

Crosby, Alfred. *America's Forgotten Pandemic: The Influenza of 1918.* Cambridge University Press, 2003.

Fissell, Mary. "Pandemics Come and Go. The Way People Respond to Them Barely Changes." *Washington Post,* 7 May 2020, https://www.washingtonpost.com/outlook/2020/05/07/coronavirus-bubonic-plague-london/. Accessed 9 December 2020.

Green, Alix. "Continuity, Contingency and Context: Bringing the Historian's Cognitive Toolkit into University Futures and Public Policy Development." *Futures,* vol. 44, no. 2, 2012, pp. 174–80.

Humphries, Mark. *The Last Plague: Spanish Influenza and the Politics of Public Health in Canada.* University of Toronto Press, 2013.

Jones, Esyllt. *Influenza 1918: Death, Disease and Struggle in Winnipeg.* University of Toronto Press, 2007.

Jones, Esyllt, Ian Milligan, and Shelley Sweeney. "Will COVID-19 Become the 21st Century's Forgotten Pandemic?" *Globe and Mail,* 5 October 2020, https://rsc-src.ca/en/voices/will-covid-19-become-21st-century's-forgotten-pandemic. Accessed 12 March 2024.

MacNeill, William. *Plagues and Peoples.* Anchor Books, 1976.

Milligan, Ian. *History in the Age of Abundance.* McGill Queen's University Press, 2019.

Quesnel, Jennifer. Interview with Volker Gerdts. "Researchers at VIDO Working on Vaccine for Deadly New Coronavirus." *CBC Radio Saskatoon Morning,* 21 January 2020.

Rosenberg, Charles. *The Cholera Years: The United States in 1832, 1849 and 1866.* University of Chicago Press, 1987.

Thucydides. *The History of the Peloponnesian War.* Edited by M.I. Finley, translated by Rex Warner, Penguin Classic, 1954.

Uyheng J, and Kathleen M. Carley. "Bots and Online Hate During the COVID-19 Pandemic: Case Studies in the United States and the Philippines." *Journal of Computational Social Science,* vol. 3, no. 2, 2020, pp. 445–68.

2

FROM COUNTER-MEMORY TO LEGISLATIVE REFORM

SEXUAL ASSAULT ACTIVISM ON SOCIAL MEDIA IN CANADA

AMANDA SPALLACCI

SEXUAL ASSAULT LAWS IN CANADA have made tremendous strides, having gone through numerous reforms since the women's movements of the 1960s to the 1980s. Activists, women's organizations, and criminal justice professionals, within and outside of these movements, worked tirelessly to demand new legislation, leading to numerous amendments and revisions to existing rape legislation throughout the 1980s. These particular reforms, and the ones that followed, show that sexual assault activism can in fact incite legal changes in Canada. Subsequently, these legal strides have helped some victims obtain justice for these crimes, which is certainly no small feat; however, feminist legal scholars continue to point out that despite these legal reforms, the criminal justice system persistently reports high rates of case attrition and low conviction rates corresponding to sexual assault reports in Canada (Craig; Gotell; Johnson). An explanation for this anomaly is that the criminal justice system and those who work within the institutions do not exist in a vacuum; as a result, prevailing social and cultural views—often presented in popular culture, including mainstream media—about sexual assault and the victims who report it inform how law enforcements responds to reports, which cases advance to an investigation and trial, and whether a judge rules in favour of a conviction. In other words, while it has been imperative that the legal system reform its sexual assault laws, we must also work to address and change the attitudes about survivors—often constructed out of sexism, classism, racism, settler colonialism, and queerphobia—and misconceptions and misinformation about sexual assault. Targeting these oppressive ideologies is not new; historically, activists created consciousness-raising documents such as newsletters, pamphlets, manifestos, and novels in an effort to address, debunk, and challenge them. While activists continue to use these various mediums, many participate in consciousness raising on social media because this digital medium enables activists to reach wider audiences and circulate their messages more efficiently than ever before.

In 2014, for example, Sue Montgomery and Antonia Zerbisias, Canadian journalists at the *Montreal Gazette* and the *Toronto Star*, created #BeenRapedNeverReported on Facebook to challenge the discursive tendency to use a popular myth about sexual violence to discredit the women accusing Jian Ghomeshi of assault—the primary myth being that if a woman is sexually assaulted, she will immediately report the crime to the police. Since the inception of this hashtag, over 8 million social media users have posted it; some posted to demonstrate solidarity, while others responded out of a shared recognition or appreciation of the hashtag because they had also been sexually assaulted and did not report to the police. If most victims do not report to the police, the statistics on the prevalence of sexual assault in Canada, based on the criminal justice system's formal archive of reports, fail to represent the pervasiveness of the issue nationally. For this reason, Mendes et al. argue that the 8 million social media posts that include #BeenRapedNeverReported produce an informal archive that documents the pervasiveness of sexual assault in Canada and, I would add, attempts to debunk one of the most pervasive misconceptions about sexual assault. Like the material consciousness-raising documents from the past that helped to persuade the criminal justice system to reform rape laws in the 1980s and 1990s, digital consciousness raising on social media also contributes to contemporary efforts to revise and amend sexual assault legislation, such as the introduction of Bill C-51, which prohibits the use of sexual history evidence in court. Scholars have thus begun to research how sexual assault activism on social media impacts legal reforms (Quinlan; Sheehy); however, *how* this digital activism works to challenge oppressive ideologies and attitudes about sexual assault and survivors remains under-theorized.

By assigning 2014 and the hashtag #BeenRapedNeverReported as its starting point and using subsequent examples of sexual assault activism on social media in Canada, this chapter considers how personal and collective forms of memory operate within and beyond the digital sphere. It engages cultural memory studies to contextualize social media testimonies of sexual assault within national oppressive ideologies or attitudes of sexual assault; put differently, this chapter asks how the personal memories of sexual assault that survivors share on social media reinforce or challenge collective memory of sexual assault in Canada.

CULTURAL MEMORY AND POLITICAL ACTIVISM

Cultural memory provides a framework to theorize the points of convergence between personal forms of remembering in the public sphere and collective memory. Memory studies scholars Emily Keightley and Michael Pickering argue that memory, expressed through personal experience, "shares a concern with the use of the past as a resource in making experience and social life meaningful, in producing, or challenging cultural norms and conventions, and in reproducing or subverting established orders of power" (151). Essentially, personal memories, which many presume are part of internal and independent processes, are inextricably linked to established forms of knowledge, a person's community, and systems of power; they are negotiated and mediated through historical-material contexts. Consequently, these memories can counter or contradict pervasive cultural narratives; these counter-memories, according to Marianne Hirsch and Valerie Smith, "serve as a challenge...to official hegemonic history" (7). This premise regarding counter-memories helps to explain the work of activists in circulating personal memories on social media: in doing so, they can disrupt the cultural silence surrounding various forms of oppression and contest national hegemonic narratives. Sometimes, these counter-memories can spark entire movements that permeate into collective memory, transforming national attitudes; however, more often than not, they are silenced and excluded because, as trauma and memory studies scholar Allen Meek explains, structures of power are sustained by inflicting trauma onto others and excluding their stories of pain from collective memory (3). Within this power dynamic, personal representations of memory function as a means to memorialize events that the nation would rather forget, but their very exclusion from collective memory also reveals the narratives, myths, and legacies that the nation seeks to uphold.

To exclude personal memories, Canadian historian Daniel Francis contends, involves perpetuating and reinforcing myths that weave a coherent story of Canada to reproduce the "values of privileged citizens who use this narrative to secure the status quo" (10). One of the tenets of Canada's story is that the nation is hospitable to all citizens because it believes in and supports that equality should be granted to all. A contemporary myth underpinning this story is post-feminism—a cultural discourse stating that women achieved gender equality during the women's liberation movements of the 1960s and 1970s and, as a result, no longer need to rely on feminism or activism. National myths such as post-feminism, according to feminist scholar Cecily Devereux, are "implemented and reinforced ideologically through education, language, religious and legal systems, popular media, literature and the full range of what Althusser has defined as state apparatuses" (180).

This myth functions like a curtain, allowing systems of power such as patriarchy, racism, homophobia, ableism, and settler colonialism to persist with impunity because feminists, who continue to expose these systems of power, are confronted with the opposing narrative that Canada no longer needs feminism because it has achieved gender equality (180). This conflict demonstrates that nationally accepted narratives and ideologies are deeply pervasive and ingrained in all Canadian institutions, making it incredibly difficult for counter-memories to be recognized and accepted as collective memory.

To challenge these national narratives and prevent their causes from being dismissed, silenced, or excluded, activists use social media's wide reach to circulate large numbers of counter-memories and personal narratives, often using other forms of consciousness raising like hashtags, and invite other users to share their similar stories. Digital memory scholars Elisa Giaccardi and Liedeke Plate state that when activists create such spaces of dynamic story sharing online, they participate in the "collection, preservation and interpretation" of personal memories (65). As activists work to transform oppressive ideologies and narratives by creating, publishing, and circulating forms of counter-memory on social media, their narratives must constantly negotiate prevailing collective forms of memory in Canada. By reading social media activism within a framework of cultural memory studies, therefore, scholars can analyze how forms of counter-memory challenge national ideals, myths, and narratives.

In this respect, Meek claims that personal memories, especially those pertaining to trauma and oppression, are always "embedded in larger ideological formations" and require a reading practice that analyzes these memories "against the grain in order to elaborate the historical contexts and political implications of trauma's role in modern media criticism" (1). In reading sexual assault activism on social media, then, scholars must also account for the historical-material contexts in which these memories are situated because, as memory studies scholar Maurice Halbwachs emphasizes, "it is in society that people normally acquire their memories. It is also in society that they recall, recognize, and localize their memoires" (38). By examining social media activism alongside contextual analysis of Canadian popular discourses on sexual assault and identifying points of convergence between the two, this chapter demonstrates how social media activism reflects, informs, and resists prevailing discourses—including the cultural denial—about sexual assault.

SEXUAL ASSAULT IN THE CANADIAN CONTEXT: 2014

Since this chapter will engage with social media activism that begins with the 2014 hashtag #BeenRapedNeverReported, the contextual work will begin the same year. Before situating Canadian public conversations about sexual assault, it is important to turn briefly to the United States' context. In 2014, leaders of the United States federal government, former president Barack Obama and then–vice president Joe Biden, signed a memorandum to create a task force named "The White House Task Force to Protect Students from Sexual Assault," which consisted of senior administration officials who would coordinate federal enforcement efforts to hold universities accountable in thoroughly investigating claims of sexual assault and creating bystander culture (2). Furthermore, Obama's task force sought to spread awareness about the prevalence of sexual violence—often stating that one in five women are sexually assaulted on college campuses—and to debunk misinformation about sexual assault by asserting that survivors rarely report sexual assault because most often they are assaulted by someone they know (2). While this Democratic government exposed the pervasiveness of sexual assault in the United States, that same year, the Conservative government in Canada repeatedly and publicly denied that gendered and racialized violence exists in Canada. Despite America's global influence, in the context of sexual assault, the Canadian government was unmoved by its neighbour's interest in these political conversations.

Although the Canadian Conservative government and the United States Democratic government espouse different values, George

Elliott Clarke defines Canada as a nation that shares "common values and harmonized policies" with the United States (27–28). Initially, then, one might presume that the Canadian government would follow the United States' lead and prioritize a similar campaign to address sexual assault in Canada, especially since Statistics Canada was actively publishing studies on sexual assault that year, such as Adam Cotter and Laura Savage's report, which stated that more than 11 million Canadians disclosed that they had been physically or sexually assaulted since the age of fifteen (n.p.). Yet Clarke also asserts that, while Canadians "ache to reproduce American practices and approaches...[they] shrink, still, from the American penchant for extremism—in religion, in political disruption, in citizenship, in practice, yep, of racism" and "in contrast, [their] cities are cleaner, [their] citizens healthier, [their] children better educated, and [their] 'visible minorities' not as viciously brutalized" (28). In other words, even though Canada aligns itself with the United States, Canadians also take pride in promoting the idea that, unlike the United States, they live in a "Peaceable Kingdom" (28). If Canadians juxtapose their national identity with the United States because they believe that Canada is a more peaceful place, it is not surprising that regardless of whether American political leaders have publicly declared sexual assault a national problem, the Canadian federal government avoided related political discourse.

Accordingly, any time members of the Canadian Press questioned the Canadian federal government about the subject of violence against women, the government remained conspicuously silent or outright dismissive. Anne Kingston reported that Stephen Harper, prime minister of Canada, "doesn't want to talk about so-called 'women's issues.'" For Kingston, Harper refused to address questions about murdered and missing Indigenous women and girls, sexual violence, or income inequality because they reveal an "inconvenient truth" that Harper preferred to ignore ("Why Stephen Harper" n.p.). Moreover, Tanya Kappo points out that, during 2014, Harper repeatedly demonstrated a "profound lack of respect for Indigenous women and girls" when he publicly stated that establishing an inquiry into the missing and murdered Indigenous women in Canada was not "really high [on the government's] radar, to be honest" (n.p.). Furthermore, when a journalist asked Harper about the murder of Tina Fontaine, a fifteen-year-old Indigenous woman, he declared that her murder should not be viewed as a "sociological problem" but rather as a terrible crime (Kennedy n.p.). This blatant denial that violence against Indigenous women is a systemic issue conceals what Leanne Simpson refers to as "a long present and a long history of ignoring Indigenous consent" (7). By relegating violence against women, particularly Indigenous women, to the realm of the private sphere as opposed to acknowledging Canada's history of settler colonialism and Indigenous exploitation, the government maintains the national narrative that Canada is a "Peaceable Kingdom." That same year, Harper introduced new legislation, Bill C-36, to criminalize sex work despite significant opposition from feminist organizations asserting that this bill would lead to increasingly dangerous and precarious conditions for sex workers. Even though Harper declared that most Canadians supported the bill, Justin Ling reported that the results from a national poll revealed that "despite [the] aggressive campaign from the government to sell its tough-on-sex agenda to voters, fewer Canadians support the new laws" (n.p.). Harper's unfounded assertion that Canadians support the criminalization of sex work supported the government's conservative stance on the purchase of sex in an effort to dismiss any opposition to the bill. In another instance, the drummer from Harper's band, who was also employed as a grade 7 and 8 teacher, was accused of sexually assaulting a minor, and according to Steven Chase, Harper's team refused to comment because "given that this individual is now facing charges, it would be inappropriate to comment any further at this time" (n.p.). Harper used rhetorical tactics— such as declaring that systemic violence is not a priority, criminalizing those who are at risk of violence, and avoiding the topic entirely— to minimize the severity and prevalence of sexual violence in Canada.

By undermining any discussion of these issues, Harper maintains the national myth that systemic sexism, racism, and settler colonialism do not exist in Canada because the nation is post-feminist, post-racial, and so on. As stated, this public-facing political denial reinforces a curtain that conceals injustice created and perpetuated by oppressive systems. Later that same year, however, a national event would disrupt this cultural denial of sexual assault in Canada: Jian Ghomeshi, well-known radio and television host, who worked for the CBC—a significant proponent of Canada's civic ideology—was charged with four counts of sexual assault and one of choking to overcome resistance.

*BEENRAPEDNEVERREPORTED: CHALLENGING CANADA'S POST-FEMINIST MYTH

In 2014, the CBC removed Jian Ghomeshi, the prominent host of Q, from his position after allegations that he had sexually assaulted and choked women surfaced in the mainstream media. On 26 October 2014, Ghomeshi addressed his dismissal from the CBC in a lengthy post on Facebook. He acknowledged that his sexual practices might not adhere to conventional notions of sex, but that these practices were always "mutually agreed upon, consensual, and exciting for both partners" ("Jian Ghomeshi's" n.p.). By evoking the notion that his partners enthusiastically consented and by asserting that these allegations are being "pursued by a jilted ex-girlfriend," Ghomeshi set a foundation to claim that the allegations were false. He used social media to challenge the narratives circulating in the news media by appealing to the widely held misconception that many claims of sexual assault are false; historically, this myth has sparked fear in the public that an alleged perpetrator would suffer devastating consequences to their career and reputation as well as serve legal prosecution because of lies put forth by a spiteful woman.

It is in large part precisely these widely held misconceptions that prevent women from reporting sexual assault or from receiving justice if they decide to report. To return to the context: while the federal government was publicly dismissing that sexual assault was a problem in Canada, Ghomeshi—a beloved celebrity-type figure in Canada—was denying the sexual assault allegations brought against him. Unsurprisingly, many citizens were quick to defend Ghomeshi and attempt to silence the complainants by evoking myths about sexual assault—such as the assumption that if a woman were truly sexually assaulted, she would immediately report to police. Statistics Canada debunks this myth by reporting that in 2014, 83 percent—the vast majority—of sexual assaults were not reported to law enforcement. Yet in an opinion piece for the *Montreal Gazette,* Montgomery recalls that as the allegations against Ghomeshi circulated in the media, she read numerous social media posts in which people questioned the women's claims: they asked why the complainants, if they truly had been assaulted, had they not immediately reported the assault to authorities. By posing such questions on social media, those posting reinforced the narrow conclusion that the women who reported Ghomeshi did so years after the alleged assaults took place only because the allegations were false.

Of course, Ghomeshi was a public figure whom many people respected, which explains why Canadians were publishing strong opinions in his defence; however, these fervent assertions perhaps represent something deeper. Sexual assault specialist Judith Herman, for instance, explains that "it is tempting to take the side of the perpetrator" because this side requires the bystander to do nothing, while the survivor "asks the bystander to share the burden of pain" by demanding "action, engagement, and remembering" from the public (7–8). In other words, the public is inclined to side with the perpetrator because it takes little effort and maintains the status quo. The public denial concerning the Ghomeshi case thus operates on two levels: first, myths and misconceptions about sexual assault are commonly employed to dismiss complaints as false, and second, these myths, like Harper's rhetorical strategies, seek to deny the prevalence of sexual violence in Canada. In order to respond to the backlash of the case and to challenge this national denial of sexual assault, journalists Montgomery and Zerbisias ended up creating the hashtag #BeenRapedNeverReported.

This hashtag demonstrates the relationship between mainstream media, social media, and sexual assault activism. As journalists,

Montgomery and Zerbisias take an interest in how the public responded to the sexual assault allegations made against Ghomeshi. Once they noticed the public tendency to attempt to discredit the complainants' testimonies, they decided to use social media to create an archive of survivor testimonies that could both reveal the prevalence of sexual violence and debunk widespread misconceptions about sexual assault. #BeenRapedNeverReported generated an archive of 8 million tweets and made visible the prevalence of sexual violence in Canada. Since the majority of sexual assaults occur in private spaces and the national narrative denies that these traumatic events ever happened, survivors were able to find a community of people with similar experiences on social media. By posting a sexual assault testimony on social media and having someone like, share, or comment on the post, survivors felt a sense of comfort, support, and solidarity in the public sphere (Mendes et al. 1292), sentiments that Loney-Howes argues survivors often struggle to obtain offline (44). Perhaps most significant is that as online witnesses engaged with their testimonies, survivors began to feel that their testimonies were believed in the public realm—a sense of validation that survivors rarely experience in such a space.

These forms of online recognition, Loney-Howes points out, not only enable survivors to feel validated but also resist the power imbalance that exists in more traditional forms of witnessing (43). For example, with respect to legal forms of witnessing, Craig argues that education and social or economic class disparities are "connected in inequitable ways to race, Indigeneity and disability" and "these factors all contribute to the profound power differential between those who control the [legal] process and those who are subject to it" (10). While victims are, to varying degrees, subordinate to legal professionals in trial settings due to the latter's position of power both in the legal context and in society, when victims' credibility is questioned during the trial, trauma may likewise impinge on their memory and their testimonies lack linear narratives and coherence (Herman 39). And rather than acknowledge that the victim's trauma is responsible for her inability to form a legal testimony that fits within the conditions set by those controlling the questioning, her testimony presumed not to be credible (Alcoff and Gray-Rosendale; Leydesdorff and Adler).

Unlike formal institutions like the criminal justice system, online spaces facilitate a community in which those who testify and those who witness "construct a different kind of power relation: one based on shared experience" rather than one that "seeks out an authority to bestow recognition upon them" (Loney-Howes 44). In challenging dominant myths about sexual violence and assault, criminology and digital media scholar Michael Salter argues, such social media spaces render claims by survivors "intelligible and meaningful even if they breach social and legal norms" (13).

However, while these spaces can certainly be more validating and empowering than formal institutions, scholars argue that online spaces may not be as liberating and inclusive as they appear because they are curated spaces with specific guidelines and parameters. Participants in #BeenRapedNeverReported, in particular, have been those who have a social media account, access to the internet, and may not be fearful of the perpetrator reading their post. Furthermore, the hashtag assumes that survivors themselves have not internalized misinformation about sexual assault and are therefore aware that sexual assault can be perpetrated by someone they know and not only by a stranger wielding a weapon, for instance. Another concern about social media activism is that often "trolls" will try to invade the conversation by attempting to discredit survivors' posts. Although trolling has devastating effects on survivors, Loney-Howes proposes that it can also be demonstrative of the "disruptive capacity" of survivor testimonies and their ability to generate "discussion and debate" (47). In other words, trolling can be a sign that the activism is circulating and permeating collective forms of remembering.

Unlike trolls, empathetic witnesses who engage with online testimonies might be motivated by compassion. Nonetheless, this is, as Deidre E. Pribram argues, "a poor foundation for political action because it removes political, social, and ideological issues to a personal realm" (8). The compassionate witness might be responding merely out of a personal sense of moral superiority for being on what they perceive to be the "right" side of the debate; this response fails to identify the systems of power that create conditions for sexual assault to occur without recourse or justice for survivors. For this reason, Marianne Hirsch and Valerie Smith argue that witnessing violence in any form requires empathy as well as critical distance (10). Moreover, even if witnesses positively engage with online survivor testimonies—by sharing, liking, or commenting on survivors' posts—these are considered "low impact forms of witnessing" (Loney-Howes 44). These forms of activism are necessary and important because, as previously stated, they validate survivors' experiences and provide a sense of support that survivors struggle to obtain in the criminal justice system. However, even though social media posts and replies might not always radically transform public attitudes about sexual assault or work to dismantle oppressive systems of power because they occur at an individual or personal level, nonetheless, in large numbers—such as the 8 million posts that featured the #BeenRapedNeverReported hashtag—social media activism, like this ground-breaking campaign, can resist the silence and denial around sexual assault. This is why since 2014, the news media and social media have continuously worked to make subsequent issues related to sexual assault more visible. This surge in visibility is attributed to a variety of factors, including individuals who recognized the importance of speaking out, newspaper editors seeking stories that would attract more readership, and social media algorithms capitalizing on trending topics.

POST-GHOMESHI ERA IN CANADA

In 2015, Justin Trudeau, a self-declared feminist, campaigned to be Canada's next prime minister and made sexual harassment, sexual assault, and domestic violence central to his campaign. Trudeau promised to provide greater support for survivors, develop a national strategy to combat gender-based violence, and launch a national inquiry into the cases of missing and murdered Indigenous women and girls in Canada. Whether or not Trudeau fulfilled these promises, his position on sexual violence is in opposition to Harper's remarks the previous year, and Trudeau's public comments on the subject bolster ongoing efforts that seek to bring the gravity of sexual assault into the public consciousness. According to memory studies scholar Astrid Erll, sociocultural contexts shape individual memories, and "a 'memory' which is represented by media and institutions must be actualized by individuals, by memories of a community of remembrance, on shared notions of the past. Without such actualizations, monuments, rituals, and books are nothing but dead material, failing to have any impact in societies" (5). By acknowledging that gendered, racialized, and settler-colonial violence exists in Canada, Trudeau, like the campaign #BeenRapedNeverReported, establishes the pervasiveness of sexual assault.

Since Trudeau and the Liberals achieved a majority government, there has been an increase in sexual harassment and assault reports at Canadian universities and in the mainstream news media, and activists continue to use online activism to address this national problem. In 2016, for example, Steven Galloway, former professor in the Creative Writing Department at the University of British Colombia, was terminated from his position after students made formal complaints of harassment against him. Following Galloway's dismissal, "An Open Letter to UBC: Steven Galloway's Right to Due Process," signed by prominent members of the Canadian literature community—most famously, Margaret Atwood—circulated in the public sphere; specifically, people shared the letter on social media, and the news media circulated the letter as well as various commentaries on the subject. It is not surprising that members of the Canadian literature community, those who are not only friends with Galloway but who are also responsible for creating stories about Canada, would want to quickly dismiss these allegations because they disrupt the notion that Canada is a "Peaceable Kingdom."

Almost immediately, an "Open Counter-Letter About the Steven Galloway Case at UBC" was posted on *Change.org*, conveying outrage that the open letter "did not express any support for the female complainant or for other female students who felt it was safe to make complaints after Steven Galloway was suspended." The counter-letter asks those who signed the open letter to withdraw their signatures "and call for a fair and open process based on recognition of realities of rape culture" (n.p.). The counter-letter was shared across social media platforms in order to generate awareness, and the news media reported that it had received over 600 signatures. On 15 December 2015, a few writers removed their signatures from the open letter, and the authors added an addendum titled "Procedural Fairness for All," stating that they did not intend to dismiss the complainants' disclosures but wanted to stress the importance of due process. This case demonstrates how those on both sides of this case used social media to circulate their letters and cultivate signatures to strengthen their position.

Similarly, in 2018, the news media reported that two students from Concordia University filed formal complaints with the school, alleging that a professor who teaches in the English Department sexually harassed them. In response to these allegations, the university conducted an external review of the English Department, and the subsequent report stated that it had an unhealthy climate with real or perceived sexual violence (Beaumont). Since the complaints, students have continued to express that the university has failed to adequately address the recommendations outlined in the report and that the university's policies and procedures for reporting sexual assault do not satisfactorily support complainants. In an effort to circumvent these barriers, students created a social media page titled "UntoldConcordia," which serves as a space where students can share their testimonies of systemic oppression at the university, including sexual assault, harassment, racism, and any form of discrimination. This social media page documents testimonies that in turn create a record of the prevalence of various forms of oppression at the university.

While some activists use social media to address toxic culture on university campuses, others use these digital platforms to protest the multiple ways in which the criminal justice system treats sexual assault complainants. In some cases, online news media outlets publish trial verdicts as well as public court transcripts pertaining to sexual assault cases. Although journalists can discredit survivors' testimonies

Amanda Spallacci

or propagate an anti-feminist agenda in their reports, there is still merit in having reports about sexual assault cases circulating in the media. Carrie Doan, for instance, explains that sexual assault cases often do not circulate in the public sphere and that, as a result, the testimonies and judgments that take place within the court are not open to the general public (295). Even though some trial transcripts are made public, citizens might not know that these documents exist or where they can find them; therefore, circulating these cases and reports in the media makes these cases, testimonies, and verdicts accessible to the public. Sometimes these cases can spark outrage at the injustice that stimulates political activism.

In 2016, for instance, a 2014 sexual assault trial in Calgary circulated across multiple online news outlets, and the articles reported that throughout the trial, Justice Robin Camp had repeatedly referred to the complainant—a young Indigenous woman—as "the accused"; he also asked her why she did not close her legs to stop the assault and remarked that pain and sex often go together (Fletcher n.p.). The judge's language in addressing the complainant and the nature of the assault demonstrates his acceptance of misconceptions about sexual assault, and his apparent disdainful remarks about the survivor reveal his racism and settler-colonial attitudes towards Indigenous people. In response, four law professors from the University of Calgary filed complaints with the Canadian Judicial Council regarding the judge's conduct during the trial, which prompted an official inquiry. The inquiry found that Justice Camp had committed misconduct throughout the trial, and the report caused Camp to formally resign from the bench. By reporting on the case, the news media had exposed the trial judge's unethical behaviour, and from this awareness steps were taken to prevent Camp from treating future complainants in a similar manner.

Likewise, in 2017, a Nova Scotia judge, Justice Gregory Lenehan, acquitted a taxi driver, Bassam Al-Rawi, of sexually assaulting his passenger, who was found unconscious and naked from the chest down in the back of his car. During the trial, a forensic alcohol specialist testified that the complainant was severely intoxicated—her blood alcohol level was three times the legal limit—which would cause her to lose awareness of her surroundings. In his ruling, the judge claimed that in order for Mr. Al-Rawi to be convicted, the Crown would have to establish beyond a reasonable doubt that the accused violated the complainant's sexual integrity without her consent. According to Hilary Beaumont, the judge asserted that "clearly, a drunk can consent" and that the complainant's lack of memory of the event, due to her intoxication, did not establish a lack of consent (n.p.). Once the trial's verdict and the judge's remarks began to circulate in the public sphere—via mainstream news media—activists distributed a letter template on social media along with instructions to submit the letter to the judiciary committee. The goal was to flood the judiciary with complaints recommending that Judge Lenehan be removed from the bench; in the end, 121 complaints were received from various individuals and organizations. The judiciary reviewed the trial and determined that it would be "dangerous and wrong to equate [the judge's] comments with judicial misconduct" and subsequently cleared Judge Lenehan of misconduct (n.p.). Despite the results of the review, this case demonstrates that once the news media reported on specifics from the trial, activists used social media to make visible the judge's misconduct towards the complainant.

These examples represent a fraction of the advocacy that has occurred across Canada since 2014. The purpose of outlining these cases, however, was to demonstrate the various forms that sexual assault activism can take on social media and how such activism seeks to disrupt the cultural denial and transform social attitudes about sexual assault in Canada. Cristine Rotenberg and Adam Cotter, for instance, state that from 2016 to 2017, reports of sexual assault increased by 24 percent nationally, possibly because of the changing conversations about sexual assault that survivors see on social media and in the mainstream news. Despite the increase in reports, however, sexual assault case attrition remains high, and Jennifer Temkin and Barbara Krahé classify this phenomenon as the "justice gap" (n.p.). In response to this gap, Jody Wilson-Raybould introduced legislation, Bill C-51, in 2017, to amend the Criminal Code and the Department of Justice Act. The proposed legislation prohibits the use of sexual history evidence already in the possession of the accused, allows sexual assault complainants a right to be represented by counsel in hearings that determine the admission of evidence regarding sexual activity, and clarifies the law as it relates to consent (Department of Justice n.p.).

On the surface, the introduction of the bill seemed to coincide with the #MeToo movement that started in the United States following Jodi Kantor and Megan Twohey's investigation into the sexual harassment allegations against Hollywood film producer Harvey Weinstein, which was published in the *New York Times*; ten days later, Hollywood actress Alyssa Milano tweeted on 15 October 2017: "if you've been sexually harassed or assaulted write '#MeToo' as a reply to this tweet." The original phrase "me too" was created in 2006 by Tarana Burke, a Black woman, and following Milano's public call on Twitter, the hashtag produced a global archive of over 12 million posts by survivors of sexual violence. Yet despite the popularity of the #MeToo Movement, Anne Kingston reported that "those on the front lines of sexual violence education and advocacy in Canada date this country's #MeToo anniversary back four years" to the hashtag #BeenRapedNeverReported ("Inside" n.p.). Furthermore, Bill C-51 was first proposed in June 2017, four months before the #MeToo movement, and it was formally passed on 10 December 2018. The new law is a testament to sexual assault activism in Canada since 2014; similar to the antirape activism and shifts in Canadian law in the 1970s, social media activism in Canada since 2014 has contributed to the nation's most recent sexual assault legislative reform.

CONCLUSION:
PUSHING FORWARD, CHANGING ATTITUDES

While the goal of Bill C-51 is to ensure that sexual assault complainants are treated fairly as they try to navigate the criminal justice system and to close the justice gap, some scholars are skeptical about the merit of legal reform. Holly Johnson states that the rape reform laws from the 1980s were supposed to improve the "prejudicial attitudes toward women in the investigation, rules of evidence, and instructions to the jury"; yet these changes have "not made a real difference in the treatment of sexually assaulted women throughout the justice system" (613). Similarly, Kate Puddister and Danielle McNab assert that Bill C-51 will not change court officials' attitudes and behaviours about either the complainant or sexual assault, and, moreover, they wonder how the justice system plans to uphold this new legislation and hold law professionals accountable. These concerns are valid; however, from a memory studies perspective, this legislation represents a tangible result of the ways that digital news media and social media can disrupt cultural denial about sexual assault in Canada.

E. Ann Kaplan and Ban Wang ask, "how do traces of trauma leave their mark on culture?" (16). This chapter sought to answer this question by demonstrating how governments, news media reports, and social media activism can both perpetuate and resist misconceptions and misinformation about sexual assault. Of course, activism still remains to be done to change attitudes about sexual assault. While governing rules and regulations are established to protect survivors, the justice gap in Canada means that there are nonetheless persistent misconceptions and cultural denial about sexual assault. Elaine Craig, for example, argues that stereotypical thinking informs the ways in which laws are interpreted and applied; therefore, closing the justice gap requires that Canada address "the much larger issue of changing social attitudes generally and reducing systemic gender inequality" (222). Until social attitudes about gender, race, settler colonialism, and sexual assault transform in Canada and systems of power are eradicated, survivors will struggle to obtain justice for these crimes. In the meantime, digital news media and social media can offer avenues for survivors to speak out and receive support.

WORKS CITED

Alcoff, Linda, and Laura Gray-Rosendale. "Survivor Discourse: Transgression or Recuperation?" *Getting A Life: Everyday Uses of Autobiography*, edited by Sidonie Smith and Julia Watson, University of Minnesota Press, 1996, pp. 198–225.

"An Open Letter to UBC: Steven Galloway's Right to Due Process." *UBC Accountable*, 14 November 2016, https://www.ubcaccountable.com/open-letter/steven-galloway-ubc/#:~:text=The%20University's%20conduct%20in%20this,irresponsibly%20in%20Professor%20Galloway's%20case. Accessed 17 April 2024.

Beaumont, Hilary. "Judge Who Said 'A Drunk Can Consent' in Sex Assault Case Cleared of Misconduct." *Vice*, 5 April 2018, https://www.vice.com/en_ca/article/a3yj4z/judge-gregory-lenehan-who-said-a-drunk-can-consent-in-sex-assault-case-cleared-of-misconduct-by-nova-scotia-judiciary. Accessed 19 May 2021.

"Bill C-51, An Act to Amend the Criminal Code and the Department of Justice Act and to Make Consequential Amendments to Another Act." Department of Justice, https://www.justice.gc.ca/eng/csj-sjc/pl/cuol-mgnl/c51.html. Accessed 18 May 2021.

Chase, Steven. "Drummer in Harper's Rock Band Charged with Sexual Assault on a Minor." *Globe and Mail*, 6 February 2015, https://www.theglobeandmail.com/news/politics/drummer-in-harpers-rock-band-charged-with-sexual-assault-on-a-minor/article16728442/. Accessed 19 May 2021.

Clarke, George Elliott. "What Was Canada?" *Is Canada Postcolonial? Unsettling Canadian Literature*, edited by Laura Moss, Wilfrid Laurier University Press, 2003, pp. 27–39.

Cotter, Adam, and Laura Savage. "Gender-based Violence and Unwanted Sexual Behavior in Canada, 2018: Initial Findings From the Survey of Safety in Public and Private Spaces." Statistics Canada, 5 December 2019, https://www150.statcan.gc.ca/n1/pub/85-002-x/2019001/article/00017-eng.htm. Accessed 19 May 2021.

Craig, Elaine. *Putting Trials on Trial*. McGill-Queens University Press, 2018.

Devereux, Cecily. "Are We There Yet? Reading the 'Post-Colonial' and *The Imperialist* in Canada." *Is Canada Postcolonial? Unsettling Canadian Literature*, edited by Laura Moss, Wilfrid Laurier University Press, 2003, pp. 177–89.

Doan, Carrie. "Subversive Stories and Hegemonic Tales of Child Sexual Abuse: From Expert Legal Testimony to Television Talk Shows." *International Journal of Law in Context*, vol. 1, no. 3, 2005, pp. 295–309.

Erll, Astrid. "Cultural Memory Studies: An Introduction." *A Companion to Cultural Memory Studies: An International and Interdisciplinary Handbook*, edited by Astrid Erll et al., De Gruyter, 2008, pp. 1–15.

Fletcher, Robson. "Federal Court Justice Robin Camp Should be Removed From Bench, Judicial Committee Recommends." *CBC*, 30 November 2016, https://www.cbc.ca/news/canada/calgary/robin-camp-federal-court-judge-inquiry-committee-report-1.3874314. Accessed 19 May 2021.

Francis, Daniel. *National Dreams: Myth, Memory, and Canadian History.* Arsenal Pulp Press, 1997.

Giaccardi, Elisa, and Liedeke Plate. "How Memory Comes to Matter: From Social Media to the Internet of Things." *Materializing Memory in Art and Popular Culture*, edited by Laszio Muntean et al., Routledge, 2016, pp. 65–88.

Gotell, Lise. "Reassessing the Place of Criminal Law Reform in the Struggle Against Sexual Violence." *Rape Justice: Beyond the Criminal Law*, edited by Anastasia Powell et al., Palgrave Macmillan, 2015, pp. 53–71.

Halbwachs, Maurice. *On Collective Memory.* Translated by Lewis A. Coser, University of Chicago Press, 1992.

Herman, Judith Lewis. *Trauma and Recovery.* Basic Books, 1997.

Hirsch, Marianne, and Valerie Smith. "Feminism and Cultural Memory: An Introduction." *Signs*, vol. 28, no. 1, 2002, pp. 1–19.

"Jian Ghomeshi's Full Facebook Post: 'A Campaign of False Allegations' at Fault." *Toronto Star*, 27 October 2014, https://www.thestar.com/news/gta/jian-ghomeshis-full-facebook-post-a-campaign-of-false-allegations-at-fault/article_4179a984-e801-5ae5-b25d-a23a41c5d945.html.

Johnson, Holly. "Limits of a Criminal Justice Response: Trends in Police and Court Processing of Sexual Assault." *Sexual Assault in Canada*, edited by Elizabeth A. Sheehy, University of Ottawa Press, 2012, pp. 613–34.

Kaplan, E. Ann, and Ban Wang. "Introduction: Traumatic Paralysis to the Force Field of Modernity." *Trauma and Cinema: Cross Cultural Explorations*, edited by E. Ann Kaplan and Ban Wang, Hong Kong University Press, 2004, pp. 1–23.

Kappo, Tanya. "Stephen Harper's Comments on Missing, Murdered, Aboriginal Women Show 'Lack of Respect.'" *CBC*, 19 December 2014, https://www.cbc.ca/news/indigenous/stephen-harper-s-comments-on-missing-murdered-aboriginal-women-show-lack-of-respect-1.2879154. Accessed 19 May 2021.

Keightley, Emily, and Michael Pickering. "Painful Pasts." *Research Methods in Memory Studies*, edited by Emily Keightley and Michael Pickering, Edinburgh University Press, 2013, pp. 151–66.

Kennedy, Mark. "Stephen Harper Blasted for Remarks on Missing and Murdered Aboriginal Women." *Ottawa Citizen*, 23 August 2014, https://ottawacitizen.com/news/national/stephen-harper-blasted-for-remarks-on-missing-and-murdered-aboriginal-women. Accessed 19 May 2021.

Kingston, Anne. "Inside the First Year of #MeToo." *Maclean's*, 5 October 2018, https://www.macleans.ca/society/inside-the-first-year-of-metoo/. Accessed 19 May 2021.

Kingston, Anne. "Why Stephen Harper Doesn't Want to Talk About 'Women's Issues.'" *Maclean's*, 11 September 2015, https://www.macleans.ca/politics/ottawa/why-stephen-harper-doesnt-want-to-talk-about-womens-issues/. Accessed 19 May 2021.

Leydesdorff, Selma, and Nanci Adler. "Introduction: On Evidence and the Value of Personal Testimony." *Tapestry of Memory: Evidence and Testimony in Life-Story Narratives*, edited by Nanci Adler and Selma Leydesdorff, Routledge, 2013, pp. ix–xxix.

Ling, Justin. "New Poll Shows Canadians Don't Like Stephen Harper's Prostitution Bill." *Vice*, 15 January 2015, https://www.vice.com/en_ca/article/dpk5by/new-poll-shows-canadians-dont-like-stephen-harpers-prostitution-bill-273. Accessed 19 May 2021.

Loney-Howes, Rachel. "Shifting the Rape Script: 'Coming Out' Online as a Rape Victim." *Frontiers: A Journal of Women Studies*, vol. 39, no. 2, 2018, pp. 26–57.

Meek, Allen. *Trauma and Media: Theories, Histories and Images*. Routledge, 2009.

Mendes, Kaitlynn, et al. "Digitized Narratives of Sexual Violence: Making Sexual Violence Felt and Known Through Digital Discourses." *New Media and Society*, vol. 21, no. 6, 2019, pp. 1290–1310.

Montgomery, Sue. "Opinion: #BeenRapedNeverReported Started a Global Discussion About Rape." *Montreal Gazette*, 4 November 2014, https://montrealgazette.com/opinion/columnists/opinion-beenrapedneverreported-started-a-global-discussion-about-rape. Accessed 19 May 2021.

"Open Counter-Letter: Steven Galloway Case at UBC." *Open Counter-Letter Galloway*, https://sites.google.com/ualberta.ca/counterletter/home. Accessed 20 April 2021.

Pribram, E. Deidre. *Emotions, Genre, Justice in Film and Television: Detecting Feeling.* Routledge, 2011.

Puddister, Kate, and Danielle McNabb. "#MeToo: In Canada, Rape Myths Continue to Prevent Justice for Sexual Assault Survivors." *The Conversation*, 5 March 2019, https://theconversation.com/metoo-in-canada-rape-myths-continue-to-prevent-justice-for-sexual-assault-survivors-110568. Accessed 19 May 2021.

Quinlan, Elizabeth. "Introduction: Sexual Violence in the Ivory Tower." *Sexual Violence at Canadian Universities: Activism, Institutional Responses and Strategies for Change*, edited by Elizabeth Quinlan et al., Wilfrid Laurier University Press, 2017, pp. 1–26.

Rotenberg, Cristine, and Adam Cotter. "Police-reported Sexual Assaults in Canada Before and After #MeToo, 2016–2017." Statistics Canada, 8 November 2018, https://www150.statcan.gc.ca/n1/pub/85-002-x/2018001/article/54979-eng.htm. Accessed 19 May 2021.

Salter, Michael. "Justice and Revenge in Online Counter-Publics: Emerging Responses to Sexual Violence in the Age of Social Media." *Crime, Media, Culture*, vol. 9, no. 3, 2013, pp. 225–42.

Sheehy, Elizabeth A. "Introduction." *Sexual Assault in Canada*, edited by Elizabeth A. Sheehy, University of Ottawa Press, 2012, pp. 7–22.

Simpson, Leanne Betasamosake. *A Short History of the Blockade: Giant Beavers, Diplomacy, and Regeneration in Nishnaabewin.* University of Alberta Press, 2021.

Temkin, Jennifer, and Barbara Krahé. *Sexual Assault and the Justice Gap: A Question of Attitude.* Hart Publishing, 2008.

"The White House Task Force to Protect Students from Sexual Assault." *WhiteHouse.Gov*, https://www.whitehouse.gov/sites/whitehouse.gov/files/images/Documents/1.4.17.VAW%20Event.Guide%20for%20College%20Presidents.PDF. Accessed 15 May 2020.

3

"I MAKE *IN REM*— AGAINST THE WORLD— THE FOLLOWING ORDER"

SURVIVOR AGENCY AND REFUSAL IN THE INDEPENDENT ASSESSMENT PROCESS'S DIGITAL MEMORY

CAROLINE HODES

THE FEAR OF DIGITAL TECHNOLOGY as a tool with the potential to increase policing and surveillance often forms the basis of criticism suggesting that its rapid and efficient electronic processing and sharing of large amounts of information will facilitate state incursions into personal lives (Ball and Snider; Cosgrove; Deleuze; Graham). These criticisms are matched by those who offer celebratory narratives suggesting that the creation and availability of digital media will not only democratize state and independent archives by providing increased access to public information, but usher in a revolutionary era in which direct democratic participation is the norm, and church and state will be made accountable for their collective crimes (Rheingold; Schuler). The question that emerges from each of these accounts is to what extent does the mediation of information via digital technology lead to both yet neither of these outcomes simultaneously?

In this chapter, I examine a case that tests a limit between two spheres that are endemic to both the law and the debates surrounding the dangers and virtues of digital technology: the public and the private. In this case, representation in settings where testimonial speech is recorded, preserved, and verified through documentary evidence and transcribed into text creates a peculiar series of files that can be understood to produce collective memory due to the iterative nature of the law. However, they also describe personal experiences that ought to remain private. What happens when courts become spaces of memory work that promise privacy and confidentiality even while demanding the expansion of the self to stand in for others? How is agency both circumscribed and used to challenge institutional constraints through this process?

With respect to these questions, the Supreme Court ruling in *Canada (Attorney General) v. Fontaine* (2017) is notable for a number of reasons. First among these is the court's decision to uphold a destruction order for thousands of residential school records; second is the court's admonition of its own decision as "having no significant precedential value" (para. 35). The court thereby creates an exception out of this case that brings the oppositional structure of public and private to its crisis. Reading these proceedings along their archival grain provides a valuable inroad into how litigants become digital memory agents whose claims collectively and publicly demonstrate how law exceptionalizes the memory of its own originary violence—the violence of settlement—yet meticulously documents the crimes of both church and state through a series of administrative acts.

Although this case complicates the digital debate, the labyrinthine nature of its preservation transforms it into an object, a site of memory, that has been thrown into a partial, public and transnationally available digital archive that is no more easily accessible than its paper counterparts (Hodes). Jennifer Wemigwans has observed that despite the Truth and Reconciliation Commission (TRC) of Canada's inclusion of a section on "Media and Reconciliation" in its final report, it "completely missed any discussion of the internet" (6). The proceedings examined in this chapter are illustrative of two consequences of this omission: significant gaps in the truth and legal impediments to reconciliation.

THE CASE AND THE FILES

On 15 December 2006, the superior courts in nine Canadian provinces approved the Indian Residential Schools Settlement Agreement (IRSSA), thereby concluding what has been described as "the largest and most complex class action settlement in Canadian History" (*Fontaine* 2014 ONSC 4585 para. 1). Residential school survivors initiated lawsuits beginning in the 1980s, and by 2005 the number of cases had grown to an estimated 18,000 (TRC 560). In 2006, these cases were merged into a single class action named after Phil Fontaine, who acted as the representative plaintiff for both the residential school survivors and the Assembly of First Nations (AFN). Despite successfully negotiating the IRSSA, adversarial proceedings continued as part of the Independent Assessment Process (IAP), a mechanism through which residential school survivors could apply for compensation above the minimum amount granted to all class action members. *Fontaine v. Canada* is, therefore, the name given to the files produced as a result of these proceedings.

Three sets of files are central to this chapter. The first was subject to Justice Perell's destruction order at the request of the AFN, Independent Counsel for the IAP Claimants, and the Catholic entities party to the IRSSA. The courts ruled that the files at issue in the case were highly confidential and were meant to remain in the control of residential school survivors as part of the IRSSA. They are accessible only if the survivors provide their explicit, informed consent because they document the impact, type, and details of the violence experienced by those who volunteered to be a part of the process. Despite being part of what is described as a non-adversarial, highly confidential process, Canada's appeal of Justice Perell's destruction order made these files the subject of both media controversy and public, adversarial litigation—a process that generated its own set of files that ended up digitized and available online.

The second set of files comprise the court records of both sets of proceedings. These are subject to the open court principle, making them accessible to the public. To obtain some of them, I travelled to the Ontario Court of Appeal registry in Toronto, where I located a range of different documents and correspondence outlining the arguments of the parties, testimony, and the exhibits introduced into evidence with respect to the third set of files.

The third set of files was not directly the subject of Justice Perell's destruction order or the Supreme Court of Canada's 2017 decision; however, they put into question the reach of the destruction order and whether documents produced in civil proceedings pertaining to residential schools could be subject to it (*Fontaine* 2018 paras. 185–88). These are referred to as the "Cochrane files" named after the town in which civil proceedings were held against Canada and the Catholic Church for the abuses at St. Anne's residential school prior to the IRSSA negotiations. They include Ontario Provincial Police (OPP) records that were part of both the civil proceedings against Canada and criminal proceedings against the staff. The lawyer acting on behalf of St. Anne's survivors requested these files to support them in their IAP hearings.

The proceedings under consideration in this chapter do two things. First, the IRSSA and judicial interpretations of its contents and authority establish various limits on issues of public and private law, property, access, publication, reproduction rights, and classification protocols that are central to the debates surrounding digital technology. The second thing that these proceedings make clear is the agency of residential school survivors to both refuse and to force the reinvention of the limits set out by settler-colonial law.

Throughout the proceedings, the IRSSA is identified as a contract that creates new rules and new institutions. Therefore, the file that sets the limits also brings forth the files at issue in the case and some of the institutions that lay claim to them. Conversely, those same files are used by survivors to force specific interpretations of the IRSSA, thereby generating new files in the form of orders and decisions that both enforce, recreate, and extend the limits of the agreement to different regulatory regimes outlined in various kinds of legislation. The files that both create and are the subjects of these proceedings therefore point to the intersections of memory, history, digitization, survivor agency, and state power that were left out of the TRC's 2015 report and they reinforce the mutually constitutive relationship between the material and the symbolic in law's digital archive.

The Destruction Order

The IAP hearings were meant to be inquisitorial and non-adversarial: they were closed to the public and presided over by specially trained adjudicators who were expected to conduct them in ways that were respectful to claimants and that provided an environment conducive to hearing a full description of their experience. Counsel for Canada and perpetrators were not permitted to cross-examine claimants. The proceedings were all transcribed in the event of the need for re-hearing and to facilitate report writing. The transcriptions of the adjudicators' decisions were all redacted to remove the names of perpetrators. Only claimants were entitled to have copies of their transcripts; however, if they consented to it, their testimonies and the adjudicators' decisions could be preserved and memorialized (*Fontaine* 2016 ONCA paras. 8 and 48).

There is no explicit protocol in the IRSSA outlining what was to become of the supporting documents that were produced as evidence after the hearings concluded. As a result, two requests for direction were brought to the Ontario Superior Court of Justice. In the first, the Chief Adjudicator, Independent Counsel for the Survivors, the AFN, the Catholic entities party to the IRSSA, and the Sisters of St. Joseph who owned and operated St. Joseph's residential school all sought the destruction order. The TRC, the National Centre for Truth and Reconciliation (NCTR), and the government of Canada all requested that the IAP documents be archived at Library and Archives Canada with redacted copies of the IAP hearings also archived at the NCTR (*Fontaine* 2014 ONSC 4585 paras. 93 and 94). In the second, the parties requested an order that would establish a notice program to inform claimants of the option to archive their documents, but each had different stipulations regarding who needed to consent and who would administer the program.

In response, Justice Perell issued a destruction order for the documents after a fifteen-year retention period, during which time the survivors could decide whether they wanted their documents preserved. He also elaborated on the terms of the notification program that would instruct survivors on how to opt in to archiving their documents. At the time of the hearing, the TRC had gathered approximately 6,200 oral statements; by contrast, 37,847 people had submitted applications through the IAP. Of the 7,000 IAP claimants who had chosen to volunteer their testimony to the TRC, 40 percent wished to anonymize it (*Fontaine* 2014 ONSC 4585 paras. 207, 208, and 244).

The Attorney General of Canada, the TRC, and the NCTR cross-appealed Justice Perell's directions, thereby turning the files produced through an inquisitorial and private process into the subjects of public, adversarial litigation—the results of which are digitally archived and publicly available. In the 2016 Ontario Court of Appeal ruling, Chief Justice Strathy articulated that prior to 2012, it was considered "common practice for adjudicators to give assurances to claimants and alleged perpetrators that their testimony would be kept confidential to the people in the hearing room" (para. 49). When it became apparent that the government of Canada and the TRC's requests for the documents would be before the courts, the Chief Adjudicator issued a direction to all adjudicators requesting that they not "give iron clad assurances of confidentiality" but instead advise claimants and the other participants in the hearings that the information would be handled securely and only be seen by those who needed to see it (*Fontaine* 2016 ONCA para. 49), thereby breaking the first in the long line of broken promises that shape both these proceedings and those surrounding the Cochrane files.

Both the TRC and the Attorney General of Canada argued that the IAP documents were under government control and thereby ought to be archived as part of the memorial function of the TRC, an argument that, if upheld in court, would have breached the confidentiality promised to survivors. The government of Canada made an additional series of arguments that also reproduced the originary violence of residential schooling by casting doubt on the credibility of survivors. They argued that the documents ought to be preserved in order to ensure "public confidence in the integrity of the IAP," "transparency in the use of public funds" (*Fontaine* 2016 ONCA para. 219), and to "protect itself from re-litigation of released claims" (*Fontaine* 2014 ONSC 4585 para. 237). Finally, in an additional cross-appeal, the Catholic entities who were party to the IRSSA were supported by Independent Counsel for the survivors in their attempt to argue that the survivors should not be the only ones to decide whether to archive their documents, an argument that would have, if upheld in the courts, granted perpetrators a veto over the survivors' choices, a position further complicated by the fact that some of the perpetrators are also survivors themselves.

The submissions of the AFN and the Chief Adjudicator both supported the destruction order. They argued that the personal accounts of abuse belong to the survivors alone and if their documents are to be archived, a notice plan that would ensure their free, prior, and informed consent would have to be put into place. At the Ontario Court of Appeal, Chief Justice Strathy, writing for himself and Justice MacFarland, upheld the destruction order, the retention period, and the notice plan, thereby granting residential school survivors' control over their documents. Nevertheless, in a dissenting opinion, Justice Sharpe instead followed Canada's submissions, concluding that the documents were public records subject to public law and that they thus ought to be archived.

Despite disagreements in the outcome, all the appellate court judges unanimously dismissed the Catholic entities' cross-appeal. In October 2017, the Supreme Court of Canada dismissed Canada's arguments and upheld Chief Justice Strathy's ruling. Turning their attention to the survivors who had died prior to the ruling, the Supreme Court of Canada articulated that despite the possibility that the order would be inconsistent "with the wishes of deceased claimants who were never given the option to preserve their records...the destruction of records that some claimants would have preferred to have preserved works a lesser injustice than the disclosure of records that most expected never to be shared" (*Canada* para. 62).

The court's stated desire to "work a lesser injustice" in their final ruling, however, did not take into account the structural violence inherent in the movement of the IRSSA between public, private, and treaty domains that required the ruling in the first place. In its role as adversary to the survivors, Canada, with the support of the TRC and Justice Sharpe, attempted to legally sanction a breach of contract to justify the expenditure of public resources and preserve public memory. In order to prevent a total breach of contract by giving the survivors control over their own documents, and preserving some vestige of the confidentiality they had originally been promised, in the end, the IRSSA simultaneously became analogous to a private, commercial contract and a treaty. The result of this was the reduction of redress to the corporate form where the IRSSA became a distinct legal entity that is separate from its creators, beneficiaries, and signatories, and it exists in perpetuity. As such, the IRSSA as a commercial contract absolves those party to it through limited liability where personal responsibility becomes deferent to the terms of the contract simultaneous to the removal of government control over the documents. In creating a commercial contract out of the IRSSA while also invoking treaty relationships, the honour of the Crown, a legal principle that requires the federal government of Canada to act with honour, integrity, good faith, and fairness in its dealings with Indigenous Peoples, became a vehicle through which the courts could presume Canada's integrity and legitimacy at the same time as providing the survivors with a means to challenge both.

The Contract and the Exception: Both Public and Private

Justice Perell's destruction order both unselfconsciously records the existence of files describing detailed memories of the crimes of individuals, church, and state at the same time as it leads to their eventual destruction if the survivors either choose to have their records destroyed or are unaware of the option to preserve and archive them. Despite the public outcry and the divisions among survivors that the order generated, this process neither preserved nor destroyed memory; instead, it reconstituted it through a series of administrative acts. The complexity of this process becomes most apparent through the disagreements between the judges about whether to apply public law, private law, or both, beginning with Canada's challenge to the TRC's standing to request directions from the courts. Tracing the movement of the IRSSA between public, private, and treaty, the digital record of this tangled set of proceedings reveals how rules can be generated by the courts through the production of an exception that is brought into public memory by the wishes and challenges of survivors, who acted as the primary claimants.

Despite Canada and the TRC sharing an interest in archiving the IAP documents, Canada submitted a separate request for direction, asking the Ontario Superior Court to strike out the TRC's previous request on the grounds that it did not have the standing or legal capacity to ask the courts for an interpretation of the IRSSA (*Fontaine* 2013 para. 2). Justice Goudge concluded that the TRC did not lack standing, and in doing so, he situated the IRSSA somewhere between public and private law.[1] In contrast to Justice Goudge's simultaneous application of public and private law, Chief Justice Strathy instead relied primarily on precedents that were the result of private commercial litigation (*Fontaine* 2016 ONCA para. 96). He concluded that Justice Perell's decision should stand (*Fontaine* 2016 ONCA paras. 84–89) and that "there will be no future cases like this one" (*Fontaine* 2016 ONCA para. 96). This conclusion led Justice Sharpe to question Justice Strathy's reasoning and his choice of standards of review in a case that involved the expenditure of public resources and that would impact the production and preservation of public memory.

In his dissent, Justice Sharpe instead supported Canada's argument, concluding that the IAP documents were government records. For him, Chief Justice Strathy had made a mistake by using the court's authority to limit the use of documents to the purposes for which they were produced (*Fontaine* 2016 ONCA para. 317): that is, in civil litigation, courts are generally bound by a rule that they are "not to use...documents...for any purpose other than securing justice in the civil proceedings in which [they] were compelled," irrespective of whether they contain incriminating or confidential information (*Fontaine* 2016 ONCA para. 275). This is generally referred to as the "implied undertaking rule." Justice Sharpe took issue with Strathy's decision to rely on *Andersen Consulting* to extend this rule to the IAP documents as *Andersen* is a piece of private commercial litigation that Justice Sharpe deemed to be inappropriately applied to what he considered a question of public law.

The *Andersen* Court answered the question of whether the government could retain control of documents containing "a great deal of sensitive commercial information which should not be made available to [a company's] competitors" (*Andersen* para. 3). The Federal Court decided that the documents were subject to the rule that they not be used in any other context as they were compelled prior to being in the government's possession, thereby negating government control. Chief Justice Strathy decided that because the IAP files were obtained and created through a court-controlled process, they could only be used in that context: once it "had run its course the documents had to be returned [to the survivors] or destroyed" (*Fontaine* 2016 ONCA para. 196).

In contrast, Justice Sharpe was unequivocal that the IRSSA fell squarely within the ambit of public law and that the case before them was "radically different than the decision of an arbitrator resolving a dispute between two private commercial entities" (*Fontaine* 2016 ONCA para. 293). Describing it as "a contract with an overwhelmingly public law flavour" (*Fontaine* 2016 ONCA para. 294), he concluded that the IRSSA

> is an agreement that bound the government of Canada to establish one of the most important public inquiries in Canadian history and to spend over two billion dollars of public funds...The agreement relates to a pressing issue of public policy and the righting of a dreadful historical wrong. (*Fontaine* 2016 ONCA paras. 292 and 294)

Despite the role of private commercial litigation in upholding the destruction order at the Court of Appeal and in keeping with Justice Sharpe's account of the "public law flavour" of the agreement, Justice Perell had originally chosen to follow the Chief Adjudicator's submission that the IRSSA, while not a treaty, is "at least as important as a treaty." As such, the interpretation of the agreement ought to be consistent with the honour of the Crown (*Canada* para. 14; *Fontaine* 2014 ONSC 4585 para. 88).

As a legal principle, the honour of the Crown has been derided as not being of much help "in resolving specific issues about specific rights" (*Lefthand* para. 75), as "the alchemical conjuring of state sovereignty" (Borrows 537–96), and as a concept that transforms Canada into a "benevolent patriarch" charged with the role of "protecting the Indians [from] greedy settlers and racist provincial governments" (Valverde 967). The courts generally interpret this legal principle to mean that "the Crown must act with honour and integrity, avoiding the appearance of sharp dealing" in negotiations with Indigenous Peoples (*Haida Nation* para. 19). In Justice Perell's formulation, the IRSSA becomes comparable to agreements that have accrued constitutional status through section 25 of the *Charter* and section 35 of the *Constitution Act*, leading him to conclude that given the choice between "an honourable interpretation and a dishonourable interpretation...it would be wrong to interpret the IRSSA in a way that dishonours Canada" (*Canada* para. 14; *Fontaine* 2014 ONSC 4585 para. 88).

Like the movement of the IAP proceedings from private to public through the process of appeal, in Justice Perell's directions, the IRSSA moves from the confines of contract and private commercial law into the realm of public, constitutional law through being understood as a treaty. Each judge's choice to apply private or public, or both private and public law dramatically changed the result. In the end, the decision to collapse public into private reduces redress to the corporate form by relying on private, commercial litigation to create a contract that exists in perpetuity out of the IRSSA, yet such a judgment simultaneously grants Canada limited liability for its responsibility in what the House of Commons later unanimously voted to name genocide by retaining pretenses to reconciliation and a concern with state accountability through the invocation of treaty and the honour of the Crown.[2] Through this process, regardless of whether the survivors choose to archive their stories, they remain in the national imaginary as present absences documented in digitally available public records. Nevertheless, while the IRSSA, the proceedings, and the transmuted memories of the survivors who testified in the IAP hearings may be simultaneously public and private, the IAP documents themselves, as explained in what follows, are neither public nor private.

"I Make *In Rem*—Against the World—the Following Order": Neither Public nor Private

Justice Perell invoked the ability to control the files *in rem* to issue his destruction order (*Fontaine* 2014 ONSC 4585 paras. 17 and 19). *In rem* is Latin for "against a thing." These rights are proprietary rights that not only implicate the survivors in the sense that they are enforceable against them if a suit is brought to determine that they are not the rightful owners of their own documents, but the rights are also enforceable against the rest of the world, including all parties and non-parties to the IRSSA. In this formulation, both parties to the IRSSA and non-parties can bring an action against survivors for the control of their documents, placing the documents in a liminal space that is neither public nor private (*Fontaine* 2014 ONSC 4585, para. 338).

At the Ontario Court of Appeal, Chief Justice Strathy made it clear that the IAP was never a federal government program (*Fontaine* 2016 ONCA para. 168). He elaborated that despite Canada's status as a defendant in the class action, it was the only entity with the administrative and fiscal infrastructure to carry it out. For this reason, it was vital to all parties to the IRSSA that "the court and not Canada be in control of the process" to "ensure that the defendant, *qua* administrator, [was] not able to manipulate the administration of the settlement for its purposes" (*Fontaine* 2016 ONCA paras. 161 and 170). He thereby rejected the outcomes of two access-to-information rulings. The first concluded that a government institution can control a record irrespective of whether it is in physical possession of it if "a senior official of the government institution...should be able to obtain a copy of the record" (*Fontaine* 2016 ONCA para. 160). The second concluded that irrespective of the confidentiality agreements outlined in contracts, they may still be under government control as "the *Access to Information Act...* applies to any record or information in a record which happens to be within the custody of the government regardless of the means by which that custody was obtained" (*Fontaine* 2016 ONCA para. 161).

Instead, Justice Strathy concluded that the IRSSA gives control to the IAP claimants and their documents inhabit a liminal space between public and private, where they are governed by neither sphere's legal conventions (*Fontaine* 2016 ONCA para. 188). As such, the documents are controlled by the survivors under the supervision of the courts because the IRSSA took "the preservation of the history of residential schools out of the hands of Canada, which bore responsibility for [them], and [put it] into the hands of the survivors under the oversight of an independent body" (*Fontaine* 2016 ONCA para. 229).

As a result, through the agency of survivors, without whom none of these files would exist, the judges in these cases are prompted to reconsider how the IRSSA is implemented and interpreted. In the next set of proceedings under consideration in this chapter, the requests for direction made by and on behalf of survivors draw out the structural divisions in the pre-existing law that delimit the possible discourse around what should be done with their records while they simultaneously challenge the legitimacy of the state, the honour of the Crown, and the legal system in the process.

DIGITAL MEMORY MAKERS:
DAMNING, TOXIC, AND SCANDALOUS ALLEGATIONS

In his order, Justice Perell identified the "collective purpose" of the IRSSA as one that addressed "the fact that the Indian residential school system was a systemic violation of human rights that had significant impact on the collective rights of Aboriginal peoples" and as such, "went against the goal of achieving privacy and confidentiality for individual Claimants and for Defendants" (*Fontaine* 2014 ONSC 4585 para. 143). This contradiction not only shaped the disagreements outlined in the proceedings discussed earlier but also draws into question the honour of the Crown. Canada's failure to disclose the Cochrane documents and make truthful reports, in addition to characterizations of its conduct in court as less than honourable, are the subjects of the second set of the *Fontaine* proceedings that I will discuss in greater detail here.

The IAP was originally supposed to privilege oral testimony over documentary evidence in addition to prohibiting cross-examination of the claimants. Justice Perell described it as a process intended to be respectful and conducive to hearing the experiences of survivors (*Fontaine* 2015 para. 71). In a dramatic contradiction to these earlier acknowledgements (*Fontaine* 2014 ONSC paras. 64 and 67), in both the proceedings concerning lawyer Fay Brunning's alleged misconduct and those surrounding the disclosure and production of OPP files that precipitated it, Justice Perell describes "the IAP's search for truth" as one that is in service of adjudication, "not for the purposes of reconciliation" (*Fontaine* 2015 para. 69).

In this formulation, like its documentary record, the IAP itself moves from a private, inquisitorial process into a public, adversarial one (*Fontaine* 2015 para. 3). The complexity of implementing the IRSSA, combined with ongoing court proceedings and the challenges that arise from what Justice Perell referred to as Canada's multifarious and conflicting roles as administrator, funder, and adversary to the survivors, have thereby resulted in misunderstandings and what Justice Perell acknowledged as "ongoing acrimony and bitterness" (*Fontaine* 2017 ONSC para. 5). All of this shapes the outcomes and escalation in the requests for direction concerning the disclosure of the OPP files and requests for re-hearings of St. Anne's IAP claims.

Brunning has been representing St. Anne's IRS survivors since 2012. St. Anne's IRS was an institution whose staff were among the perpetrators who had committed some of the most egregious forms of violence against students (*Fontaine* 2018 para. 14). Brunning successfully obtained re-hearings for a number of IAP claimants as well as court orders requiring Canada to disclose OPP files in support of IAP claimants who had been forced to attend the school. These proceedings, however, culminated in a series of allegations against Brunning and the survivors that reproduce settler-colonial law's originary violence at the same time as they record it in a digital archive. In January of 2018, Justice Perell released a case management direction admonishing Brunning for what he and the Crown variously referred to as "damning," "scandalous," "toxic," and "discredited" allegations that "slandered the court" (*Fontaine* 2017 Factum of the Respondent para. 5), a violent conclusion to an almost thirty-year battle for some kind of redress for the survivors of St. Anne's.

Between 1902 and 1976, First Nations children from Winisk/ Peawanuck, Attawapiskat, Fort Albany, Moose Factory, and Moosonee were removed from their homes and forced to attend St. Anne's residential school. In 1992, the Keykaywin Conference took place in Fort Albany, providing survivors a forum to disclose what had happened to them during their time at the school. There, they began the process of seeking redress for the extensive abuse they had been made to suffer. In the context of what had been disclosed as part of later IAP hearings, Justice Perell described their stories as "horrific" (*Fontaine* 2018 para. 22). This school was both funded by the federal government of Canada and run by Canada directly from 1970 to 1976 (*Fontaine* 2018 paras. 12 and 14). Between 1992 and 1997, the OPP took witness statements from hundreds of survivors and gathered the necessary documentation to initiate criminal proceedings. Ontario's Ministry of the Attorney General brought criminal prosecutions forward in Cochrane, Ontario, where charges were laid against teachers, staff, and supervisors (*Fontaine* 2018 para. 18); other perpetrators died before their trials (*Fontaine* 2017 ONSC paras. 23–26). In 2000, 154 students brought civil proceedings against Canada and the Catholic Church entities. As part of the Cochrane civil proceedings, Canada filed a motion to obtain the OPP records to proceed to trial. That same year, the OPP was ordered to release the documents to Canada (*Fontaine* 2017 ONSC paras. 27–32) in order for the state to construct its response. These OPP documents contain such deeply incriminating evidence that the Canadian government spent $3.2 million between 2013 and 2020 fighting the survivors of St. Anne's, only to be forced to produce what have been described as the "heavily redacted" documents that were in its possession (Johnson).

The same year that Justice Perell issued the destruction order for the IAP documents, he also provided a production order in a request for direction concerning Canada's failure to disclose the files that it had obtained as part of both the civil and criminal proceedings against it, the Catholic Church entities, and the staff at St. Anne's as part of the Cochrane proceedings (*Fontaine* 2014 ONSC 283). The following year, he heard another request for direction concerning Canada's failure to disclose an assault that took place in a girl's dormitory at Bishop Horden Residential School that resulted in criminal charges leading to the dismissal and the replacement of the supervisors at the school (*Fontaine* 2015). Canada's obligations under the IRSSA include the requirement that it produce documentation pertaining to students and staff, and any allegations of sexual or physical abuse that were made against staff, and all documents mentioning sexual and physical abuse that had taken place at the school (*Fontaine* 2017 ONSC 2487 para. 60). Failure to disclose is considered to be a breach of the IRSSA and thereby a breach of contract.

In the first case, Justice Perell outlined that the IRSSA grants the court jurisdiction to order Canada to produce any court and police records that it has in its control to facilitate the process. He elaborated that if the records in Canada's control would facilitate IAP hearings, using its discretion, the court could ignore the rule that documents compelled and produced in one case cannot be used in different cases

(*Fontaine* 2014 ONSC 283 para. 12). As a result, he ordered Canada to produce the over 12,000 documents that were in its possession. In the second case, the claimants drew attention to the incomplete narrative that Canada had produced, omitting the assault at Bishop Horden Residential School and the criminal proceedings that followed. Again, Justice Perell found Canada to be in breach of contract and compelled the state to conduct additional searches with the RCMP to locate documents relevant to the assault (*Fontaine* 2015 para. 80). Following each order, Canada produced the documents at issue. Despite the OPP being a non-party to the IRSSA, Justice Perell ordered the police to produce the documents that were not also part of the collection that the government had in its possession, subject to review by the court's lawyer, who would assess whether any of them were privileged or otherwise immune from production (*Fontaine* 2014 ONSC 283 para. 241).

Until this point, Brunning, a sole practitioner with a part-time legal assistant and limited resources who had been working almost exclusively for St. Anne's survivors for the five years prior, had successfully secured the Cochrane trial transcripts and OPP documents and obtained orders for Canada to conduct additional investigations and produce a more accurate narrative of St. Anne's residential school. She had also successfully reopened IAP hearings, securing compensation for IAP claimants who had previously been denied. Less than a year before, she was given an additional 8,000 pages of discovery, relevant information that her opponents are required to produce pre-trial, and filed more requests for direction in support of other IAP claimants who had come to her seeking the reopening of their claims. She eventually secured assistance from members of another law firm, but the events leading up to the appellate court decision in her appeal to access discovery transcripts in the cases preceding the IRSSA reveal yet another level of structural violence, further drawing both the honour of the Crown and the IAP process itself into question.

In December of 2017, Justice Perell heard an additional set of requests for direction from IAP Claimant C-14114 and Angela Shisheesh. In their written submissions, they both contended that Canada's legal positions constituted "an abuse of process and a breach of the Department of Justice's (DOJ) professional obligations" (*Fontaine* 2018 para. 10). They also submitted that "the courts of Ontario and British Columbia are biased toward Canada and not doing their job in enforcing the IRSSA" (*Fontaine* 2018 para. 10). Addressing what he referred to as "these damning allegations" (*Fontaine* 2018 para. 11) in his ruling, Justice Perell dismissed all but one of the requests (*Fontaine* 2018 para. 9).

Claimant C-14114 requested the reopening of her IAP application, orders directing the operation of the IAP, and an order "compelling Canada to make 'admissions'" about what the school staff had done and, in her case—a case of student-on-student abuse—its role in creating the conditions and environment for this abuse (*Fontaine* 2018 para. 190). Similarly, Angela Shisheesh was seeking compensation with respect to the IAP and against a law firm that had represented her prior to the implementation of the IRSSA. She questioned the firm's legal competence, as they had not advised her to wait for the outcome of the settlement negotiations because, despite being eligible for the common experience payment under the IRSSA, she was not eligible to make an IAP claim as she had already been compensated in the context of the Cochrane civil actions against St. Anne's (*Fontaine* 2018 paras. 29–32). She also asked if the destruction order, retention period, and option to archive IAP documents extended to the Cochrane and other civil action files.

Justice Perell dismissed all of Claimant C-14114's requests, paying particular attention to the request for admissions that he defined as statements "acknowledging the truth about something" (*Fontaine* 2018 para. 199). In Justice Perell's assessment, as "voluntary acts of free will," admissions could not be compelled, coerced, or made compulsory, nor could they be mandated by a judge (*Fontaine* 2018 para. 199). This led him not only to conclude that the evidence showed that Canada had kept its promise to make admissions as part of an unenforceable obligation or "agreement to agree" (*Fontaine* 2018 para. 200), but also to characterize Claimant C-14114's interpretation of the word "admissions" as one that was "incongruous, self-contradictory [and] oxymoronic" (*Fontaine* 2018 para. 199). He also dismissed all but one of Angela

Shisheesh's requests on the grounds that the court had no jurisdiction to decide on those matters. With respect to her third request regarding the destruction order, he required her to begin again and to produce a freshly amended request for direction that focused exclusively on that question (*Fontaine* 2018 para. 9).

The repeated failures to reopen IAP hearings and Justice Perell's order against disclosing the discovery documents in the pre-IRSSA cases led Brunning to send a series of emails describing both Claimant C-14114's and Angela Shisheesh's characterizations of Canada's legal position. These emails drew the honour of the Crown into question and articulated that the court was biased in favour of the Crown. Despite Justice Perell's admonition of the second claim as one that discredits the court, he himself had articulated four years earlier that given a choice between "an honourable interpretation and a dishonourable interpretation...it would be wrong to interpret the IRSSA in a way that dishonours Canada" (*Canada* para. 14; *Fontaine* 2014 ONSC 4585 para. 88). In keeping with Justice Perell's earlier statement, Brunning wrote:

> While the Courts presumes [*sic*] the Government is always being truthful, and the Court does not require evidence from Canada, this Claimant and myself did not make up these facts. It took a lot of courage for this very vulnerable and suffering survivor, to go to the Court, and the Court neglected to enforce its own orders against Canada for her re-hearing. (*Fontaine* 2018 para. 27)

In her factum outlining the arguments that she made on behalf of this survivor and one other claimant who was also seeking redress from the court because of their treatment throughout the IAP, she wrote:

> IRSSA class member/IAP claimant C-14114 reserves her objection that the Government of Canada ("Crown"), being only [sic] other "party" participating in IAP

Claim C-14114, is being given preferential treatment by
the Superior Courts...St. Anne's IRSSA class members
have already proven concealment of documents by
the Crown and failure to make truthful reports, which
have proceeded before the Ontario IRSSA Judge since
September 2013. (*Fontaine* 2018 para. 12)

In January of 2018, Justice Perell responded with a case management direction admonishing Brunning for the "scandalous," "toxic,"
and "discredited" allegations that both he and the Crown concluded
had "slandered the court" (*Fontaine* 2017 Factum of the Respondent
para. 5). Brunning later filed a recusal motion against Justice Perell for
reasonable apprehension of bias.[3] He did not recuse himself. Instead,
Canada sought costs against Brunning for the recusal motion, and in
January of 2019, Justice Perell ordered her to personally pay Canada
$28,911.04. This series of decisions underscore the conclusions of Edwin
Metatawabin—former chief of Fort Albany First Nation, one of the organizers of the Keykaywin Conference, and a St. Anne's survivor—that
Justice Perell's orders may have sent a "chill to other survivors and
lawyers" whose claims were still in process (Barerra n.p.). They also
show the tenacity and resilience of survivors who refuse to acquiesce
in the face of the Canadian state's ongoing and ruthless attempts at
concealing records essential to their claims against it.

CONCLUSION

As lawyer Patricia Barkaskas has articulated, many Canadians assume
that the IRSSA and the IAP were part of a good and worthy process
designed to address the truth of past and ongoing settler-colonial
violence; that they provided ways to seek pathways to justice and healing
for Indigenous Peoples and communities. In keeping with her experiences with these mechanisms for redress, however, this chapter tells
a story of broken promises, settler-colonial law's violence, Canada's

concealment of documents and its failure to tell the truth in its role as adversary (see Barkaskas and Hunt).

This is not the only story recorded in these fragments of the *Fontaine* proceedings. While the memory of law's founding violence moves from presence to representation through abstraction in the files that record it, this is not part of what Jacques Derrida might refer to as an "amnesiac loss of consciousness" about its own origins ("Force of Law" 55). The legal proceedings that were generated and called upon as a result of Justice Perell's destruction order may not have accrued what the courts deem to be "precedential value," but these hearings and court proceedings create as much as they preserve memory through the agential acts of survivors that are transmuted into both physical and digital files. They illustrate the simultaneously symbolic and material force of law's digital archive to facilitate state incursions into the private and personal lives of survivors at the same time as they demand accountability and restitution for the crimes of both church and state; yet they neither permit government control nor signify the democratization of the archive and they in no way signal an end to settler-colonial law's originary violence. As digital memory agents, survivors of both residential schools and these legal proceedings, no matter their wins or losses, have created a digital record of resistance, resilience, and refusal in the face of the Canadian state's necropolitical regimes of colonial power.

NOTES

1. See *Fontaine* 2013 per Justice Sharpe at paras 34 and 56: "[The] Settlement Agreement...is not a commercial agreement that arose after a short sharp negotiating session between two corporate entities...I am not sure the Settlement Agreement can be said to be simply a private contract...There are arguably aspects of the Settlement Agreement that seek to structure the relationship between Canada and Aboriginal People...the TRC itself...is established by an Order-in-Council which sets out its mandate. These two considerations raise the possibility that the Settlement Agreement can be viewed through the lens of public law as well as private law."

2. See House of Commons Debate 8970 and 8981.
3. The reasonable apprehension of bias is distinct from a finding of actual bias in law, as the threshold for its determination is lower. To establish a reasonable apprehension of bias, the threshold question is whether a reasonable person with full knowledge of the circumstances of the case and the role that judges swear to uphold would perceive the judge's actions/statements/rulings to be biased in some way or in favour of one party over the others.

WORKS CITED

Ball, Kirstie, and Laureen Snider, eds. *The Surveillance Industrial Complex: A Political Economy of Surveillance.* Routledge, 2013.

Barkaskas, Patricia, and Sarah Hunt. "Truth Before Reconciliation: Reframing/Resisting/Refusing Reconciliation." *YouTube*, Institute for the Humanities, Simon Fraser University, 10 March 2017, https://www.youtube.com/watch?v=mB_7odACIpI. Accessed 17 March 2024.

Barrera, Jorge. "Judge Says Lawyer 'Slandered Court' for Favouring Canada in St. Anne's Case." *CBC News*, 16 January 2018, https://www.cbc.ca/news/indigenous/judge-st-anne-s-residential-school-lawyer-reprimand-1.4490498. Accessed 6 May 2021.

Borrows, John. "Sovereignty's Alchemy: An Analysis of Delgamuukw v. British Columbia." *Osgoode Hall Law Journal*, vol. 37, no. 3, 1999, pp. 537–96.

Cosgrove, Lisa, et al. "Digital Phenotyping and Digital Psychotropic Drugs: Mental Health Surveillance Tools that Threaten Human Rights." *Health Human Rights*, vol. 22, no. 2, 2020, pp. 33–39.

Deleuze, Gilles. "Postscript on the Societies of Control." *October*, vol. 59, Winter 1992, pp. 3–7.

Derrida, Jacques. "Force of Law: The 'Mystical Foundations of Authority.'" *Deconstruction and the Possibility of Justice*, edited by Drucilla Cornell et al., Routledge, 1992, pp. 3–67.

Graham, Stephen. "Spaces of Surveillant Simulation: New Technologies, Digital Representations, and Material Geographies." *Society and Space*, no. 16, 1998, pp. 483–504.

Hodes, Caroline. "The Case, The Registry and the Archive: Reflections on Truth, Reconciliation and Retrieval." *Settler Colonial Studies*, vol. 10, no. 2, 2020, pp. 149–75.

House of Commons Debate. Ms. Leah Gazan (Winnipeg Centre, NDP), 4th Parliament, 1st Session Official Hansard Report, vol. 151, no. 119, 27 October 2022, https://www.ourcommons.ca/Content/House/441/Debates/119/HAN119-E.PDF. Accessed 28 March 2024.

Johnson, Rhiannon. "Ottawa has Spent $3.2 M Fighting St. Anne's Residential School Survivors in Court Since 2013." *CBC News,* 20 November 2020, https://www.cbc.ca/news/indigenous/ottawa-st-anne-residential-school-court-costs-1.5809846. Accessed 6 May 2021.

Rheingold, Howard. "The Great Equalizer." *Whole Earth Review,* vol. 71, no. 6, 1991, pp. 95–104.

Schuler, Douglas. *Liberating Voices: A Pattern Language for Communication Revolution.* MIT Press, 2008.

Truth and Reconciliation Commission of Canada (TRC). *The Final Report of the Truth and Reconciliation Commission of Canada.* Truth and Reconciliation Commission of Canada, 2015.

Valverde, Mariana. "'The Honour of the Crown is at Stake': Aboriginal Land Claims Litigation and the Epistemology of Sovereignty." *UC Irvine Law Review,* vol. 1, no. 3, 2011, pp. 957–74.

Wemigwans, Jennifer. *A Digital Bundle: Protecting and Promoting Indigenous Knowledge Online.* University of Regina Press, 2018.

CASES

Andersen Consulting v. Canada, (2001) 2 FC 324.

Canada (Attorney General) v. Fontaine, (2017) SCC 47.

Fontaine v. Canada (Factum of the Respondent AG Canada in the matter of request for directions by IAP Claimant H-15019 pertaining to St. Anne's Residential School and in the matter of the request for directions by Edwin Metatawabin and by IAP Claimant K-10106, 26 October 2017).

Fontaine v. Canada, (2018) ONSC 103.

Fontaine v. Canada (Attorney General), (2017) ONSC 2487.

Fontaine v. Canada (Attorney General), (2016) ONCA 241.

Fontaine v. Canada (Attorney General), (2015) ONSC 3611.

Fontaine v. Canada, (2014) ONSC 4585.

Fontaine v. Canada (Attorney General), (2014), ONSC 283.

Fontaine v. Canada (Attorney General), (2013) ONSC 684.

Haida Nation v. BC (2004) SCC 73.

R. v. Lefthand (2007), ABCA 2016.

4

VIRTUAL MUSEUM TOURS

QUEER NOSTALGIC PASTS AND UTOPIC FUTURES IN CANADIAN NIGHTLIFE MEMORIES

BRAIDON SCHAUFERT

OLD ANTI-QUEER ARGUMENTS are currently finding new life in American state legislators. Florida House Bill 1557 bans discussion of sexual orientation and gender identity in elementary school under the banner of parental rights. In practice, so-called parental rights deny queer children respect and safety in navigating their queerness in an anti-queer country. In Texas, dozens of new pieces of legislation target trans children by banning trans-affirming practices like removing deadnames from birth certificates and by blocking access to sports and health care. Religious exemptions are part of this wave of legislation and threaten to legalize the denial of services to queer people on the basis of others' personal moral beliefs. Under this new anti-queer regime in Texas, health care providers and parents or guardians of trans children who provide trans-affirming care, medical or otherwise, can be punished by law as child abusers. The longstanding moral panic around children and gender fuels this new round of anti-queer bills.

Given the highly visible and public-facing role of drag performers, right-wing politicians and leaders put drag at the centre of this moral panic around queerness and children. Drag Queen Story Hour, a popular event in which drag queens read to young audiences in public libraries to bolster literacy and teach acceptance, have been made into political theatre by right-wing anti-queer forces framing these events as indoctrination. Specifically, these politicians, fringe conspiracy theorists, and conservative media figures have co-opted the word "groomer" from feminists describing the sexualization of girls within rape culture to now label all queer people as pedophiles. Story Hour is hardly a force for major cultural change, yet its opponents have staged it as a battle for the purity of a new generation. The visibility of drag performers make them a simplified and reductive metonym of queer cultural and political life at large. Protesting Drag Queen Story Hour means protesting the existence of queer people in public space and spaces that include children. These more spectacular protests are symptoms of legislative conversations behind closed doors in which the elimination of queer people from public space is considered and debated.

Florida's Bill 1557 and Texas's transphobic legislation do not exist in a vacuum and are products of a larger reactionary, conservative, and neofascist movement sweeping North America. Several American states have banned critical race theory in grade schools out of a concern that CRT blames white students for racial inequality. This misunderstanding of CRT is produced from purposeful historical forgetting. At the same time CRT is systematically banned in many states, the list of banned books centring Black and queer experiences grows larger. The Supreme Court's recent decision to overturn *Roe v. Wade* empowers Republican states to ban access to abortion, endangering the lives of women, trans men, and all people with a uterus. *Roe v. Wade*'s fate foreshadows threats to *Obergefell v. Hodges*, the Supreme Court decision that mandates all states to grant marriage licences to same-gender marriages, and *Loving v. Virginia*, the decision that deems unconstitutional any bans on interracial marriage. While legislative assaults rage in courtrooms, public information on monkeypox recycles AIDS stigma as it frames the infectious disease as a sexually transmitted infection spread among men who have sex with men. This context is the perfect storm for anti-queer sentiments in America that do not acknowledge the porous, fictional, and fabricated border between the United States and Canada.

It is within this context that I situate this chapter on queer cultural memory in digital spaces. Canadian anti-queer politicians like Jason Kenney and Andrew Scheer shape public opinion. So-called Freedom Convoys—right-wing protesters against COVID-19 precautions that became a terrorist insurgent movement—embolden sexist, homophobic, transphobic, and racist beliefs. Drag Queen Story Hours are protested across Canada, like in America, as a threat to children. These laws, protests, and reactionary movements are products of historical forgetting, which is why digital means of preserving memory are crucial in affirming the existence of queer people in time and place. The presentation and preservation of memory is not an easy task, and this chapter emphasizes the fraught and contested practice that is nonetheless integral to reckoning with historical violence. The digital museums preserving the queer history of Edmonton and Toronto I focus on in this chapter are nostalgic for places, drag performers, and musicians that once existed. Pulling these memories to the present preserves an important legacy; however, nostalgia can itself be reactionary. This chapter grapples with ambivalence of these digital museums in the face their necessary function.

QUEER MEDIA

In a January 2021 episode of the reality television series *RuPaul's Drag Race*, Tamisha Iman, a forty-nine-year-old drag queen from Atlanta, Georgia, tells her competitors that her drag daughter became famous when a recording of her performance went viral after being uploaded to YouTube in 2005. The other queens instantly recognize the video and its star when Tamisha explains that her daughter dressed as Wonder Woman and entered the stage by falling from the ceiling and landing in splits. With thirty years of experience doing drag, Tamisha's invaluable contributions to the art of drag include founding the Iman Dynasty and acting as house mother to seventy-five children (a third of whom are deceased). "Tandi is the one who made the lasting impression," Tamisha says about the YouTube video. "If you see my daughter, then guess what? You know what the art of drag is all about" ("Phenomenon"). Tandi Iman Dupree made that lasting impression in a five-minute performance to Bonnie Tyler's song "Holding out for a Hero" at the 2001 Miss Gay Black America Pageant. After her famous entrance, Tandi performs several more splits and dips (dance moves that have become synonymous with drag queen lip-synchs), and is closely synchronized with her dance partner Dee St. James, who is dressed as Superman to complement the superhero theme. Her performance is a stunning showcase of talent from start to end. The YouTube video of the pageant, titled "Best Drag Queen Entrance Ever," has 2 million views, 34,000 likes, and 2,500 comments. "If [Tandi] was still alive," Tamisha explains to RuPaul later in the episode, "she would be one of your girls because she was a phenomenal entertainer" ("Phenomenon"). Memories like this one of Tandi, preserved and accessed online, deserve consideration for their impacts on North American digital cultures, queer social movements, and the politics of memory.

Evidently, a successful and profitable show like *Drag Race* owes an unpayable debt to these performers at pageants and balls. Black drag queens like Tandi made impressions on the private memories of audiences, competitors, families, and friends, and rare performances have been recorded and made public in documentaries like *The Queen* and *Paris is Burning*. As "Best Drag Queen Entrance Ever" demonstrates, drag performance was a part of early internet virality at YouTube's inception and continues to casually circulate now on social media apps like Twitter, Instagram, and TikTok, which incorporate *Drag Race* into popular discourse as GIFs, memes, and gossip. The episode in question briefly showcases Tandi's entrance but does little to contextualize the performance by informing viewers of its original time, place, and purpose. Competitions like the Miss Gay Black America Pageant, in which both Tandi and Tamisha made careers, are organized around winning titles that recognize and validate competitors who experience structural homophobia and anti-Black racism. Queens lit by television lights, performing scripts, and exposed in high definition by close-up camera shots create standards of drag far removed from those of the live pageants and balls, even as *Drag Race* endlessly appropriates them, and the show's popularity often actually hinders entertainers not associated with RuPaul's commercialized drag family. Rather than using Tamisha's memory of Tandi to equate a drag queen's impact with the success of *Drag Race*, however, I want to draw focus to collective memory and discuss the historic contexts of drag performances in Canada.

In doing so, however, it remains important to note that *Canada's Drag Race* premiered in the summer of 2020 in an attempt to replicate the popularity of the American version. The spin-off features contestants, judges, and guest hosts exclusively from Canada and incorporates Canadian popular culture, stereotypes, and histories into familiar challenges. Around the emergence of *RuPaul's Drag Race* as a brand starting in 2012, Canadian television began raising the profile of its drag culture through episodes of *Outspoken Biography* (2015) and *Canada's a Drag* (2018). At the same time, digital archives created by activist-historians began collecting local stories and anecdotes for what have become official queer histories of Canada's urban centres. These histories trace the rise and fall of gay nightclubs as the social sites that made queerness public, defendable, and organized. *Edmonton City as Museum Project (ECAMP)* and *Then & Now: Toronto Nightlife History* are two such archives that exist as multimedia websites offering virtual exhibits on nightlife using historical facts and anecdotal stories. These two digital museums are notable for archiving histories of two cities that have recently been the setting of protests at Pride parades, with activists in both Toronto and Edmonton having protested Pride parades for permitting uniformed cops to march and for commercializing a ceremony that began as a riot. *ECAMP* and *Then & Now* offer potential historical anchors for the present struggles in these cities by creating knowledge on the contexts out of which they emerge. My aim is to identify and work against the neoliberal impulse latent in these online museums in order to locate other anchors that can produce more radical outcomes to these present struggles.

Activist-historians present these nightlife histories nostalgically as times when gay bars were lively, both in the sense that they were spaces of vitality and because they made social life possible for a population of queer people forced into secrecy. Nightlife factors heavily into queer histories because gay bars "provided places to meet friends and sexual partners, and shaped individual group identity" (Armstrong and Crage 728). These bars later declined in prominence as gay rights campaigns successfully integrated *some* gays and lesbians into larger publics and as digital technologies in the twenty-first century created new methods of connection away from the physical space of the club. Returning to the notion of nostalgia, Alexandra Juhasz defines the memory practice as "a kind of duration trouble in that one defiantly wants something to endure that cannot and has not" (322). Nostalgia is thus a productive memory form for queer theorists because of how it troubles linear time and creates community. For Nishant Shahani, it constantly makes and remakes community through its personal and public nature, and *ECAMP* and *Then & Now* in particular as nostalgic media "[enable] an affective rationality through the revival of shared cultural makers" (Shahani 1217). I seek to unpack how digital museums present their stories, the politics that they reinforce in the present, and what Lisa Lowe refers to as their "past conditional temporality" (175). Concerned that fixed, immobilized, and settled histories reinforce the present status quo of systemic oppression, Lowe argues that "it is possible to conceive the past, not as fixed or settled, not as inaugurating the temporality in which our present falls, but as a configuration of multiple contingent possibilities, all present, yet non-inevitable" (175). *ECAMP* and *Then & Now* offer opportunities to construct pasts for a better future rather than historical narratives that preserve this status quo.

DIGITAL NIGHTLIFE

Virtual Exhibits:
Edmonton City as Museum Project

Edmonton City as Museum Project is a website that collects stories from Edmontonians and curates them as virtual exhibits in an online museum. As an initiative of the Edmonton Heritage Council, *ECAMP* is publicly funded and invested in the city's marketable image. It "explores the history of our city through story. *The stories that connect us, the stories that divide us, and the stories that nurture an appreciation of our differences as Edmontonians*" ("About"). As part of its objective of "prioritizing histories that, in the past, have been excluded from representations of Edmonton's history" ("About"), *ECAMP*'s featured exhibits include "Women's Histories," "Indigenous Perspectives," Childhood Experiences," and "Edmonton's Italian Community." The exhibit "Queer Histories" consists of various articles retelling notable events pertaining to queer culture, including "History of Edmonton's Gay Bars: Part 1–Part 5," "The Imperial Sovereign Court of the Wild Rose," "The Pisces Bathhouse Raids," "Flashback and the Gay Drag Races," "Queers on Campus," and "Womonspace: Creating Space for Edmonton's Lesbian Community in the 1980s." These exhibits combine anecdotal writing with historiography in addition to incorporating photography. Various advertisements for the nightclub Flashback from the 1980s, for example, showcase employees, patrons, and drag queens together to reconstruct the nights of "Drag Races," "the Bimbolympics," and "Mr. and Mz. Flashback" in Michael Phair's piece. Longstanding activist and *ECAMP* contributor Ron Byers explains that "Queer Histories" is "an effort to capture some of our history before it gets lost forever" ("Q&A"). The fact that the city's queer population, which survived the AIDS epidemic in the 1980s and 1990s, is aging creates an urgency to write and preserve the stories of those decades. "Without a queer history," Byers asks in an interview, "how do our youth learn who we are as a community? How we were then and now will shape where we will be down the road" ("Q&A").

While this orientation toward the future establishes the stakes of the online museum, the vagueness of this statement weakens the project's potential to address present struggles and leaves me wondering what kind of future *ECAMP* imagines.

This lack of vision for the future and reluctance to take a stance on the present contrasts with the certainty and comprehension of the history that it presents. Historically, queers could only gather privately at house parties until Bill C-150 partially decriminalized homosexuality in Canada and made Edmonton's first gay bar, Club 70, legal. Ron Byers and Rob Browatzke open their "History of Edmonton's Gay Bars" with an account of this club after explaining that "same-sex relations have been a part of life on the expansive prairies since time immemorial" ("Part 1"). The physical space of a nightclub becomes a narrative device in these exhibits that makes queer history knowable. Club 70, for example, straddled the private and public spheres as a private social club exclusively for the protection of patrons willing to openly identify as gay or lesbian. By the mid-1970s, protectionist restrictions became too stifling for queer patrons looking to socialize beyond the private club members, and the first iteration of Flashback opened as a space for both queers and their allies ("Part 2"). Flashback—in its three different iterations, all in the Oliver neighbourhood—owes its success to challenging the Alberta Liquor Control Board and to advertising itself outside of private membership. Flashback would go on to form a symbiotic relationship with The Roost, a gay bar across the street in Oliver, as the two clubs—with Boots later joining them as a third bar—mapped out queer nightlife in the 1980s ("Flashback"). This map would eventually be integral to community work once the Edmonton police and the RCMP raided the Pisces Health Spa, after a tip that the bathhouse was operating as a brothel, and arrested several men before photographing them undressed. After this raid, the city's bars developed into spaces of collective action that would eventually evolve into the city's annual Pride festival ("The Pisces Bathhouse").

Virtual Exhibit:
Then & Now

Toronto journalist and disk jockey Denise Benson's *Then & Now: Toronto Nightlife History* began in 2011 as a written segment on different nightclubs in Toronto for the newspaper *The Grid*. After *The Grid*'s folding in 2014, Benson created the website *Then & Now* to archive those stories and expand on them through more interviews, photographs, and DJ sets. According to Benson, "the history of a city's nightlife reveals its pulse" ("Series"); therefore, each article focuses on one nightclub with Benson organizing the writing around five recurring headlines: "Years in operation," "History," "Why it was important," "Who else played/worked there?" and "What happened to it." Benson draws on her career as a journalist as well as her experiences as a lesbian DJ working at these clubs to write their histories. Like *ECAMP*, *Then & Now* incorporates photographs of the clubs, drag queens, and advertisements, all donated by former patrons and employees, and adds the audio element of playlists that DJs played, making the website "a rich multimedia experience that conveys a vivid sense of time and place" ("Series"). While each article focuses on the history of a single nightclub, other spaces weave through stories and are hyperlinked to other articles. For instance, a toggle menu organizes exhibits by tags that include musical genre, the decades from 1970 to 2010, and "gay" and "lesbian," creating a more flexible, variable space for users beyond a linear historical narrative.

Then & Now weaves together stories about Toronto nightlife to create a map of queer geographies and timelines in the city. Bars had been strictly organized by sexual identity until the gay disco, Club David's, opened in 1975 and advertised itself to all genders and sexualities as a "bisexual" space. Open to patrons sixteen and older, Club David's became a site for young and questioning members of the queer community until it burned down and its owner was murdered in 1978 ("Club David's"). Meanwhile, Stages, in contrast to Club David's, opened in 1975 to create a more sex-positive environment amid the atmosphere of violent homophobia in the city. Then, nightlife changed again as

Chez Moi opened as a lesbian bar in 1984, the first to advertise itself to queer women other than the "women's nights" of the other gay bars that otherwise defaulted to gay men ("Chez Moi"). Nightlife proliferated at this time around Queen's Park, a prominent cruising spot, as more bathhouses and bars opened to give gay men more options for social and sexual activity: Komrads, for instance, offered a dance floor and rallying spot for the gay liberation movement to react to "Operation Soap," the police raids of bathhouses in 1981. Later, bars segregated again during the AIDS epidemic in the 1980s and 1990s as HIV/AIDS stigma kept queer and straight patrons from sharing intimated spaces like dance floors ("Komrads"). In addition to tracing a historical and geographical narrative of Toronto's nightlife, Benson's stories feature drag entertainer and celebrity cameos, including Tina Turner impersonator Randy Cole, Club David's Miss Starlight Pageant, Vicki Sue, movie star Divine, drag troupe The Imposters, George Michael, Dee-Lite, and more. These virtual exhibits delineate the physical and geographical changes in the city from queer nightclubs on Yonge, Bloor, and Hayden to the edges of Queen's Park before solidifying Church and Wellesley as Toronto's gay village, where bars like Woody's and Crews & Tangos still operate. Benson also draws attention to the histories of musical genres played at clubs, often using "disco" as a synonym for queer dance spaces that would decline with the genre's overexposure before evolving into the new wave and house genres. Each article ends in an explanation of the bar's fate—usually, by the new millennium, their replacement with condos.

QUEER TIME AND MEMORY

Temporality is a central preoccupation within queer theory as a critique of homonormative timelines. While temporal homonormativity designates nightlife to the years before marriage and family, these emerging histories of discos, dancing, cruising, drugs, and excess disorganize time while reconceptualizing what counts as historical. For queer theorist Eve Kosofsky Sedgwick, queer refers to "the open mesh of possibilities, gaps, overlaps, dissonances and resonances, lapses and excesses of meaning when the constituent elements of anyone's gender or anyone's sexuality aren't made (or can't be made) to signify monolithically" (53). In general, queer temporality is a sense of time that unfolds in opposition to the linearity, productivity, and predictability of "straight time" (Pryor 10). In its attention to anti-normativity, queer time rejects, refuses, or fails the straight line of straight time since "queer and trans people have always been at the vanguard of radical ways of working, playing, fucking, organizing, educating, parenting, making home, making art, and creating ritual that defy normative patterns of clock, biological, and nuclear family time" (5). *ECAMP* and *Then & Now* emphasize queer temporalities in their activist-history work by focusing on nightclubs, late-night spaces, dance floors and musical genres, drag houses and performances troupes, as well as chosen families over nuclear. Historical attention to abandoned nightclubs, forgotten drag pageant winners, and DJs playing outdated music evokes a kind of "queer embrace" of "backwardness in many forms: in celebrations of perversions, in defiant refusals to grow up, in explorations of hauntings and memory, and in stubborn attachments to lost objects" (Love 7).

In the context of queer temporality and memory, nostalgia underwrites the narratives that activist-historians like Benson and Byers contribute to their respective digital museums. In Alexandra Juhasz's words, *ECAMP* and *Then & Now* are products of nostalgia's "duration trouble" by "defiantly [wanting]" the long-gone nightlife to "endure" in the present (322). Rather than duration trouble, Elizabeth Freeman uses "temporal drag" to name a kind of "*temporal* transitivity" (63, emphasis in original) in nostalgia that is associated with "retrogression, delay, and the pull of the past on the present" (62). Instead of emphasizing the "gender-transivity" most commonly associated with drag in the context of queer subcultures, temporal drag is "a *productive* obstacle to progress, a usefully distorting pull backward, and a necessary pressure on the present tense" (64, emphasis in original). Bringing Juhasz and Freeman into conversation, temporal drag is the work that nostalgia does in the realm of memory in that it drags the memory of a lost object to the present in an attempt to have that object endure. For Nishant Shahani, "nostalgia for an 'outmoded' history disrupts the linear and straight lines of progressive history. It offers queer collectives a way of reclaiming its otherness—of returning to intimacies of exile in the past, to recognize its continuities in the present, in order to ultimately imagine a more radically democratic future" (1228). The concurrent assimilation of gays and lesbians into normative society and the acceleration of internet technologies have created a discontinuity between a queer present and a queer past, one for which Shahani sees nostalgia as a possible remedy. Rather than "the swirling empty space of the present" (*Twilight Memories* 28), online museums can recreate the radical anti-normative queer consciousness of the past through remediation.

The remediation of nightlife memory on websites with comment sections in particular bridges private and collective memory. In *The Future of Nostalgia*, Svetlana Boym argues that "unlike melancholia, which confines itself to the planes of individual consciousness, nostalgia is about the relationship between individual biography and the biography of groups or nations, between personal and collective memory" (xvi). In the cases of *ECAMP* and *Then & Now*, the personal memories of activist-historians construct an accessible cultural memory of these clubs as refuges from homophobia, sites of both resistance and joy, and places of grief during the HIV/AIDS epidemic. The interactivity of these virtual exhibits through comment sections demonstrates how these online museums invite public forms of nostalgia. A commentator on *Then & Now*'s "Boots," for instance, remembers the club as "a noisy, smoky home away from home for many people" and says that "reading this article brought thoughts and faces back to mind that have been absent for far too long." Another commenter tells Benson that her article "is a beautiful blast from the past and a reminder of our friends who aren't here anymore." These are intimate memories tied directly to the nightclub spaces that fostered the sociality needed for political resistance against police brutality and other forms of discrimination. DJ Pamandon, for example, explains that "Komrads was the place to celebrate our political 'wins'...We celebrated and we had a political voice at Komrads"

("Komrads"). The closing of many bars like Komrads, often for condo development, suggests that places of resistance are no longer needed, in turn reinforcing the assimilatory politics of contemporary gay rights efforts. For Juhasz, "one generation's yearning could fuel another's learning, if we could look back together and foster an escape from melancholia through productive communal nostalgia" (Juhasz 323).

With respect to *ECAMP*, its inclusion of some YouTube videos from Edmonton's Flashback combines the audio and visuals of this space to produce even more potent forms of nostalgia. The "Queer Histories" exhibit on *ECAMP* links to two YouTube videos of the drag performance troupe Flashback Follies performing at the nightclub. Both videos were uploaded by MonaghanVideoEngine, and the first, "Flashback Gay Club Edmonton," depicts drag queen Mrs. K performing on New Years' Eve in 1983 to Dolly Parton's "A Lil Ole Bitty Pissant Country Place" from the film adaptation *The Best Little Whorehouse in Texas* (1982). The selection of a song from a musical about a brothel in the United States' conservative southern region is a crude, campy reference to Alberta's own political climate of religious conservativism that is deeply entrenched in the colonial imagination of the settled west. Mrs. K lip-synchs while dressed and styled after Dolly Parton and surrounded by other performers emulating the style of Texas under Flashback's disco ball. The second video captures the Flashback Follies recreating the "Time Warp" from *The Rocky Horror Picture Show* (1975) in what has now become a staple of camp and an oft-repeated performance. While never viral like Tandi Iman Diamond's Miss Gay Black America performance, these recordings are nonetheless significant "because we once loved, and recorded it, we have proof that we did and others will" (Juhasz 326). These videos share memory across generations through YouTube as the love for this era drags these performances from the 1980s onto the internet to inform a more collective queer identity.

Joseph Deleon argues that "YouTube can reanimate video and video archives, building on nostalgic spectatorship online to help audiences claim their queer history and feel a part of a queer community across time and space" (16). Historical videos that endure, however, can also take on a haunting quality. YouTuber Andre Tardif's video "Flashback Nightclub (1981–82)," for instance, splices together several performances from unnamed drag queens filmed over a year on Super 8 mm film. The original film was digitized for uploading purposes, and in the process, the original audio was replaced with the sound of clicking hardware. The result is an unintended contrast between the movements of lively, exaggerated drag queens and the cold sound of a machine. Juhasz writes that "editing at its most Eisensteinian enlivens dead things through the clash of the cut" (326). Dead things enlivened through "video archives, production, editing, and viewing," for Juhasz, are "necessary components of social justice movements that while rooted in nostalgia strive to ensure that remembered abuses will not happen in the present or future" (326). Reanimated and enlivened dead things in Andre Tardif's Flashback montage become more Frankensteinian than Einsteinian, however, through its haphazard edits and the shadows from Super 8 film's inability to adequately capture Flashback's lighting. Rather than sharing the time and place of Flashback with people who never had access to it, the video reveals the unbridgeable gulf between the past and present. Bound up within this video are thus deeper ironies than the digital museums preserving nightlife are willing to address, including an ambivalence toward technology.

Technology itself is ghost-making, as the overall decline of gay bars across North America is largely a consequence of digital technology rendering those spaces obsolete. All of the bars and nightclubs in these virtual museums have been closed, creating the essential loss that produces nostalgia. Fondly remembering the nightclub Boots, a commenter responds to Benson's article on the nightclub by saying, "it was never empty when I was there, I always had a great time and met so many new people. Back then strangers would always ask you to dance, it was easy to meet men, unlike today. Gay men weren't afraid to approach strangers back in the 80's/90's. What happened to gay men?" ("Boots"). Catherine Nash and Andrew Gorman-Murray partly answer this question in their analysis of LGBTQ+ urban enclaves by explaining that "gay villages are in decline because of increased internet and social media use, allowing LGBT and queer individuals to find other like-minded individuals without the need for expressly LGBT and queer spaces such as gay villages" (88). Paradoxically, the same devices that access *ECAMP* and *Then & Now* on the internet are the ones that helped make the physical space of the club obsolete. The internet means that virtual museums can become "virtual and floating [entities]" that transcend "the physical museum complete with hushed galleries, curated exhibits and tangible objects" ("About"). A virtual museum can honour the sights and sonic tones of queer dance culture in noisy nightclubs by loudly giving sound to a subculture historically forced into the silence of the closet. Yet conceptualizing memories as "floating" in digital space risks eroding their contexts. "Rather than conceiving of digital memory as fluid and floating free of their contexts of production," Merrill and colleagues explain, it is important to "anchor digital memory in material and social contexts" (7–8). The unacknowledged irony of the *digital* in digital memory contributing to the closing of these nightclubs' physical doors speaks to greater possible contradictions around politics, futures, and utopias in these, precisely, *digital* exhibits.

UTOPIAN FUTURE MEMORIES

Queer theorists working on nostalgia, memory, and history emphasize the past's connection to the present in order to strategize paths toward possibly better futures. The activist-historians contributing to *ECAMP* and *Then & Now* do memory work by using "practices, cultural forms, and technologies" to drag the past into the present and towards the future (Smit et. al. 3120). For Shahani, memory work is crucial for social justice because "what happened in the past must be repeated in the present in order to secure the (historically informed) future" (326). In this sense, repetition through nostalgia offers a potential remedy for the cultural "amnesia, anesthesia, or numbing" that Andreas Huyssen argues is a consequence to rapid modernization (*Present Pasts* 16). Attachments to clubs, queens, and disco dance music, "objects otherwise condemned

Braidon Schaufert

to be thrown away, to become obsolete" (*Twilight Memories* 28), create temporal literacy through an awareness of the past, the present, and possible future. I bring *ECAMP* and *Then & Now* into conversation with each other because they endeavour toward similar historiographic goals, use digital methods to preserve memory, and are anchored in cities that have had Pride parades protested in the *present*. Our ways of knowing these present situations in Toronto and Edmonton are simultaneously more informative and less comprehensive than the historical knowing offered in *ECAMP* and *Then & Now*; those online exhibits have singular authorial voices while the narratives of Edmonton and Toronto's recent events circulated through social media and their more ephemeral informational capacities. Digital ephemera like Facebook events, Instagram stories, and Snapchats spread information to organize and mobilize action in the moment, but online news media often contain broken links to deleted tweets and content from deactivated accounts. Bearing this tendency in mind, I have assembled versions of these protest events using available information in order to parallel the past mediated in these online museums with the present, but their accounts inevitably and intentionally fail at comprehensiveness.

Contested Presents

Co-founded by Yusra Ali and Janaya Khan in 2014, Black Lives Matter Toronto (#BLMTO) is an organization meant to "forge critical connections to work in solidarity with black communities, black-centric networks, solidarity movements, and allies in order to dismantle all forms of state-sanctioned oppression, violence, and brutality committed against African, Caribbean, and Black cis, queer, trans, and disabled populations in Toronto" ("Black Lives Matter—Toronto"). In 2014 and 2015, #BLMTO had been active in efforts to hold Toronto Police Services accountable for the murders of Jermaine Carby and Andrew Loku. In doing so, they blocked traffic flows, protested police board meetings, and led demonstrations outside of Toronto City Hall and police headquarters (Battersby). In June 2016, police chief Mark Saunders made "a historic apology" for police discrimination in the queer community and unveiled a mural symbolizing new relations on 425 Church Street ("Apologizes"); however, the mural's unveiling ceremony was protested by #BLMTO for being a publicity stunt (Vendeville). Relatedly, after the Pulse Nightclub shooting in Florida on 12 June 2016, the promise of increased policing at Pride in Toronto threatened the safety of Black attendees at the festival (Perkel). As the "Honoured Guests" of Pride, #BLMTO led the parade but blocked its movement after a moment of silence for the Pulse victims. Rather than marching, activists released rainbow-coloured smoke bombs and rallied behind a list of demands that included banning police from marching in uniform ("Black Lives Matter—Toronto"). Pride director Mathiew Chantelois agreed to the demands, but told press in the days following that he did so in bad faith to move the parade forward (Wilson).

As a result of these protests, Toronto Pride 2016 sent ripples across North America as more Pride organizers were forced to grapple with increasing demands to remove cops marching in uniform. Edmonton's 2018 Pride parade was protested by members of two advocacy groups: Shades of Colour, a public interest group "that exists to advocate for queer and trans Black folks, Indigenous folks, and people of colour" (Shades of Colour, Facebook Page), and RaricaNow, "a non-profit organization with the sole aim of Promoting Human Rights for all LGBTIQ+ refugees and newcomers in Canada" (RaricaNow). These groups demanded that the Edmonton Pride Society Festival (EPSF) reallocate funds to spaces for queer and trans Black and Indigenous people of colour and remove police and military from marching (Shades of Colour, "Pride Demands"). These demands challenged the EPSF through to 2019 as Shades of Colour and RaricaNow expected systemic changes to the festival's organization. On 4 April, the EPSF blocked these advocacy groups from attending a board meeting and called in security when tensions rose. Days later, on 11 April, news media received a leaked email from the EPSF's board of directors stating that Pride would be cancelled "in light of the current political and social climate" (Heidenreich, "Festival Cancelled"). The vague rhetoric around the current climate caused many to assume the cancellation was a consequence of Jason Kenney's newly elected anti-queer United Conservative Party rather than the EPSF's inability to reflect Edmonton's needs. Shades of Colour called the cancellation "a disavowal of deep systemic problems in the framework of [the] EPFS" and an "attempt to direct the discontent arising from the cancellation of the Pride Festival onto communities that have done nothing but speak their truth" (Shades of Colour Community YEG, "Pride Cancelled"). With no Pride parade or festival, Shades of Colour and RaricaNow co-organized the "Edmonton Stonewall 50th Anniversary March and Rally," a grass-roots march with no corporate sponsorship emphasizing the history of Black queer and trans activism in North America.

Memory Work/Future Work

Challenges to Pride are challenges to queer memory work, given Pride's status as one of the most famous commemorative vehicles for political demonstration. These contemporary protests to Pride (rather than what were once Pride protests) are also intrinsically linked with the memories preserved in *ECAMP* and *Then & Now*, since police raids and brutal-ity run across the geography of the nightclubs, cruising spots, and public spaces mapped by those online museums. These Pride festivals in Canadian cities take for their model the commemorative marches launched in the years after the Stonewall riots. The week-long riots in 1969, provoked by longstanding police raids on the bar, are so significant that "almost [the] entire corpus of gay and lesbian history can be read as an attempt to deconstruct the Stonewall narrative" (Kissack 105). Rather than understanding the riot as the origin of the gay rights activism that spread across North America, however, Armstrong and Crage empha-size viewing the Stonewall story "as an *achievement* of gay liberation" (725). They recontextualize Stonewall as a success not because it was a unique event but because of the memory work done to raise its impact. Other previous or concurrent uprisings, such as the Compton riot in San Francisco, were similar in form but activists with power did not put resources behind their commemoration. The successful commemoration of the Stonewall riots through a large protest the year after their occurrence—in addition to annual gay Pride parades ever since—was the result of "affluent, educated, and politically connected [white] gay men" who "mobilized resources, ran newspapers, and engaged in extended legal challenges" (Armstrong and Crage 744). As a famous example of memory work, Stonewall thus continues to be a highly visible illustration of Lisa Lowe's concept of past conditional temporality.

In terms of recent memory work on the riots, the distinction between Roland Emmerich's feature film *Stonewall* (2015) and Tourmaline's independent short *Happy Birthday, Marsha* (2018) exemplifies how presentations of the past inform the priorities of the present. *Stonewall* provoked critique for mischaracterizing the events of the riot and centring the fictional character Danny Winters, a white, gay, cis man played by Jeremy Irvine, as the original brick thrower. The creation of Winters symbolizes a homonormative politics that Lisa Duggan says "does not contest dominant heteronormative assumptions and institutions, but upholds and sustains them, while promising the possibility of a demobilized gay constituency and a privatized, depoliticized gay culture anchored in domesticity and consumption" (50). This reconstruction of the Stonewall past has an orientation "toward upward mobility" and participates in "reinstating white privilege" threatened by a queer sexual identity (Puar 151). In contrast to *Stonewall*, Tourmaline's short film, *Happy Birthday, Marsha*, depicts the night leading up to the riot by reimagining the birthday of Marsha P. Johnson, the Black trans woman present at the riots yet erased from Emmerich's film. Rather than using narrative to construct the illusion of historical accuracy for an event that already has "discrepancies between popular and scholarly stories" (Armstrong and Crage 743), *Happy Birthday, Marsha* takes obvious liberties with facticity. Johnson's birthday is 24 August, not 28 June, but the detail does not matter next to the film's project of centring the Black queer trans woman written out of mainstream historical representations of queer history. Folks "marginalized by class, gender-presentation, and often race," Armstrong and Crage explain, "were more willing than others to confront police, and were important in the riots at both Compton's and the Stonewall Inn" (744). Obscured in *Stonewall* is that the "radical impulses moderate quickly," as affluential white gays and lesbians "coalesced around a gay rights/gay pride political agenda" (744). Thus, reorienting the Stonewall narrative in *Happy Birthday Marsha* recommits the politics today toward challenging police brutality and anti-Black racism.

Returning to the idea of nostalgia, its potential to inscribe certain futures is part of queer theory's broader preoccupation with futurity. The "omnipresence of futurism in queer politics" (Best 1) is a product of debates between antisocial or anti-future queer theorists and scholars working on utopias. Lee Edelman's *No Future: Queer Theory and the Death Drive* makes the provocative claim that queers should reject "reproductive futurism" (3) since norms are reinforced by thoughts and actions for the future. The "Child" is "the emblem of futurity's unquestioned value," and the "future is mere repetition and just as lethal as the past" (31). Edelman argues for reveling in anti-futurity as a way to counter normativity, yet this anti-futurity does not account for the ways in which queers are differently proximate to this finality depending on how they are racialized; some subjects may choose to live a life in opposition to the future while others have that choice, along with a future, taken from them. In contrast to *No Future*, José Esteban Muñoz in *Cruising Utopia* contends "that if queerness is to have any value whatsoever, it must be viewed as being visible only in the horizon" (11). For Muñoz, queerness is the practice of rejecting the "here and now" (1) in service of a future that is radically different and better. The scholarship on nostalgia that uses "moving backwards" as part of the "reparative process" of using "collective memory as the base materials for imagining a different future" (Shahani 1227) is thus firmly rooted in the utopian impulse of queer theory rather than the antisocial ones.

Tavia Nyong'o's scholarship on disco in "Disco and its Discontents" helps conceptualize the utopia that might be imagined in virtual museums on the history of nightlife. Nyong'o writes about "the utopian scenario of a disco that did not know itself as disco, and that in lacking this name could simply move, feel, flow, and be oceanic" (109).

Drawing on "Civilization and Its Discontents," disco-that-did-not-know-itself-as-disco, according to Nyong'o, resists the racialized and sexualized binary between civilized and primitive egos in Freud's work. The utopian in underground nightclubs is "grounded in the experience of the oceanic feeling-tone of love, ecstasy, and oneness" (106). The "oceanic feeling-tone" in Nyong'o's article refers to Freud's writing on the "adult psyche of the unbounded plenitude we have all experienced as infants, a state in which polymorphous sensuality, unspoiled by the sense of a division between self and other that we later accrue, still holds sway" (105). This sensation is most potent in the "plateau of bodily disorganization" of "collective, dance-floor ecstasy" (109). While the "artificial, machinic, and/or technological" would eventually become "ambivalent icons of capitalism, whiteness, and homosexuality" (111), Nyong'o's work on Donna Summer's career, for instance, works to situate disco in "a genealogy of afrofuturism" that moves "the analysis of black music beyond primitivist frameworks" (110). Afrofuturist sound and the legacy of gay dance music names "disco" as the utopian impulse informing *ECAMP*'s and *Then & Now*'s vigour to preserve the spaces that played disco and its evolutions, hosted disco's dancers, and allowed for experimentation at the edge of binaries.

CONCLUSION

The lesson that proximity to power shapes commemoration even within marginalized groups bears on *ECAMP* and *Then & Now*, both of which focus on nightclubs in Edmonton and Toronto and how they participated in narratives of their cities that made their urban spaces appear more vibrant and therefore more attractive. These virtual museums further the argument that memories are important to a politics of futurity, but a politics of futurity that goes unnamed while neoliberalism goes unchallenged. The memories of activist-historians are crucial in these cities that have had Pride parades protested for their homonormative politics. After the Stonewall riots in America and the bathhouse raids in Canada,

Pride parades became the most institutionalized commemorative vehicle in the gay rights movement. While the protests in Toronto and Edmonton are part of larger, ongoing tensions throughout each city born from the alliance between assimilatory queer activists and institutionalized police forces, the act of blocking the parade is symbolic of challenging memory and remediation more generally. These virtual museums gesture toward the "oceanic feeling-tone" of the discotheque utopia, but they are ultimately inscribed by more normative, liberal futurity. Black Lives Matter Toronto and the assemblage of activist groups in Edmonton demand new memory forms that take what *ECAMP* and *Then & Now* have started and indulge in pasts that can produce better futures.

After the global pandemic temporarily closed the doors to all nightclubs, memories of those spaces so integral to queer public sociality are even more precious. The oceanic feeling-tone of Nyong'o's utopic disco is at odds with our socially distanced COVID-19 present, but we have an opportunity to enter a social world different than the one that we left. *ECAMP* and *Then & Now* use digital technology to preserve memories of nightclubs in a process that I claim has an ironic relationship to the technologies that made those spaces obsolete by moving sociality away from the public and back to the private sphere that online platforms now facilitate. This is memory work on subjects that typically fall by the wayside of a history that renders them either banal, secretive, frivolous, or trivial, but, as these online museums demonstrate, these subjects have indeed shaped queer struggles. Both museums have a sense that their memory work is oriented toward the future, and I posit them in relation to present struggles in each city. Those struggles are symbolized by protests at Pride festivals by queer Black and Indigenous activists and queers of colour over alliances between organizers, city police, and corporations. This relationship is especially important to consider as cities start incorporating queer narratives into their official histories: rather than being co-opted into the neoliberal frameworks of vibrant and diverse cities, queer memory work must maintain a rigorous critique of the present so that queer nightclubs can open their doors to better futures.

WORKS CITED

"About the Edmonton City as Museum Project." *City Museum Edmonton,* https://citymuseumedmonton.ca. Accessed 31 December 2020.

Armstrong, Elizabeth A., and Suzanna M. Crage. "Movements and Memory: The Making of the Stonewall Myth." *American Sociological Review,* no. 71, 2006: pp. 724–51.

Battersby, Sarah-Joyce. "From Jermaine Carby to Andrew Loku: A Timeline of Black Lives Matter in Toronto." *The Star,* 16 April 2016, https://www.thestar.com/news/gta/2016/04/16/from-jermaine-carby-to-andrew-loku-a-timeline-of-black-lives-matter-in-toronto.html. Accessed 15 April 2021.

Benson, Denise. *Then & Now: Toronto Nightlife History,* http://thenandnowtoronto.com. Accessed 29 December 2020.

Best, Stephen Michael. "Game Theory: Racial Embodiment and Media Crisis." *Living Color: Race and Television in the United States,* edited by Sasha Torres et. al., Duke University Press, 1998, pp. 219–38.

"Black Lives Matter—Toronto." *Black Lives Matter Toronto,* https://blacklivesmattertoronto.ca. Accessed 15 April 2021.

Boym, Svetlana. *The Future of Nostalgia.* Basic Books, 2001.

Byers, Ron, and Rob Browatzke. "History of Edmonton's Gay Bars, Part 1: The Beginning." *City Museum Edmonton,* 23 September 2020, https://citymuseumedmonton.ca/2020/09/23/history-of-edmontons-gay-bars-part-1-the-beginning/. Accessed 31 December 2020.

Byers, Ron, and Rob Browatzke. "History of Edmonton's Gay Bars, Part 2: A Flashback to Flashback." *City Museum Edmonton,* 30 September 2020, https://citymuseumedmonton.ca/2020/09/30/history-of-edmontons-gay-bars-part-2-a-flashback-to-flashback/. Accessed 31 December 2020.

Deleon, Joseph. "Nelson Sullivan's Video Memories: YouTube Nostalgia and the Queer Archive Effect." *The Velvet Light Trap,* vol. 86, Fall 2020, pp. 16–26.

Duggan, Lisa. *The Twilight of Equality? Neoliberalism, Cultural Politics, and the Attack on Democracy.* Beacon Press, 2003.

Edelman, Lee. *No Future: Queer Theory and the Death Drive.* Duke University Press, 2004.

Emmerich, Roland, director. *Stonewall.* Roadside Attractions, 2015.

"Flashback Nightclub (1981–82)." *YouTube,* uploaded by Andre Tardif, 13 March 2020, https://www.youtube.com/watch?v=Nh1jft-TslQ. Accessed 20 May 2021.

Freeman, Elizabeth. *Time Binds: Queer Temporalities, Queer Histories.* Duke University Press, 2010.

Heidenreich, Phil. "2019 Edmonton Pride Festival Cancelled." *Global News*, 10 April 2019, https://globalnews.ca/news/5154261/2019-edmonton-pride-festival-cancelled-email-april/. Accessed 20 May 2021.

Holota, Victoria. "The Pisces Bathhouse Raid." *City Museum Edmonton*, 28 May 2015, https://citymuseumedmonton.ca/2015/05/28/the-pisces-bathhouse-raid/. Accessed 31 December 2020.

Huyssen, Andreas. *Present Pasts: Urban Palimpsests and the Politics of Memory*. Stanford University Press, 2003.

Huyssen, Andreas. *Twilight Memories: Marking Time in a Culture of Amnesia*. Routledge, 1995.

Juhasz, Alexandra. "Video Remains: Nostalgia, Technology, and Queer Archive Activism." *GLQ*, vol. 12, no. 2, 2006, pp. 319–28.

Kissack, Terence. "Freaking Fag Revolutionaries: New York's Gay Liberation Front, 1969–1971." *Radical History Review*, no. 62, 1995, pp. 104–34.

Love, Heather. *Feeling Backward: Loss and the Politics of Queer History*. Harvard University Press, 2007.

Lowe, Lisa. *The Intimacies of Four Continents*. Duke University Press, 2015.

Merrill, Samuel et al., eds. *Social Movements, Cultural Memory and Digital Media: Mobilising Mediated Remembrance*. Palgrave Macmillan, 2020.

Muñoz, José Esteban. *Cruising Utopia: The Then and There of Queer Futurity*. NYU Press, 2009.

Nash, Catherine Jean, and Andrew Gorman-Murray. "Recovering the Gay Village: A Comparative Historical Geography of Urban Change and Planning in Toronto and Sydney." *Historical Geography*, no. 43, 2015, pp. 84–105.

Nyong'o, Tavia. "I Feel Love: Disco and its Discontents." *Criticism*, vol. 50, no. 1, 2008, pp. 101–12.

Perkel, Colin. "Toronto Pride Celebration Will Go Ahead amid Tighter Security: Organizers." *Global News*, 13 June 2016, https://globalnews.ca/news/2757717/toronto-police-to-reassess-security-for-pride-month-in-wake-of-orlando-shooting/. Accessed 15 April 2021.

"Phenomenon." *RuPaul's Drag Race*, season 13, episode 3, *VH1*, 15 January 2021.

Phair, Michael. "Flashback and the Gay Drag Races." *City Museum Edmonton*, 16 September 2014, https://citymuseumedmonton.ca/2014/09/16/flashback-and-the-gay-drag-races/. Accessed 31 December 2020.

Pryor, Jaclyn I. *Time Slips: Queer Temporalities, Contemporary Performance, and the Hole of History*. Northwestern University Press, 2017.

Puar, Jasbir. "The Cost of Getting Better: Suicide, Sensation, Switchpoints." *GLQ*, vol. 18, no. 1, 2011, pp. 149–58.

RaricaNow. Homepage. https://raricanow.org. Accessed 15 April 2021.

Sedgwick, Eve Kosofsky. *Tendencies.* Duke University Press, 1993.

Shahani, Nishant. "'Between Light and Nowhere': The Queer Politics of Nostalgia." *Journal of Popular Culture*, vol. 46, no. 6, 2013, pp. 1217–30.

Smit, Rik, et al. "Activating the Past in the Ferguson Protests: Memory Work, Digital Activism and the Politics of Platforms." *New Media & Society*, vol. 20, no. 9, 2017, pp. 3119–39.

Shades of Colour Community YEG. Facebook Page. Retrieved 16 April 2021 from https://www.facebook.com/shadesofcolour.yeg/. Accessed 12 January 2023.

Shades of Colour Community YEG. "Pride Cancelled 2019." Facebook, April 2019, https://www.facebook.com/notes/673241583618844/?fref=mentions. Accessed 14 January 2023.

Shades of Colour Community YEG. "Pride Demands 2019." Facebook, March 2019, https://www.facebook.com/shadesofcolour.yeg/posts/1210132735820879?ref=embed_post. Accessed 14 January 2023.

"Toronto Police Chief Mark Saunders Apologizes for 1981 Gay Bathhouse Raids." *CBC*, 22 June 2016, https://www.cbc.ca/news/canada/toronto/police-apology-raids-1.3647668. Accessed 15 April 2021.

Vendeville, Geoffrey. "Black Lives Matter Protesters Interrupt Pride Mural Unveiling by Toronto Police." *Toronto Star*, 25 June 2016, https://www.thestar.com/news/gta/2016/06/24/black-lives-matter-protesters-interrupt-pride-mural-unveiling-by-toronto-police.html. Accessed 15 April 2021.

Wilson, Cody. "Pride Organizer Says He Has Not Agreed to Exclude Police Floats from Parade." *CP24*, 4 July 2016, https://www.cp24.com/news/pride-organizer-says-he-has-not-agreed-to-exclude-police-floats-from-parade-1.2971974. Accessed 15 April 2021.

5

COUNTER-CARTOGRAPHIES AND ACTIVIST ARCHIVES

NAVIGATING PETROCULTURAL MEMORY IN BRIAN HOLMES'S *PETROPOLIS*

JORDAN B. KINDER

AS RESISTANCE TO THE EXPANSION of the Canadian oil sands megaproject gained momentum in the early 2010s, activists Jesse Fruhwirth and Melanie Jae Martin identified the formation of a new, geographically dispersed yet conceptually coherent movement: Blockadia. In a think-piece written for *Yes! Magazine* in 2013 titled "Welcome to Blockadia!," Fruhwirth and Jae Martin describe how oil sands expansionism, whose momentum is achieved largely through pipeline projects, has ushered in a new network of resistance whose sights are set on halting such expansion (Fruhwirth and Jae Martin). The Canadian oil sands megaproject refers primarily to the three largest oil sands deposits—Athabasca, Cold Lake, and Peace River—that mostly reside in Treaty 8 territory across northern Alberta and western Saskatchewan. Described by some as "the single largest and most destructive industrial project on earth" (Berman), the sands also comprise the largest single industrial project in history (Vettese). These sands are deemed "unconventional" resources because they contain bitumen deposits that require significant processing to become anything like oil as we might commonly imagine it. Unlike conventional deposits of crude oil, oil sands extraction demands vast amounts of financial and external natural resources not only in the initial stages, but throughout the entire production process. In upgrading and refining the bitumen into a usable commodity, financial and material inputs are consumed at a scale and intensity far beyond bitumen's conventional counterparts.

Movements of resistance to the oil sands megaproject point to such terms of scale and intensity as causal factors in the unevenly experienced deleterious social and ecological consequences of oil sands development. It is this scale of impact from whence Blockadia came. As Lakota historian and activist Nick Estes wrote in the wake of the #NoDAPL movement,[1] pipelines proliferate and deepen colonial forms of ecological violence, "but in the process, they are also connecting and inciting to action disparate communities of the exploited and dispossessed" (253). The very condition of expansionism, then, has immanently ushered in a network of solidarity among land and water protectors across North America and the planet more broadly.

Our welcome to Blockadia in 2013 and the network of solidarity that Estes describes each contain latent cartographic imaginaries. These cartographic imaginaries serve two ends: both the reproduction *of* and resistance *to* settler colonialism and extractive capitalism. As pipelines spread across landscapes and territories, so too do clusters of resistance emerge that are bound conceptually and materially. Engaging these cartographic dimensions of pipeline politics, Chicago-based cultural critic and artist Brian Holmes released an interactive digital mapping platform in conjunction with the "Petcoke: Tracing Dirty Energy" exhibition hosted by the Museum of Contemporary Photography at Columbia College in 2016 (Holmes *Petropolis*). Titled *Petropolis*, the project has two main features. First, it fuses images of the infrastructures of North American "fossil economy," a term that refers to "an economy of self-sustaining growth predicated on the growing consumption of fossil fuels" (Malm

Fossil 11), including vast swaths of pipeline networks and railways, natural resource deposits, mining projects, refineries, and upgrading facilities that connect it to the globe. Second, it spatially and temporally ties these infrastructures to points of disruption against them, archiving the myriad multimedia documentation of on-the-ground acts of resistance as well as artistic production that engages the politics and materialities of oil. Connecting Canada's oil sands with the Chicago metropolis, what Holmes identifies as "the single largest market for the environmental disaster known as the Athabasca Tar Sands" ("What Can Art" 427), the project offers a kind of cognitive map through which audiences can navigate across varied scales and temporalities. Literary and cultural theorist Fredric Jameson describes effective cognitive maps as those that formally make legible the totalizing scales and contours of contemporary capitalism as they relate to individual experience (356). Holmes's description of *Petropolis* reveals the ways in which the project tarries with these scales and contours of extractive capital anchored to the petroleum industry in particular. The project, he writes, is an "online cartographic archive exploring the petroleum industry and its discontents at local, metropolitan, continental, and global scales" ("What Can Art" 429).

This chapter navigates the spatial and temporal dimensions of *Petropolis* by exploring the project as a form of counter-cartography and an activist archive that mediates and memorializes resistance to Canadian extractivism. Extractivism names the ideological impetus of a capitalism whose mechanisms of value generation fundamentally rest upon extractive processes. Writer and activist Naomi Klein succinctly describes extractivism as a "nonreciprocal, dominance-based relationship with the earth, one purely of taking" (148). Nonreciprocity, dominance, and taking are forces of extractive capitalism and settler colonialism that I interrogate in my journey through *Petropolis*. These forces are maintained and reproduced through what I call Canada's "extractive state apparatus," or the state and extra-state actors that enable and perform extractivism. Beginning at the site of extraction, I focus on the flows of oil that originate in the oil sands, where 96 percent of Canada's proven reserves sit—the third largest in the world. I explore how *Petropolis*

Jordan B. Kinder

challenges cartography as an extractive practice by charting the infrastructural underbelly of extractive capital. I navigate *Petropolis* from *the site* of extraction to *the routes* of positive and negative possibility represented in the project, with a stop at *the blockade* along the way.

Throughout this journey, I employ cartographic metaphors of navigation to draw attention to the movement of *Petropolis* as an interactive medium. The course I follow and the stops I make represent only one path among many, and my engagement follows a kind of "choose-your-own-adventure" methodology inspired by questions of scale. First, at *the site*, I offer a brief account of the Canadian extractive state apparatus through its consolidation in the oil sands megaproject and I interrogate the cartographic dimensions of extractive capitalism and settler colonialism. Moving to *the blockade*, I read the archive of resistance that *Petropolis* brings together through its collective documentation of Blockadia, with particular attention to coalitions of Indigenous and non-Indigenous allies at this movement. Finally, I scale out by following *the routes* of *Petropolis*, paths that name the networked assemblages of reproduction and resistance that harbour and express modes of "petrocultural memory." A phrase that I develop to anchor my exploration of *Petropolis*, petrocultural memory synthesizes the concept of petrocultures, which describes the bounded relation between cultures of modernity and oil, with the notion of cultural memory. Petrocultural memory names collective modes of remembering oil culture that include a range of affects, from literary and cultural theorist Stephanie LeMenager's notion of petromelancholia—which she describes as "the grieving of conventional oil resources and the pleasures they sustained" (18)—to the human and nonhuman solidarities that underwrite Blockadia, as well as those not yet known in our oil-saturated present. My journey through *Petropolis* questions what it means to memorialize dominant relations—extractive capitalism and settler colonialism—*while* they remain at the fore of our material and cultural lives, and in doing so proposes digital, interactive media as one avenue through which petrocultural memory can be mobilized toward realizing a future beyond these relations.

THE SITE:
EXTRACTIVE SPACE AND COUNTER-CARTOGRAPHIES

Some thirty kilometres north of Fort McMurray's city centre sits the first commercial oil sands megaproject, right beside the flows of the Athabasca River. Established in 1967, the project was spearheaded by Great Canadian Oil Sands Limited, a subsidiary brought into being by the US-based Sun Oil Company. The plant remains operational to this day by Suncor, which was formed in 1979 when Sun Oil Company merged its eastern, Montreal-based Canadian retail and western Canadian, production-oriented commercial operations to become the standalone corporation Suncor Inc. (Vassiliou 489). Suncor's official promotional lore frames the construction of the Great Canadian Oil Sands plant, which arguably ushered in the oil sands as we know them today, as a tale of overcoming adversity as Canadians. "The skeptics said Canada's oil sands could never be developed commercially," the history section of the company's website states. "In 1967," it continues, "Suncor Energy proved them wrong" ("History"). Narratives of overcoming such as these construe the oil sands as a collective, national achievement accomplished in the face of adversity, which in turn cement resource extraction as a foundational component of Canadian national identity that obscures the settler-colonial impetus of extraction.

Like the construction of the Great Canadian Oil Sands plant itself, resistance to the expansion of Canada's fossil economy took shape as Blockadia emerged in the shadow of a much longer history of resource extraction, settler colonialism, and national imagining. After all, settler colonialism and extractive capitalism were central pillars to the formation of the Canadian settler state then, and they remain central to the settler state's continued existence now. Critical discussions of this relation-ship between extractive capitalism and settler colonialism often cite the historical legacy of the fur trade, the infrastructural network of trade that this economy both generated and relied upon, and the extractive econo-mies that emerged from it as anticipating Canadian confederation's mate-rial embodiment in the Canadian Pacific Railway (CPR). The CPR further

Jordan B. Kinder   105

cemented extraction as the modus operandi of the Canadian settler state. These extractive legacies were so materially and culturally instrumental to Canadian identity that political economist Harold Innis famously deemed Canada a "staples" economy—that is, an economy premised on the widespread export of raw materials (385).

Beyond the consideration of the degree to which resource extraction has shaped national identity, however, these "staples" also rely on external relations unaccounted for in capitalist schemas of value, despite playing a determinant role in the production of that value in the first place. In Marxist terms, the concept of primitive accumulation provides some explanatory power here. Primitive accumulation describes the process through which non-capitalist relations become capitalist. Marx, for instance, famously cites England's enclosure of the commons as an example of primitive accumulation (877–95). Orthodox readings of this process relegate primitive accumulation to originary moments of capitalism's emergent stronghold, whereas thinkers such as Yellowknives Dene political theorist Glen Coulthard challenge these narrow, historical readings by positing primitive accumulation as continuous, evidenced in part through the ongoing dispossession of land experienced by Indigenous peoples (13). This dispossession historically materialized through the creation of so-called Crown land in the constitution of Canada and today in the continued destruction of lands and waters across both ceded and unceded territory in the establishment of productive landscapes that fuel extractive capitalism. The stakes of this ongoing process cannot be overstated. In their introduction to a special issue of the *South Atlantic Quarterly* on "Getting Back the Land," editors Shiri Pasternak and Dayna Nadine Scott chart out the stakes and consequences of this staples view on Indigenous peoples and the questions of jurisdiction that arise—questions whose answers reveal that "Canada's claim to exclusive territorial authority across all the lands and waters is a failed project" (205). These relations of extraction made possible by dispossession are so deeply engrained in Canadian identity that even the first major oil sands project symbolically nodded to the embedded, co-constitutive relation between extraction and the Canadian national

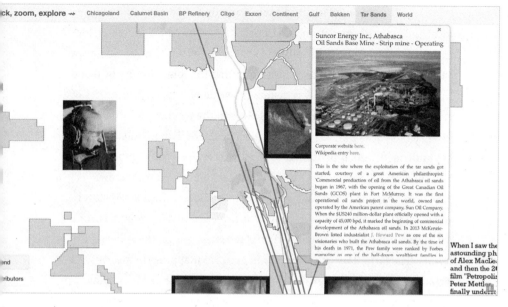

FIGURE 5.1.
Detail of Suncor's Athabasca oil sands base mine.
(Brian Holmes, *Petropolis*. Used with permission.)

imaginary—the "Great *Canadian* Oil Sands." This is all to say that *the site* remains a formative locus where dispossession has taken and continues to take place.

Although *Petropolis* largely focuses on Chicago as the corridor through which a plethora of pipeline and railway routes coalesce to upgrade, refine, exchange, and disperse oil across the planet, its predetermined views offer parameters through which to set one's sights on the centres of production by region and corporation to generate a critique of oil sands expansionism. In Figure 5.1, these views are outlined in the options spread along the top control panel. From "Chicagoland" to the "World," Holmes's predetermined parameters offer lines of sight that tell a larger geographical story of planetary extraction and circulation filtered through Chicago and other North American hubs that position Canada's oil sands as a main character.

When zoomed in on, these parameters tell a deeper, more localized story of extraction and impact. The view of the oil sands, for instance, exposes the predominance of extractivism. Homing in on the "Tar Sands" displays the region surrounding the municipality of Wood Buffalo, which immediately registers the scale of impact. These sites of extraction—described as tar sands leases in the legend—dominate the view as blotches or stains on the landscape. Here, Holmes also gathers multimedia documentation of the territory, including embedded YouTube videos related to the 2016 Fort McMurray wildfire known as "the Beast," a series of aerial photographs by Boston-based artist and photographer Alex MacLean, and a cut from filmmaker Peter Mettler's 2009 documentary *Petropolis: Aerial Perspectives on the Alberta Tar Sands*. The latter two are exercises in cultural mapping themselves, primarily due to how they make the scale of oil sands extraction and its consequences legible to audiences through an aerial aesthetics.

Maps were and continue to be a medium for settler-colonial world building. In what is now called Canada, this world building was expressed through state-sponsored surveys such as the 1841 Geological Survey and the Dominion Land Survey in 1871, the latter of which was "the largest survey to ever take place in the history of the world" (Bélanger et al. 452). Pierre Bélanger, Christopher Alton, and Nina-Marie Lister describe these surveys as a process of "crafting uneven cartographies of colonization" (452). "To be mapped and settled, either for provincial farms or municipal towns or Indian reserves," they write, "land first had to be surveyed, and then drawn, placed on a map to draft and craft the imagination of settler space, on paper" (454). The figure of the grid was wielded as a choice instrument of dispossession, an epistemological weapon to reconceptualize space for the extractive state apparatus. In doing so, maps served to "erase the history, memory, and premise of Indigenous foundations" (459). As an extractive technology, the settler-colonial cartographic imaginary expressed through the grid "masked, obscured, and erased the political embodiment of the ground and its history" (493).

At *the site*, the grid reappears as a spatial taxonomy for extraction in the form of leases. Figure 5.1 details how the landscape is parcelled in these ways. For Michi Saagiig Nishnaabeg theorist Leanne Betasamosake Simpson, the extractivism that underwrites the dominant settler imaginary ultimately undermines place-based knowledges that are crucial to good relations with Indigenous Peoples. In a brief critical analysis of Arctic mapping done in the 1970s by architecture firm Van Ginkel Associates Ltd. for Canadian Arctic Gas Pipeline Ltd. as part of its preliminary work on the never-realized Mackenzie Valley natural gas pipeline, I argued that such cartographies translate complex landscapes and relations into reductive ones legible to extractive capitalism (Kinder). Extending the scope of this critique, Western cartographic practices, such as those that informed the Geologic Survey and the Dominion Land Survey, made legible complex ecosystems for manipulation by the governing resource logics of empire. It is perhaps unsurprising that under the banner of resisting these dominant, settler-colonial cartographies, the Inuit, Wet'suwet'en, Gitxsan, and Coast Salish "have [published] or [endorsed] publication of their own atlases" (Rundstrom 316). Offering a more granular account of the power of counter-mapping in the early pages of her 2017 book, *As We Have Always Done: Indigenous Freedom Through Radical Resistance*, Simpson describes formative experiences working with Elders of the Anishinaabeg reserve community of Long Lake #58 in northern Ontario to "gather the individual cognitive, territorial maps Elders held in their heads into a collective, a visual re-mapping and translation of some aspects of Indigenous Knowledge into a form that would be *recognized* by industry and the state" (14). Simpson's reflections substantiate how mapping can also serve as a process of resistance and resurgence. "I wrote down on large topographical maps every place-name for every beach, bay peninsula, and island they could remember—hundreds and hundreds of names," she writes (14). The mapping "also recorded pain," Simpson continues, which included

> [the] prisoner-of-war camp, the internment camp,
> and its school that some Nishnaabeg kids attended so
> they could continue to live with their families and not
> go to residential school. The 150 years of clear-cuts.
> The hydro-electric dams, the direction the lake was
> supposed to flow. The flood, the road, the railway
> tracks, the mines, the pipeline, the hydrolines. The
> chemical sprays, the white people parks and camp-
> grounds. Deaths. (15)

For Simpson, this "map of loss" produced clarity: "Colonialism or settler colonialism or dispossession or displacement or capitalism didn't seem complicated anymore" (15). Where settler-colonial cartographies impose the grid upon landscapes to undermine complex relations, the mapping Simpson describes collectively emerged instead *from* these relations in a way that makes legible the modes of violence expressed through settler colonialism.

As a form of non-Indigenous counter-cartography or counter-mapping itself, *Petropolis* complements Indigenous counter-mapping by employing cartographic methods to produce a cultural object that challenges the dominant registers and power relations of mapping. Although initially "a task taken up primarily by indigenous peoples who often find themselves in a perpetual state of emergency," counter-mapping is defined generally as community-based or -oriented mapping practices that "seek to represent places in a manner that not only counters the maps made by state and corporate authorities but also reveals the hegemonic politics inherent in those maps they are countering" (Rundstrom 314). In this way, *Petropolis* undermines the extractive spatiality produced by dominant mapping practices both in terms of form and content by making legible the spatial and temporal machinations of extractive capitalism as expressed in the petroleum industry. *Petropolis*'s affordances as an interactive digital medium extend the range of possibilities in how it counter-maps. Although static in the sense that it relies on a static database—one that hosts and hyperlinks to paratextual materials outside of the platform's confines—*Petropolis* remains dynamic in its myriad possibilities of engagement by visitors. Through such engagement, visitors participate in the process of counter-cartography itself by generating their own paths of legibility that form the collective building blocks of petrocultural memory.

THE BLOCKADE:
ACTIVIST ARCHIVES AND
EMERGENT PETROCULTURAL MEMORY

The counter-mapping strategies at play in *Petropolis* lay bare the material and symbolic relations between sites of extraction and sites of resistance as a way of figuring and confronting ongoing legacies of extractive capitalism in explicit registers and settler colonialism in more implicit ones. While *Petropolis* is an example of non-Indigenous counter- cartography, its counter-mapping strategies express spatial dimensions of cultural memory by producing an activist archive of Blockadia that lays out nodes of resistance both near and far in proximity from what I described in the previous section as *the site*, or the primary sites of production that extract, upgrade, and transport bitumen. As an activist archive, these nodes of resistance primarily focus on blockades of sites of production and circulation, offering a spatio-temporal snapshot of particular demonstrations that contribute to the shaping of petrocultural memory.

In archiving activist efforts in such spatial and temporal ways through *the blockade*, Holmes employs rhetorics and aesthetics that echo protest placards from the streets. "It's Time to Break," the icons that signify protest read (Figure 5.2). What break is being proposed via this declaration? "It's Time to Break" is a direct call to action that foregrounds the necessity of transition. Framing transition as rupture in this way unapologetically evokes images of a kind of revolution—that is, a kind of breaking with the established order, the status quo, or what is often referred to as "business as usual." More precisely, the break

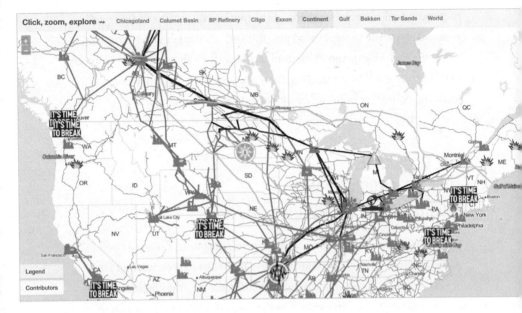

FIGURE 5.2.
Continental view with resistance nodes labelled
"It's Time to Break."
(Brian Holmes, *Petropolis*. Used with permission.)

articulated in this dimension of *Petropolis* is a direct invocation of the positioning that inspired a series of collective, coordinated demonstrations across the planet in May 2016. Under the banner of "breaking free" from fossil fuels, these demonstrations disrupted the operations of oil sands infrastructure through nonviolent civil disobedience actions such as blockades. According to Oliver Milman of *The Guardian*, organizers with Break Free described the events as comprising "the largest ever global civil disobedience against fossil fuels" (qtd. in Milman). The website that first coordinated and later documented these actions details the aims, principles, and scope of the demonstrations in retrospect: "Each action was unique: from the coal fields of Germany, to the oil wells of Nigeria, to defiant actions against [a] new coal power plant in Indonesia and the Philippines—and many places beyond" ("May 2016"). And though these actions were uniquely localized, their messaging was consistent: "keep fossil fuels in the ground. Build a just transition to a new kind of 100% renewable economy. Do it now" ("May 2016"). By proposing that a just transition for the future requires keeping it in the ground in the present, the rupture proposed here occurs through a fundamental break from the fossil economy.

Some of the North American actions that *Petropolis* archives were specifically mobilized against the reach and expansion of Canada's oil sands. From the "Continent" parameter, these coordinated actions come more clearly into view. Beside the BP refinery situated in parts of Whiting and Hammond, Indiana, and East Chicago, Illinois, for instance, a video produced by the independent, horizontal media organization Unicorn Riot titled "#BreakFree2016 Midwest Action Against Climate Change" is embedded in the "It's Time to Break" icon. In the video, a reporter asks a demonstrator what it feels like to be marching next to "one of the biggest tar sands refineries in the world" (Unicorn Riot). The demonstrator responds by saying that it "feels incredible because tar sands is the dirtiest form of oil" (Unicorn Riot). Other actions, like in Albany, New York, saw community members gather to block a rail corridor that transports crude oil (350.org).

Clicking on the icon situated near Vancouver, British Columbia, in Burnaby brings up video documentation of a demonstration at the terminal of then–Kinder Morgan's Trans Mountain pipeline. The expansion of this pipeline has been one of the most contentious oil sands pipeline projects to date. According to the Canada Energy Regulator, the project will upgrade and twin the existing 1,147-kilometre line, increasing capacity from 300,000 barrels per day to 890,000 (Government of Canada 2020). In 2018, the government of Canada purchased the pipeline from Kinder Morgan for $4.5 billion, which served as a bailout for Kinder Morgan on the one hand and a full backing of the project by the Canadian extractive state apparatus to see it come to fruition. The now federally owned TMX continues to face immense opposition from Indigenous and environmental groups such as the Tiny House Warriors, a Secwepemc-led movement of land and water protectors who are occupying their traditional, unceded territory along the path of the pipeline.

The embedded video is from the environmental non-governmental organization Greenpeace Canada's YouTube channel. Titled "Greenpeace & First Nations Action In Vancouver—Break Free From Fossil Fuels," the video documents the blocking of land and sea traffic surrounding the Trans Mountain pipeline terminal that sits on unceded Coast Salish territory (Greenpeace Canada). Although the video is extremely brief at fifty-five seconds, it speaks to a larger coalition of Indigenous and non-Indigenous activists that came together at *the blockade.*

A spatio-temporal snapshot of demonstrations stemming from what was described by organizers as the largest global civil disobedience against fossil fuels to date, however, can only say so much about the deeper legacies of resistance that eventually culminated in Blockadia. Beyond what is gathered in these more metropolitan nodes of resistance that sit at the terminal points of oil sands transmission or other monuments of the oil and gas industry, the momentum of Blockadia is simultaneously dispersed and concentrated. Greenpeace Canada's documentation of the alliance between Indigenous activists and non-Indigenous allies offers a glimpse of this momentum, while Holmes's linking to Standing Rock Sioux Tribe's resistance efforts against the Dakota Access Pipeline—whose red, blue, and yellow seal can be seen at the centre of Figure 5.2—offers further detail.

Coalition efforts such as these against yet-to-be-built infrastructure are arguably some of the most powerful and promising challenges to disrupting and dismantling the fossil economy. Beyond the Break Free demonstrations, *the blockade* in *Petropolis* traverses not only built pipelines, but proposed or incomplete ones as well. Represented by a dotted line, these proposed or in-construction pipelines have a threatening, spectral presence that has since become more concrete. Since writing this chapter, the futures of these projects have to some degree become more certain, or about as certain as future relations of the fossil economy can be. Enbridge's Northern Gateway, for instance, has been cancelled, as has TC Energy's Energy East and, at the behest of US President Joe Biden, TC Energy's Keystone XL, yet the government of Canada's TMX is almost fully completed. Meanwhile, struggles over the Dakota Access Pipeline continue in the wake of its completion in 2017. Blockadia has played significant roles in the outcomes of these cancelled pipelines and in the continued resistance against those in construction or whose construction is on the horizon. What is so promising about these coalitions is how Indigenous voices are centred in the context of an environmental movement that, to put it gently, has not always been in sync with the interests of Indigenous communities and, in some cases, actively against those interests. Indigenous researcher and activist Dina Gilio-Whitaker details this complicated historical relationship in her 2019 book, *As Long as Grass Grows: The Indigenous Fight for Environmental Justice from Colonization to Standing Rock.* Gilio-Whitaker describes this relationship as ambivalent due in part to the modern environmental movement's genealogical link with the earlier preservation movement, which was tied to settler colonialism and white supremacy. Blockadia—alongside the global resistance against extractive capitalism and the fossil economy more broadly—has provided ripe conditions for genuine solidarities that support Indigenous sovereignty in the struggle for environmental justice to emerge, which Holmes's activist archive makes clear.

THE ROUTES:
PETROCULTURAL MEMORY AGAINST EXTRACTIVISM

A desire to memorialize that which is still in historical motion emerges from an internalization of the now common argument that dominant, Western frames of reference to linear time have been fundamentally disrupted and require us to collectively refigure these temporalities. A linear temporality that cleanly delineates the present from the past and future, in other words, no longer maps onto empirical historical experience, if indeed it ever did. As part of a series on climate change directed towards a ranging public audience, the National Aeronautics and Space Administration (NASA) set out to answer the question of whether or not it is too late to prevent climate change. "Even if we stopped emitting greenhouse gases today," the article's opening paragraph states, "global warming would continue to happen for at least several more decades, if not centuries." "There is a time lag between what we do and when we feel it," the paragraph concludes (NASA). Human ecologist Andreas Malm describes the consequences of this fact on broader experiences of history. Malm tells us that in the wake of global climate change—a condition of the present that has resulted from the past accumulation of greenhouse gases in the atmosphere—we no longer reside in the present as such. Instead, we reside "[in] the heat of this ongoing past" (*Progress* 5). This point is instructive, if not politically immobilizing. The consequences of climate change—influenced in large part by the burning of fossil fuels— reveal that conventional temporal markers of past, present, and future are no longer adequate.

Linearity is perhaps the temporal counterpart to the grid in the ways that it flattens complex social and ecological relations. Put otherwise, linear time is a problem precisely because in its naturalized form it eschews other temporal relations, an inheritance of dominant Western frameworks that reify the teleological notions of progress so central to the mythologies of ongoing projects of settler colonialism and extractivism. In his 2015 book *Fossil Capital: The Rise of Steam Power and the Roots of Global Warming*, Malm describes the consequences of this explosion by arguing that, after a well-established "spatial turn" in critical theory, time is having its "revenge" (6). "For every year global warming continues and temperatures soar higher, living conditions on earth will be determined more intensely by the emissions of yore, so that the grip of yesteryear on today intensifies," Malm writes (9). After we reach a point of no return—a sort of climate rubicon—we experience "the final *falling in of history on the present*" (9). We arguably have yet to pass this rubicon; however, to date, the material consequences of the "revenge" of the past that is so jarring to the experience of linear time have been unevenly felt. This "explosion" of linear time occurring in the heat of climate change demands linear time's redress. As Potawatomi environmental justice scholar and philosopher Kyle Powys Whyte writes, "anthropogenic climate change is an intensified repetition of anthropogenic environmental change inflicted on Indigenous peoples via colonial practices that facilitated capitalist industrial expansion" (156). For Whyte, Indigenous knowledges—understood as "systems of monitoring, recording, communicating, and learning about the relationships among humans, nonhuman plants and animals, and ecosystems that are required for any society to survive and flourish in particular ecosystems which are subject to perturbations of various kinds" (157)— offer solutions to adequately address climate change when recognizing that these solutions must in the first instance be decolonial ones.

Alongside and in support of the centring of Indigenous knowledges in pursuit of self-determination as an integral component of addressing climate change, archives, in many ways, are well-suited to the task of confronting the explosion of linear time since they often tell us as much about the present and future as they do about the past. And like climate change itself, an archiving of an unfolding present troubles linear time while drawing attention to the possibilities of temporalities otherwise. In a more speculative closing chapter to her path-breaking 2014 book *Living Oil: Petroleum Culture in the American Century*, LeMenager thinks through the temporal implications of a "petroleum archive" grounded in an analysis of three oil museums that stoke petrocultural memory. LeMenager's interventions are "at once personal records of travel and close readings of museums devoted to petroleum as an everyday object, a habitual practice, and a resource destiny" (143). Travelling to the Page Museum at the La Brea Tar Pits in Los Angeles, California, the Oil Sands Discovery Centre in Fort McMurray, Alberta, and a series of energy museums in east Texas, LeMenager finds visions of our oil futures that speak to the conditions of the present. At the tar pits, LeMenager sees potential traces of the emergence of a "post-oil museum." A "post-oil museum," for LeMenager, "is simply a place where the cultural meanings of petroleum and fossil fuel more generally are on display, as a reflection on the age of conventional oil that we are now exiting" (145). Vocabularies of the museum and archive converge here to chart a series of possibilities for likewise approaching *Petropolis* as a virtual "post-oil museum."

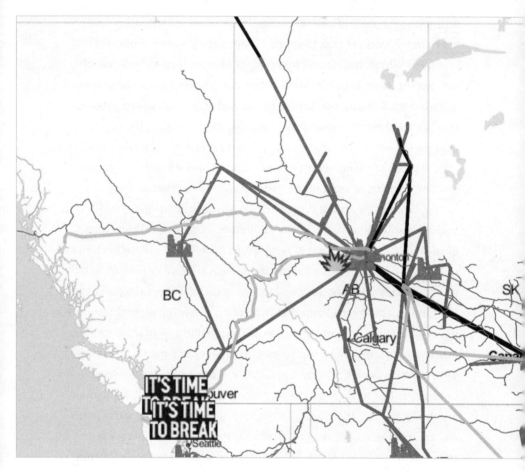

FIGURE 5.3.
Detail of pipeline networks from Athabasca oil sands and resistance sites.
(Brian Holmes, *Petropolis*. Used with permission.)

Petropolis is, as I have suggested throughout this chapter, a kind of petroleum archive in itself that opens up avenues for generating and tarrying with petrocultural memory. To read it as such brings into view the project's key sites of intervention: the sites of extraction and flows of oil through infrastructure and the nodes or communities of resistance in solidarity with one another that follow this expansion of fossil capital. In light of LeMenager's speculative impulse to read the petroleum archive in terms of the futures or ways forward that it offers, the counter-cartographic, activist archive that Holmes constructs and which is co-constituted by visitors who navigate *Petropolis* offers two competing *routes* as a dialectical pair, containing between them realizations of a range of possibilities. One *route* hinges upon the reproduction of "business as usual," where many of the spectral, dotted pipelines solidify and materialize, growing the infrastructural network seen so clearly in Figure 5.3. The other *route* sees the momentum of Blockadia finally topple the fossil economy. From the perspective of the present, it is not entirely clear which route will be favoured. What is clear is that Holmes is committed to the latter, and this emergent critique in *Petropolis* rests upon the shared experiences of petrocultural memory that the project promotes.

Emergence and process are thus registers through which *Petropolis* performs its critique of extraction on the one hand and its affirmation of resistance efforts geared toward the building of futures otherwise on the other. This critique and affirmation is performed through engagement with *Petropolis* as an interactive media object. The affective experience of stoking petrocultural memory, in other words, is generated through the navigation of scales and temporalities in *Petropolis*. The narrative against extractivism that emerges is contingent on the path that the audience chooses. Given the ways that the past now bears on the present as a snapshot of the contours of our petrocultural present, *Petropolis* will gather more determinant meaning further into the future as petrocultural memory becomes a widespread affective condition.

CONCLUSION

With better or worse outcomes, a future beyond oil is imminent. The routes we take and have taken to arrive at that future will determine its shape. For the series of potential routes that land squarely in the category of "worse," this future will come from the ruins of a system bent on its own destruction for the temporary benefit of a privileged few, a system that cultural theorist Michael Truscello describes in his work as the suicidal tendencies of capitalist states (8). That, it might go without saying, is the bad post-oil future. For those paths that promise more just relations leading up to and at the terminal point of the fossil fuel exit route, this future will come into being as a result of a collective undertaking.

Regardless of which future comes to the fore, from this speculative future vantage point, *Petropolis* will serve as an indicator of the emergence of petrocultural memory. Although *Petropolis* is in many ways more robust in its archiving of the structures and infrastructures of fossil capital than it is in its mapping of resistance, its positioning in support of the latter is clear. Returning to Holmes's own line of inquiry in his metacritical reflection on *Petropolis* is productive here. "What," he asks, "can art do about pipeline politics?" One of the most generative aspects to Jameson's theorization of cognitive mapping that I recounted in the early pages of this chapter is in the way that such mapping serves both to critique existing relations and to promote relations otherwise. *Petropolis* does both by stoking petrocultural memory vis-à-vis the spatial and temporal contours of "the petroleum industry and its discontents" (Holmes "What Can Art" 429) up to 2016, a period whose consequences are still unfolding. In a worse post-oil future, *Petropolis* will be a stark reminder that the fossil economy did not go unchallenged. In a post-oil future for the better, *Petropolis* will serve as a testament to the powers of collective resistance in shaping the future on our own terms.

NOTE

1. #NoDAPL is a Twitter hashtag that refers to a larger movement against Energy Transfer Partner's controversial Dakota Access Pipeline. The movement is a Sioux-led resistance effort that culminated in the establishment of a blockade encampment at Standing Rock in 2016 that drew international attention and private security and police repression.

WORKS CITED

350.org. "Break Free 2016—Albany, NY. 2016." *YouTube*, https://www.youtube.com/watch?v=h2GhHMCdyDc. Accessed 11 March 2024.

Bélanger, Pierre, et al. "Decolonization of Planning." *Extraction Empire: Undermining the Systems, States, and Scales of Canada's Global Resource Empire, 2017–1217*, edited by Pierre Bélanger, MIT Press, 2018, pp. 438–519.

Berman, Tzeporah. "The Oil Sands Are Now the Single Largest and Most Destructive Industrial Project on Earth." *NOW Magazine*, 10 April 2014, https://nowtoronto.com/the-oil-sands-are-now-the-single-largest-and-most-destructive-industrial-project-on-earth. Accessed 19 May 2021.

Coulthard, Glen. *Red Skin, White Masks: Rejecting the Colonial Politics of Recognition*. University of Minnesota Press, 2014.

Estes, Nick. *Our History Is the Future: Standing Rock versus the Dakota Access Pipeline, and the Long Tradition of Indigenous Resistance*. Verso Books, 2019.

Fruhwirth, Jesse, and Melanie Jae Martin. "Welcome to Blockadia!" *Yes! Magazine*, 12 January 2013, https://www.yesmagazine.org/environment/2013/01/12/welcome-to-blockadia-enbridge-transcanada-tar-sands. Accessed 19 May 2021.

Gilio-Whitaker, Dina. *As Long as Grass Grows: The Indigenous Fight for Environmental Justice from Colonization to Standing Rock*. Beacon Press, 2019.

Government of Canada, Canada Energy Regulator. *NEB—Project Background*, 29 September 2020, https://www.cer-rec.gc.ca/en/applications-hearings/view-applications-projects/trans-mountain-expansion/project-background.html. Accessed 19 May 2021.

Greenpeace Canada. "Greenpeace & First Nations Action In Vancouver—Break Free From Fossil Fuels." *YouTube,* 2016, https://www.youtube.com/watch?v=ykioNfVQ1-g. Accessed 17 April 2024.

"History." *Suncor*, https://www.suncor.com/en-ca/about-us/history. Accessed 22 December 2020.

Holmes, Brian. *Petropolis*, https://ecotopia.today/petropolis/map.html. Accessed 16 April 2024.

Holmes, Brian. "What Can Art Do about Pipeline Politics?" *South Atlantic Quarterly*, vol. 116, no. 2, 2017, pp. 426–31.

Innis, Harold A. *The Fur Trade in Canada: An Introduction to Canadian Economic History*. 1956. University of Toronto Press, 2000.

Jameson, Fredric. "Cognitive Mapping." *Marxism and the Interpretation of Culture*, edited by Cary Nelson and Lawrence Grossberg, University of Illinois Press, 1988, pp. 347–60.

Kinder, Jordan B. "In Absence of...A Cool Future." *Canadian Centre for Architecture*, April 2020, https://www.cca.qc.ca/en/articles/72631/in-absence-ofeveryday-truths. Accessed 19 May 2021.

Klein, Naomi. *This Changes Everything: Capitalism Vs. The Climate*. Simon and Schuster, 2014.

LeMenager, Stephanie. *Living Oil: Petroleum Culture in the American Century*. Oxford University Press, 2014.

Malm, Andreas. *Fossil Capital: The Rise of Steam Power and the Roots of Global Warming*. Verso, 2015.

Malm, Andreas. *The Progress of This Storm: Nature and Society in a Warming World*. Verso, 2018.

Marx, Karl. *Capital: A Critique of Political Economy, Volume One*. 1867. Translated by Ben Fowkes, Penguin Books, 1990.

"May 2016: Break Free from Fossil Fuels." *May 2016: Break Free from Fossil Fuels*, https://breakfree2016.org. Accessed 19 May 2021.

Milman, Oliver. "'Break Free' Fossil Fuel Protests Deemed 'Largest Ever' Global Disobedience." *The Guardian*, 16 May 2016, https://www.theguardian.com/environment/2016/may/16/break-free-protest-fossil-fuel. Accessed 19 May 2021.

NASA. "Is It Too Late to Prevent Climate Change?" *Climate Change: Vital Signs of the Planet*, https://climate.nasa.gov/faq/16/is-it-too-late-to-prevent-climate-change. Accessed 19 May 2021.

Pasternak, Shiri, and Dayna Nadine Scott. "Introduction: Getting Back the Land." *South Atlantic Quarterly*, vol. 119, no. 2, 2020, pp. 205–13.

Rundstrom, R. "Counter-Mapping." *International Encyclopedia of Human Geography*, Elsevier, 2009, pp. 314–18.

Simpson, Leanne Betasamosake. *As We Have Always Done: Indigenous Freedom through Radical Resistance*. University of Minnesota Press, 2017.

Truscello, Michael. *Infrastructural Brutalism: Art and the Necropolitics of Infrastructure.* MIT Press, 2020.

Unicorn Riot. "#BreakFree2016 Midwest Action Against Climate Change." *Vimeo,* 2016, https://vimeo.com/167070242. Accessed 11 March 2024.

Vassiliou, Marius S. *Historical Dictionary of the Petroleum Industry.* Scarecrow Press, 2009.

Vettese, Troy. "At All Costs." *Jacobin,* 13 July 2016, https://jacobinmag.com/2016/07/alberta-wildfire-tar-sands-petroleum-energy-oil-crisis/. Accessed 19 May 2021.

Whyte, Kyle. "Indigenous Climate Change Studies: Indigenizing Futures, Decolonizing the Anthropocene." *English Language Notes,* vol. 55, no. 1, 2017, pp. 153–62.

6

SOCIALLY MEDIATIZED IDENTITIES VERSUS THE LAW OF THE HEART

POSTHUMAN MEMORY IN SOPHIE DERASPE'S *ANTIGONE*

RUSSELL J.A. KILBOURN

IN THIS CHAPTER I read Quebecois filmmaker Sophie Deraspe's 2019 film *Antigone* as the vibrant expression of a youth-cultural identity specific to the experience of new immigrants living in Quebec's Laval region. This identity is in fact the "property" of an amorphous, if not entirely faceless, mass of teenagers who constitute a kind of collective secondary character that manifests in the film's ingenious remediation of the discourses of smartphone-supported social media within its encompassing adaptation of the original Greek tragedy.[1] This group identity is distinct from the film's protagonist, the titular Antigone (Nahéma Ricci), who, although also a teen in addition to being a refugee, actively sets herself apart from both this collective youth-cultural identity and from the mainstream hegemonic entity of the Canadian bureaucratic state. I analyze Deraspe's cinematic adaptation of Sophocles' *Antigone* in the context of posthuman memory inflected through transmediated, socially mediatized youth-subcultural identities. That my invocation of the term "posthuman" here also implies post-Canadian is only one of several ironies arising from an analysis of Deraspe's multivalent and polyvocal film. My reading is grounded in the film's adaptation of Sophocles' Antigone's character-defining refusal to compromise her radically observant adherence to "proper" religious practice: the original Antigone wishes to ensure that her brother Polynices, killed on the battlefield, on the wrong side of a civil war, receives the semblance of a proper burial. The film translates this key aspect of character and plot into its protagonist's almost fanatical adherence to personal, family-centred values and her steadfast refusal to capitulate to the law of the state.

Antigone is the only character to whose interior life we have access; despite the traumatic nature of her uprooting and move to Canada at the age of three, the film grounds her fidelity to family, home, and the past (childhood in Algeria) in a series of flashbacks to pasts both recent and distant, and in one climactic dream scene.[2] Deraspe's Antigone thus embodies intersectional memory as the nexus of a variety of mnemic vectors: Canadian, Quebecois, North African, immigrant, and diasporic, none of which takes precedence because all are subordinate to family. Her relation to memory, and the identity that it determines, is therefore powerfully "posthuman." According to Cecilia Åsberg and Rosi Braidotti, critical posthumanism is exemplified in feminist theory, "long critiquing the centrality of the figure of Man for its gender chauvinism." Woman, arguably, is the ultimate posthuman subject.[3] Despite one of its richest strains emerging from feminist philosophy, however, posthumanism has yet to fully account for the experiences of women and young people alike. By the film's conclusion, Antigone sacrifices everything to remain with what is left of her family, even as the story more broadly asserts the possibility of creating new or alternative collective identities through the appropriation, repurposing, and revaluation of the material and mediatic traces of colonialism, cultural assimilation, generational disparity, and gender inequity. *Antigone* asserts this posthumanist possibility through its exploitation of HD digital video technology, which also facilitates the presentation of a model of transindividual memory that runs counter to the protagonist's moral-ethical stance, representing another kind of posthuman identity that is as familiar as it is generic.

MEMORY IN THE MAKING

Contemporary memory theory privileges the agential "present-tenseness" of memory; its emergence out of action or reaction in the present rather than the return of some authentic or inauthentic past; its performance or construction; its malleability and productivity. The obvious touchstone here is Richard Terdiman's tidy definition of memory as "the past made present" (7). As Michael Rothberg makes clear, the notion of memory as a "making present" means that memory is "[not] strictly separable from either history or representation" and yet it "nonetheless captures simultaneously the individual, embodied, and lived side and the collective, social, and constructed side of our relations to the past" (3–4). Liedeke Plate and Annette Smelik, moreover, emphasize memory's performative dimension: "Memory is work—creative work—doing or carrying out the act...[It is] an embodied act grounded in the here and now, generating memory in the act of performing it" (2–3). "Memory," to quote Spallacci and Cormier in this volume's introduction, "is performative rather than reproductive," and thus demands "a reconsideration of [its] agency." These approaches, however, must be accommodated to memory's ongoing archival function. Contemporary cultural memory emerges at the intersection of present-tense performance or performativity (whether conscious, or agential, or not) and the archival function, because there is no memory without the materiality of a medium (Erll 114). In a very different example from Canadian cinema, the work of Isuma (now Kingulliit) Productions, since the 2001 release of *Atanarjuat* at least, has been exploiting, *avant la lettre*, a "YouTube approach" to performing, preserving, and passing on cultural knowledge. This approach is predicated on an understanding of "traditional" oral culture dependent upon a living chain of people and independent of mass media technologies of reproduction, simulation, storage, and distribution. But this is already at odds with the more recent acceptances of post-literate orality taken up by scholars and also as enacted in the Isuma films themselves. In these productions, the medium of film, or digital video, gives form to a diegetic world in which objects (tools, foodstuffs, clothing, etc.) and practices alike materialize a body of knowledge. In this manner, this knowledge, a culture's living mnemic legacy, is enacted, preserved, and passed on. The rise of social media presents a superficially similar set of practices in the contemporary obsession with learning by watching instructional videos that someone, somewhere, has posted on YouTube (Kilbourn 199).

In a different cultural context, Deraspe goes further by constructing a second-order representation of social media in action: *Antigone*'s "choral" segments remediate an already heavily mediated modality in social media as memory-in-action. The constitutive ephemerality of such techno-cultural memory is placed into dynamic, dialectical relation with the more retrograde modality of memory embodied by Antigone. In the end, because of the film's formal construction, Antigone's perspective seems to triumph, although her ultimate fate is ambiguous; the film concludes in a subjective, anti-realist register, opening out as if to address the viewer directly.

REMEDIATING ANTIGONE

Premiering in September 2019 at the Toronto International Film Festival, *Antigone* was crowned best Canadian feature, then selected as Canada's contender for best international feature at that year's Oscars. *Antigone* tells the story of a teenage Algerian refugee in working-class Laval. Fleeing the sectarian violence that killed her parents, Antigone came to Quebec from Kabylia at the age of three with her siblings and grandmother. She is now a straight-A student in a new relationship with Hémon (Antoine DesRocher), a classmate and the son of a local politician. Eteocles (Hakim Brahimi), Antigone's older brother, is shot by police when they arrest Polynices (Rawad El-Zein), her younger brother; both are involved with the Habibi, an Arabo-Quebecois street gang. Antigone's world is thrown into chaos, her sense of identity inextricably connected with the well-being of her family. She concocts a plan to break Polynices out of jail by disguising herself as him and taking his place, thinking that, as a minor, she will escape serious punishment. Instead, she faces jail time, and Polynices' deportation to North Africa. Her court-appointed lawyer secures a lighter sentence and the prospect of citizenship, as Antigone and her family are only permanent residents; the court hearing is disrupted, however, when Polynices is re-apprehended, rendering Antigone's sacrifice pointless and presenting her with the irresolvable choice between citizenship and family. She chooses the latter and deportation with her brother and grandmother, back to their village in northern Algeria.

The film opens with a prelude that turns out retrospectively to be a flash-forward to the scene of Antigone's arrest by the Montreal police. The short, single-take scene—a medium close-up of Antigone facing the offscreen police photographer, occupying the position of the film camera—concludes with a line keyed to the film's central theme: advised to call her parents, Antigone responds, "My parents are dead." The opening scene proper follows with the Hipponome family gathered at home for a communal meal for which Eteocles gives the blessing, nodding to the photograph of their deceased parents: "May the year bring peace and prosperity. Baba, Mama, and all our ancestors, keep us safe, and…" He hesitates, so Antigone finishes for him: "Keep us united." She then sarcastically imitates her other brother, Polynices', verbal mannerisms, his *joual* gangsterisms, foregrounding the centrality of an idiom, a way of speaking, to a subculture's unique identity. When he accuses her of talking like a teacher, she responds, "How should I talk, yo? I'm from the hood. I represent!…Step off. I'm from the hood!" This also foreshadows, as an unwitting dress rehearsal, Antigone's later and much higher stakes impersonation of her brother in his physicality: his clothes, hair, even his tattoos, when she disguises herself as him—and vice versa—in the audacious act of transvestitism that succeeds in springing him from jail.

Russell J.A. Kilbourn

FIGURE 6.1.
Antigone's perspective in seeing her murdered parents.

The film's first act ends with the police killing Eteocles as he moves to aid his brother, arrested in a Montreal park. When Hémon's father, Christian (Paul Doucet), the film's principal Creon character, tells the family that Polynices could be deported, Antigone translates her grandmother Meni's (Rachida Oussaada) response: "She says it's Hell," meaning the Algerian prison into which Polynices will presumably be cast upon his return. As if in response to this mnemic trigger, the scene cuts from a close-up on Antigone to the film's first flashback, the fateful scene in Kabylia. The optical point of view is hers as a three-year-old, peeking down from an upper story of a house through the filigree cast ironwork outside the window (Figure 6.1).

In a handheld shot that intensifies the intimacy of the memory, bearded men unceremoniously dump two elongated objects rolled in carpets in front of the house, Antigone's mother's red shoe conspicuous on the pavement. Deraspe economically invokes the scandal of the unburied dead in Sophocles' original, folded into a flashback sequence that gestures towards a whole catalogue of violent acts and atrocities in the name of fundamentalism. Here, not the brother's but the parents' bodies are left unburied, cast out by defacto authorities, in death a warning to anyone else with the "wrong" political or religious views. In this way, the film sidesteps the incest theme from the Oedipal myth by conflating Antigone's dead parents with the dead brothers from the original play, thereby shifting the play's foregrounded politics onto the film's background storyline.

As an adaptation of the ancient tragedy, the film interpolates a fair amount of new narrative material and reorders certain key set pieces carried over from the play. For instance, in the play's opening scene (in both Sophocles' original and Brecht's adaptation) Antigone and her sister Ismène discuss the former's decision to go against Creon, the King of Thebes', orders and bury her brother's body. In the film this is transposed to the beginning of the second act, when Antigone announces her plan to break Polynices out of prison by masquerading as him and taking his place. She asks her sister, a hair stylist, to cut her hair short, to which Ismène (Nour Belkhiria) responds, "You'll look like a boy." Here and elsewhere, the film foregrounds and complicates themes from the Oedipal myth cycle—of gender identity, interfamilial relations, and challenging cultural taboos. Antigone thus determines to save Polynices by trading places with him, by temporarily becoming him and having him become her. To the police interrogator's observation that she broke the law for her brother, Antigone responds, "I have only one left. I have to help him." This recalls one of Antigone's most famous speeches in Sophocles' play: "What law, / You ask, do I satisfy with what I say? / [Mother] and father both lost in the halls of Death, / No brother could ever spring to light again. / For this law alone I held you first in honor" (Sophocles 105). As Francesca Chaplin puts it, "[for] both the ancient and the modern Antigone, a brother must be cherished" (2). Invoking Judith Butler, Lucia Delaini reads these lines as suggesting on Antigone's part a more-than-sisterly love for Polynices: "Butler proposes a reading of this love as the exact opposite of pure, as she sees in it the clear sign of incestuous desire: but the revolutionary potential of this desire is just as incendiary...in that it challenges society's definition of kinship, normally taken for granted as natural" (74). In Butler's reading, Antigone's crime "is confounded...

by the manifestly incestuous act that is the condition of her own existence, which makes her brother her father, which begins a narrative in which she occupies, linguistically, every kin position except "mother" and occupies them at the expense of the coherence of kinship and gender" (72).[4] Deraspe's adaptation sublimates the myth's incestuous echoes, focusing instead on the significance to Antigone of family and kinship ties beyond every other concern, putting her own understanding of a kind of primal, moral-ethical "law" over any paternalistic law of the land. This primal law is also quasi-maternal, moreover, as Antigone in effect takes upon herself the role of mother to her remaining siblings, sacrificing herself in order to keep the family together at any cost. For Antigone, to perform her role as sister and daughter, and as surrogate mother, is what it means to be a human being. As Butler puts it, "[to] become human, for some, requires participation in the family in its normative sense" (22). And yet this very humanity is the basis of Antigone's posthuman identity.

Toward the end of the film's second act, as Ismène and Meni help Polynices to escape, a Laval city bus pulls up near the jail, with a banner on the side advertising "Oedipe Roi," a production by Theatre Anaphore. This intra-diegetic allusion to the second play in Sophocles' Theban trilogy asks the attentive viewer to remember the ancient mythic cycle behind the original tragedy that comes inevitably to form the background to every *Antigone* adaptation, including Deraspe's film. What might be called the laws of intermediality determine that, like it or not, the original play's themes permeate and influence the meanings of any contemporary remediation. This in turn suggests that, in a sense, the curse on the house of Oedipus, the one that brings him to his fore-ordained fate, continues to operate here: no matter her actions, Antigone cannot escape this curse. In the radically contemporary, Canadian-Quebecois-Algerian setting of Deraspe's film, Antigone's parents are nameless, faceless Algerians, "Baba" and "Mama," invoked only in a single, fleetingly glimpsed, family photo. They are always already absent, shapes rolled in carpets and dumped in front of Antigone's childhood home the night before her departure to political asylum in Canada. The only curse, so to speak, acting upon the family Hipponome is one as old as Oedipus: the all-too-human curse of armed men who seek power over others. After all, in the film's backstory, briefly glimpsed in Antigone's subjective flashbacks, Algeria was convulsed by civil war, Islamic insurgents fighting first the secular government and then one another, innocent civilians swept up in the violence. This form of the family curse carries over in Canada, transposed onto their relations with a system with which Meni, the grandmother, was ill-equipped to cope, as she failed to complete the necessary paperwork to secure her grandchildren's Canadian citizenship. But the threat or curse represented by men, by the masculinist principle of will to power through violence, also manifests within her family in the form of Eteocles' and Polynices' membership in the Habibi, whose black and orange colours visually offset Antigone's red-white-and blue palette,[5] that of the French flag, of liberté, égalité, and, most importantly for Antigone, fraternité.[6] For she willingly gives up the first two in order to secure the last, for herself and what remains of her family at the end.

DISCOURSE, REPRESENTATION, IDENTITY

Antigone is punctuated at key intervals by three (or four)[7] montage sequences that disrupt the narrative flow, providing a kind of diffuse, conflictual commentary upon the action. What Seana Stevenson calls the film's "social media montages" provide "a fascinating modernization of the Greek Chorus" (para. 3).[8] In Sophocles' play, the chorus stands in for or represents "the old citizens of Thebes" (21), and in Bertolt Brecht's 1944 adaptation of the play, they are referred to simply as "the elders." In the film, ironically, the citizen's chorus becomes a polyphonic aggregation of youthful voices, hip hop and electronic music, rapidly edited images, animation, and narcissistic social media self-promotion. To this aggregate identity is counterposed the individual protagonist, a distinction from the original play that Deraspe reimagines for the digital era. As one of the most famous ancient Greek tragedies, Sophocles' *Antigone* is an exemplar of the interplay of individual drama (Antigone's) and the chorus as voice of the collective (Rancière 5). The historical origins of this double perspective are ancient; in Greek tragedy, the chorus "is an emotional bridge between spectators and actors" (Sophocles 20), representing the audience as a collectivity, set over against the tragic protagonist, with whom the individual spectator would identify—up to a point. According to Jacques Rancière, "theatre remains the only place where the audience confronts itself as a collective...It involves an idea of community as self-presence, in contrast to the distance of representation" (5–6). The analogy with contemporary social media as mode of so-called self-expression is obvious and, like all analogies, also dangerous. Rancière refers here to theatrical performance, but I propose another, double analogy, with the collective spectatorial experience of film viewing, on the one hand, and the embodied performance of memory, on the other—a performance and an embodiment, however, which, like everything else in a film text, are irreducibly mediated at one or more removes. Film as a medium is precisely the triumph of representation over self-presence. In what might be a productive complication of current memory theory, such a memory performance captured in film is eminently reproducible; as Plate and Smelik remind us, memory "is work—creative work...an embodied act grounded in the here and now, generating memory in the act of performing it" (3). But while the memory work performed in *Antigone*'s social media interludes represents the iconic "here and now-ness" of memory as performance, as cinematic sequences such interludes also represent the indexical "there and then-ness" of representation as *re*-presentation. Antigone's engagement with memory via the dual temporal levels of the flashbacks, by contrast, is both more conventional and more radical; for her, the presentness of memory as performance is outweighed, ethically and affectively, by the irreducible pastness of memory as loss and absence.

As a contemporary Quebecois production with one foot firmly in the ancient past, *Antigone*'s choral interludes lay bare its investment in investigating the relations between and among various valences and modalities of twenty-first-century cultural memory. The choral sequences embody the double-logic of remediation in the interplay of immediacy and the hypermediacy characteristic of the Web 2.0 graphical interface. In this they cut to the heart of *Antigone*'s exploration and exemplification of posthuman memory in the most progressive and productive post-Enlightenment Humanist sense. This critique is centred in Antigone, whose agency, values, body, and voice[9] represent a radically different mode of embodied subjectivity—North African (and therefore racialized), female, youth/teen/adolescent, economically disadvantaged, immigrant—grounding a complex and irreducibly contradictory identity, ironically at odds with the socially mediatized/mediated modality of collective memory that is more obviously "posthuman." I invoke this term in reference to both the ideologically and epistemologically "posthuman*ist*" subjectivity that Antigone embodies onscreen and the "posthuman" youth-subcultural memory to which her situation gives rise within the film's diegesis: where the former emerges out of a justifiable critique of the Western Enlightenment Humanist subject, the subject of individualism, the pursuit of pleasure, and the valorization of progress, the latter, posthuman memory, is the film's response to heretofore dominant modalities of collective or transubjective memory. The "human" in posthuman thus denotes not a transhumanist alternative to *homo sapiens*, but rather a counterhegemonic critique of prevailing conceptions of embodied agential political identity.

The question of posthuman versus human identity in *Antigone*—as with virtually every narrative film ever made—is grounded in Deraspe's exploitation of the close-up, an utterly conventional technique that nevertheless still inspires commentary because, used effectively, it packs a powerful visual-affective punch (Figure 6.2).

Those who criticize Deraspe's heavy reliance on close-ups of Nahéma Ricci's face forget Carl Theodor Dreyer's *Passion of Joan of Arc* (1928), a film made up predominantly of close-ups. This comparison illuminates our understanding of *Antigone* and the significant differences between Dreyer's Joan (Renée Falconetti), whose martyrdom is sustained by her faith in God, while Deraspe's Antigone (not to mention Sophocles' heroine), puts her family above all else, including

FIGURE 6.2.
Close-up shot of Antigone.

any conventional understanding of faith. Her faith, instead, resembles chthonic paganism, in which—as she tells the psychiatrist in the final act—the souls of one's departed loved ones are always present, invisible but passing judgment.

The close-up in film exemplifies the post-classical filmic discourse that Deraspe so effectively employs. A distinction has emerged since 2006 or so, epitomized in the qualitative and quantitative difference between a digital self-portrait, or "selfie," whose primary meaning is always generic, and a human face in cinematic close-up, which retains the uncanniness of the filmic image unfolding in time. This tension between an inauthentic "mask" and the authentic "face" beneath it reminds us of the subject's lingering value for our thinking of the ethical relation between self and other in the epistemological move from human to post- or even nonhuman. *Antigone* positions the eponymous protagonist as the "face" of a human whose at times ambiguous gender and unambiguous youth push it toward the posthuman in this specific sense. Her peers, meanwhile, as a collective whole, are positioned against her via their socially mediated presence as the aggregate posthuman identity whose youth-subcultural "mask"—images and text but also music—conceals a malleable and adaptable but always already commodified package of meanings. Moreover, the film's social media montages gesture toward "youth" as a social class in (unconscious) defiance of the historical-cultural-ideological legacy of the close-up as an obvious, literal valorization of the individual, even as the representative "face" of the larger group. In spite of the recent "anti-representationalist turn" in posthumanist theory,[10] representation remains a central concern in this discussion. Since the heyday of cultural studies in the 1980s and 1990s, identity has been understood as inextricably tied up with *representation*, which is understood as "the symbolic practices and processes through which...meaning and language operate" in the construction of social reality (Hall 15). Identity, in this constructivist view, is a discursive formation connected to representation: one speaks oneself into being through the tropes and schemata, the images and narratives of the available discourses, whether verbal, sartorial, musical, technical, or otherwise.

In a variety of youth-subcultural examples from the postwar 1950s to the 1990s, Dick Hebdige (*Hiding*; *Subculture*) identifies those aspects of group self-expression—hair, clothes, and technical equipment, whether vehicles or weapons, but especially musical and linguistic choices—that stand as aspects of a bona fide discourse of expressive self-fashioning. Moreover, in most cases such youth-subcultural identarian discourses also constitute modalities of political "representation." This happens, however, not in terms of official party politics, which is part of the power structures that such subcultures imagine that they symbolically resist or transgress, but in the sense, from American hip hop usage, in which each member is seen to "represent" their collective by means of specific sartorial, linguistic, or musical choices. Ever since the rise of hip hop and Black urban slang, first in the US, then in Europe and globally, these usages have come together informally in the idea of "reprezentin'," and the most significant act of representation is when one represents one's *self*—to oneself and to others; Antigone to Polynices: "How should I talk, yo? I'm from the hood. I represent!"

CHORAL INTERLUDES / SOCIAL MEDIA MONTAGES

This returns us to the question of the choral montage sequences: interludic episodes within the overarching diegetic structure of the film, which are not part of the narrative so much as self-reflexive transmedial commentaries upon it. Rather than being "authentic" examples of such socially mediatized communication, these sequences are stylized representations, fabricated by the filmmakers, at one or more removes from the "'real-life" diegetic circumstances and characters upon which they offer commentary.

The first social media montage focuses on Eteocles' death—killed by the police because they thought his cellphone was a gun, as is clear from this sequence, filmed by another youth with his cellphone; intentionally or not, the smartphone with HD video capture capabilities is weaponized, as the scene from earlier in the film plays out again from the reverse angle. With Nate Husser's moody rap track, "Catherine," overtop ("Do you cry / You got too much pride / Who gon die"), a cascade of images and videos sums up Eteocles' short life, the signifiers of his Habibi gang affiliation predominating. Deraspe also cuts in archival footage of riots that followed the 2008 police shooting in a Montreal park of Fredy Villanueva, a young Honduran immigrant, tacitly associating the actual and fictional events. Here *Antigone* takes a page from Mathieu Kassovitz's *La Haine*, whose credit sequence exploits actual TV footage of the 1993 *banlieue* riots, which erupted in the wake of the death of a young man in police custody. This layering of cultural-mnemic, historical-mediatic, fictive-cinematic, and intra-diegetic content underscores the unique status of this interludic segment as an instance of posthuman memory in the key of angry mourning.

The second choral interlude shifts into an angrier register still, as online voices compete to tell Antigone's story, irrespective of the truth. At the start of the scene Antigone meets with her court-appointed lawyer, who lists the items that she needs to worry about as they prepare her defence: "Above all," he tells her, "there's the media. Blogs, Facebook, social networks..." Emerging smoothly out of the cellphone screen in

FIGURE 6.3.
Depiction of Antigone on social media.

Antigone's hand, the second social media montage builds out of online news feeds into a commentary on her pivotal role in Polynices' prison escape. Antigone's image circulates rapidly online through highly remediated photographs and videos, some of which filter her identity through racist, Islamophobic, and misogynist discourses. Simultaneously and outside her control, she is constructed as a symbol of resistance against police brutality. Fast-paced editing, split-screens, line animations, vertical shots, and selfies evoke the use of phone cameras to capture and post videos and photographs on social media, contributing to the growth of Antigone's online persona: an explosive montage of headlines and remediated images with fabricated narratives about her "radicalized" immigrant background. The editing and cinematography here also reveal the magnitude of Antigone's posthuman identity as a symbol of rebellion, as it grows beyond her embodied self, going viral and inspiring an online community across gendered and racial lines. "That's not who I am," laments Antigone (Figure 6.3).

Across the sequence, social media's collective audience engages in a polarizing continuum of reactions that villainize, demonize, and sexualize her, even painting her as a hero. The fast-paced montage and the amateurish superimposition of a burqa, or sunglasses and a "grill," capture the socially mediatized construction of a false, racist, and misogynist identity. To Antigone's shocked response, her lawyer reminds her that images can be controlled. "Just...tell the truth," she says. "What's the truth?" he responds. "I stand behind my family"; this is Antigone's "truth," her law of the heart: "Mon coeur me dit." As Deraspe explains: "She's even willing to sacrifice herself to stay true to [the 'law' of her heart]. This is where the sentence 'Mon coeur me dit' (My heart tells me) comes from. This, to me, is Antigone" (Dunlevy). Hémon also discerns this truth in her actions, which he manipulates, both online and off, using an enlarged close-up of her face to successfully reclaim Antigone's contested identity from that of domestic terrorist "Habibitch," who deserves to be in jail, to a Joan of Arc for the twenty-first century, a public symbol with a sizeable social media following.

In the third choral interlude, Hémon shifts the narrative from the false representations and "fake news" of the second interlude to a colour-coded expression of subcultural solidarity. Antigone's posthuman identity reaches its fullest potential in a montage of photographs and videos shared online in support of her cause, featuring Hémon's drawing of her face with the slogan: "Mon coeur me dit." This interlude emerges out of the mournful melody that Meni, Antigone's Algerian grandmother, sings from her post outside the juvenile detention centre—as if Antigone were already dead, which, in a sense, following the dream scene, she is. As Christian ponders Antigone's expression of unconditional love for her wayward brother, the image shifts to Hémon's campaign to disseminate red-and-white images of Antigone's face, with "Mon coeur me dit" stenciled below. Where the first two choral montages are conflictual or cacophonic in the sense that they contain competing voices—clearly "fake" versus "true" versions of the story—the third and fourth sequences, by contrast, represent a more unified, polyphonic vision of cross-generational dissent or resistance. And yet this is a distorted reflection of Antigone's actual achievement, which is to tell her own truth, steadfastly and without compromise. The fourth and final interlude is an extension of the third; as a segue back into the main storyline, Deraspe cuts in footage of the other girls as they style and dye their hair red in solidarity with Hémon's campaign and Antigone's "Mon coeur me dit."

Antigone becomes a rallying or centripetal force, drawing people into makeshift family groups. Almost in spite of herself, her actions have a galvanizing effect upon those around her, especially other young people: the other girls in the detention centre, for instance, start out a fractious group, only to unite under Antigone's unintentional influence. But throughout, Antigone remains apart, dedicated only to her own law. When these girls rally around her, Antigone is visibly moved, yet she never allows herself to coincide with her online, socially mediated—which here means transmediated—posthuman identity.

ANTIGONE'S FLASHBACKS

Antigone's public persona, constructed in part by Hémon, is at odds with her authentic identity, which the film addresses in the flashbacks and other sequences. The second flashback occurs in the midst of Antigone's interrogation by the police inspector. As he details Polynices' involvement with the Habibi, we see Antigone in close-up, looking at the photos in the police file; this cuts straight to Polynices coming home one night, sometime before the present-tense action of the diegesis. He is limping, his face bruised and cut. Confronted by Antigone, he reveals that he has just been initiated into the gang, a privilege he actively sought. The third flashback occurs at the end of the interrogation scene, when Antigone recalls a happier time playing soccer with Eteocles. The flashback unfolds in ironic slow-motion counterpoint with the police interrogator's account of Eteocles' criminal career. At one point, Christian, like her lawyer and the police inspector before him, asks Antigone: why sacrifice yourself for your brother, a low-life criminal? How can you love him? "When I'm unsure what to do," she replies, after a protracted pause, "I think of the little boy, little Polynices, stretching his arms to be picked up. But nobody picks him up": the fatherless little boy who grows up into a teen-age gangster. If the gender politics and interfamilial relationships in the film do not appear as straightforward as this scene might suggest, it is because they run on a parallel track, never coinciding with Antigone's trajectory, as her unshakeable "faith" in family ties becomes increasingly untenable with respect to what the state asks of her, and even with respect to the significant groundswell of popular youth-based support that her act of resistance inspires.

Antigone does make a literal sacrifice on behalf of Polynices in the film, but in a different sense from her fate in the play. Where in Sophocles' story she dares to sprinkle dust over her brother's unburied corpse, a crime for which Creon sentences her to death, in the film she substitutes herself for Polynices, making of herself a literal sacrificial substitute. Instead, her punishment is deportation to Kabylia, the family's North African *patria*. The fourth flashback, in fact, is an unattributed, mobile overhead shot of the northern Algerian village, cut into the scene of Antigone in jail, in what appears to be an attitude of prayer, and her first appearance in court.

After her final, disastrous court appearance, Antigone languishes in a solitary cell, lying on the floor in exhaustion. In a high-angle upside-down medium shot, she calls quietly for her dead father and mother: "Where are you?" There is a cut to a close-up; in the darkness a man's hand is placed on the left side of her face, then a woman's, on the right. They gently stroke her hair, in silent comfort. This space is purely subjective, strikingly different from that of either the earlier flashbacks or the social media montages. This leads into the last of the interview scenes, in which Antigone faces off against the final interlocutor in a group that has varied from antagonistic (the police inspector) to supportive (the lawyer) to affectionate (Christian). Each is in effect one face of the spirit of Creon that Deraspe wisely chose to disperse across the film. This meeting is the most ambiguous and unsettling by far.

The scene begins with a straight cut from the upside-down close-up on the supine Antigone to a close-up shot of the back of a woman's head. At the sound of the door opening, the woman turns her head. "Are you Antigone?" "Yes, Madame." She introduces herself as Teresa, a psychiatrist. "Please, can you stop calling me madame?" she asks Antigone, who responds: "yes...sir." To which the analyst—obviously the film's version of the blind seer Tiresias—laughs.[11] To her question, "What happened?" Antigone replies, "nothing you haven't already read about my family." "I've read nothing," she says. "I prefer meeting face-to-face" (the French, "rapport direct," lacks the reference to the face). At this the analyst removes her thick black glasses, revealing that she, like her masculine namesake, is blind.

> Teresa [as monotone, extra-diegetic strings swell in
>   the background, generating an atmosphere
>   of dread]: "Do you know why you're here?"
> Antigone: " I have to make an impossible choice...
>   citizenship or my brother."
> "Civic life or family."
> "I'm responsible for my family."
> "You're responsible for your future."
> "I have no future."

In Antigone's view, she has no future anymore, only her family. She cannot relax, she says, "because of the dead." The dead are here, "all around...stripped of their sheath, but here." As Antigone speaks, the camera slowly arcs, right to left. A cut to Teresa, also in medium close-up, the camera moving slowly rightwards; a cut back to Antigone, the two women linked by the unmotivated camera movement that continues across each cut. As Antigone shifts into mid-frame, the light on her face changes. She gazes at the analyst across from her, now in a trance-like state. A sudden straight cut to an overhead forward tracking shot of the Algerian countryside, the landscape of Antigone's childhood—the same setting that we have seen in flashback twice before. In voiceover, Teresa asks if Antigone fears the judgment of the dead. Antigone answers that she fears their judgment more than that of the living. Her entire being is now oriented to the past, and toward those who are no longer alive. For her, memory is the land of the dead, an afterlife that is also the only real place, the only place that will welcome her now. The analyst—now a seer— out of focus, stretches her hand, in focus, toward Antigone's face, also out of focus in the right foreground. They clasp hands and, in a sudden reverse angle, she pulls Antigone toward her, into a two-shot, the latter's face in focus. A shift to the reverse angle, another two-shot, as Teresa predicts that for Antigone there is no solution: the conflict between "the law of your heart and of man is insoluble." A cut to close-up on Teresa's face, with its sightless eyes: "You shall be walled up alive."

Her awful prediction is one of the film's direct references to the source text, to the original Antigone's eventual fate, as an enraged Creon decrees that she be imprisoned in a tomb and left to starve. In Sophocles' tragic ending, offstage Antigone pre-empts one fate and fulfills another by taking her own life, her final act of independence and resistance. Here, in this scene, on the analyst's final word, "alive" (*vivant*), Antigone recoils in horror, turning to look behind her, an offscreen scream sound- ing as the camera cuts first to the reverse angle and then to Antigone, back in her cell, waking up from the nightmare. Her breath comes raggedly, as, unable to speak, she presses up against the locked door's window, her face a mask of abject fear. She gasps for air, as if walled up alive. The appearance of Teresa within Antigone's dream mediates between her conscious and unconscious lives/selves/"fates," not to speak of the male and female aspects of Antigone's identity, her past/family and her future/death. What of North Africa? In Antigone's memory, Algeria is associated with family, but as her future destination it is associated with death, whether literal or metaphorical: a living death, being "walled up alive." For Judith Butler, Antigone's fate "is not to have a life to live, to be condemned to death prior to any possibility of life" (23). Deraspe's film, however, gestures toward a different possible fate in its penultimate scene, in which Antigone has sex with Hémon in a rain-soaked forest glade. But the scene's positive, life-affirming potential appears to be undercut when Antigone in the end chooses Polynices, a real brother over a pseudo-brother.[12]

CONCLUSION

Sophie Deraspe's decision to adapt *Antigone*, Sophocles fourth-century BCE tragedy, by way of previous adaptations by Jean Anouilh and Bertolt Brecht, is an inspired one given the character and the story's ongoing resonance for generations of viewers. For contemporary audiences, Antigone's tragedy still strikes a chord, but not necessarily for the same reasons as with her previous avatars. Deraspe's film maximizes, at a distance of over two millennia, the extraordinary potential of the original character, a young woman who defies all patriarchal—and proto-paternal—authority, following only her own principles, at the cost of her freedom and personal well-being. But, unlike all other interpretations of Antigone, the film also maximizes the protagonist's youth. Even more than an enlightened feminist take on *Antigone*, Deraspe's film is a sophisticated study of contemporary youth-subcultural identities simultaneously empowered and determined—transmediated and interpellated—by social media.

Antigone ends ambiguously, even while Antigone's fate is seemingly confirmed. A medium shot of a group proceeding down an airport terminal passage, en route to the boarding gates: Meni, Polynices, and Antigone walk single file, chaperoned by several RCMP officers. Ambient airport noise drones in the background as the angle shifts to a rear view of the departing group. The mobile camera pans left with Antigone's turning head, her attention caught by a family of newly arrived refugees. The viewer will recognize this family as the same from an earlier flashback: it is Antigone's family, and she is looking at herself as a three-year-old refugee. In this simple shot, the film folds both time frames together into a single space—the transitory non-space of the airport terminal. In a brief travelling shot-reverse-shot sequence, Antigone looks at her younger self, the child leaning forward in her stroller to stare accusingly at her avatar; as past and present meet, Antigone's future seemingly collapses into this impossible moment.

The film ends with a close-up shot of Antigone's face as she stops and turns and looks behind her, addressing the camera directly, the

FIGURE 6.4.
Final close-up shot of Antigone.

distinctive whistling ringtone from the earlier courtroom scenes on the soundtrack (Figure 6.4).

She is like a latter-day Eurydice, suddenly called back by those that she has chosen to leave behind, only Antigone here is not in the position of the woman following her lover out of the underworld; rather, she is called back from the underworld by her lover, since it was Hémon who used the ringtone first in an earlier courtroom scene. This sound, like this final close-up shot, is anomalous in that it is at once diegetic and extra-diegetic, an auditory signifier audible to Antigone within the filmic world and also to the viewer-listener, who is addressed by her searching look, all other action arrested as the other actors freeze in place around her.

Antigone, in its hypermediated engagement with social media, looks not so much to the future as to the present, insofar as it instantiates youth-cultural memory as performance: memory as the past made present. At the same time, in the flashback scenes associated with its titular protagonist, the film presents a more "immediate"—which is to say mimetically grounded—representation of individual memory in action. Antigone's posthumanist, self-determined image gives her agency and overturns racist and patriarchal assumptions about her identity. Her loyalty to Polynices, however, leads her to abandon this disembodied, politically charged identity and reject her agency when she re-establishes her place within the family structure and chooses to be deported to Algeria. She rejects the transmedial posthuman identity born of a socially mediated interface, embracing instead an embodied, offline, post-digital identity that is the locus of authenticity and "truth"—a locus that finds expression in the film's recourse to the close-up on Antigone's all-too-human face.

NOTES

1. Deraspe's film exemplifies both trajectories of remediation: an older media form (cinema) transforming a newer (social media), and a newer (cinema) transforming an older (theatre) (see Bolter and Grusin).
2. In her third-act confrontation with Meni, who has decided to return to Kabylia with Polynices, Antigone exclaims "What will I do without you? You're my home!"
3. I thank Julia Empey for this insight (personal communication).
4. See Jacobs, who cites Robert Graves regarding the etymology of Antigone's name as "in place of a mother" (891).
5. Throughout the film Antigone's signature colours are red and white, with blue (and also black) introduced in the detention centre scenes.
6. The French tricolour—here, part of Quebec's French-colonialist legacy—has historically stood "in symbolic opposition to the autocratic and clericalist royal standards of the past" (*Encyclopedia Brittanica*). According to Deraspe, the use of the colour red in the film's visual design refers primarily to the colour's historical association with socialism and revolutionary politics more generally (unpub. interview). As Matthew Cormier points out, the colour scheme "is also ironic given the French (understood to be masculinist, as well) colonization of Algeria" (personal communication).
7. The fourth sequence is essentially a continuation of the third.
8. "In addition to actors and spectators, there was a third element of the performance, one older than either of these two. It was the chorus—a

Greek word that means 'dance'; the chorus of Greek tragedies sang, but it was also and had been in origin a group of dancers...[The] chorus was always there, and it has an important function: it is an emotional bridge between spectators and actors. An anonymous crowd with only a group identity—Theban citizens, inhabitants of Colonus or whatever—it functioned on stage as if the audience itself were part of the action; all the more so because, unlike the professional actors, the chorus consisted of citizen amateurs, representing their tribal group in the dramatic competition" (Sophocles 20). See also Dunlevy.

9. The latter two belonging to first-time actor Nahéma Ricci.

10. See, for example, Barad 2003; 2007 (esp. Ch. 4 on "agential realism").

11. Antigone's joke alludes to Tiresias' backstory, having the experience of living as both a man and as a woman.

12. Just before the sex scene, Christian offers to become Antigone's legal guardian, as she is still seventeen, a minor. This would have made Hémon her brother, legally speaking.

WORKS CITED

Anouilh, Jean. *Antigone*. 1944. Translated by Barbara Bray, Bloomsbury, 2009.

Antigone. Directed by Sophie Deraspe, Association Coopérative des Productions AudioVisuelles, 2019.

Åsberg, Cecilia, and Rosi Braidotti. "Feminist Posthumanities: An Introduction." *A Feminist Companion to the Posthumanities*, edited by Cecilia Åsberg and Rosi Braidotti, Springer, 2018, pp. 1–22.

Atanarjuat. Directed by Zacharias Kunuk and Norman Cohn, Igloolik Isuma Productions, National Film Board of Canada (NFB), Aboriginal Peoples Television Network, 2001.

Barad, Karen. *Meeting the Universe Halfway: Quantum Physics and the Entanglement of Matter and Meaning*. Duke University Press, 2007.

Barad, Karen. "Posthumanist Performativity: Toward an Understanding of How Matter Comes to Matter." *Signs*, vol. 28, no. 3, 2003, pp. 801–31.

Bolter, Jay David, and Richard Grusin. *Remediation: Understanding New Media*. MIT Press, 2000.

Brecht, Bertolt. *Antigone*. 1948. Translated by Judith Malina, Applause Theatre and Cinema Books, 1990.

Butler, Judith. *Antigone's Claim: Kinship Between Life and Death*. Columbia University Press, 2000.

Chaplin, Francesca. "Sophie Deraspe's 'Antigone'." *Ostraka*, 14 January 2020, https://medium.com/ostraka-a-durham-university-classics-society-blog/sophie-deraspes-antigone-d611f23ff9ab. Accessed 12 May 2021.

Delaini, Lucia. *Resistance and Truth-telling:* Antigone *in Twentieth-Century Literature*. 2015. Crossways in Cultural Narratives, Erasmus Mundus, MA Thesis.

Deraspe, Sophie. Personal interview. March 2020.

Dunlevy, T'Cha. "From Greek Tragedy to Bill 21, Quebec Film *Antigone* Bridges Millenniums." *Montreal Gazette*, 8 November 2019, https://montrealgazette.com/entertainment/local-arts/from-greek-tragedy-to-bill-21-quebec-film-antigone-bridges-millenniums. Accessed 12 May 2021.

Erll, Astrid. *Memory in Culture*. Translated by Sara B. Young, Palgrave Macmillan, 2011.

"Flag of France." *Encyclopedia Britannica*, https://www.britannica.com/topic/flag-of-France. Accessed 12 May 2021.

La Haine. Directed by Mathieu Kassovitz, Canal+, Cofinergie 6, Egg Pictures, 1995.

Hall, Stuart. "The Work of Representation." *Representation: Cultural Representations and Signifying Practices*, edited by Stuart Hall, Sage, 1997, pp. 13–64.

Hebdige, Dick. *Hiding in the Light: On Images and Things*. Routledge, 1989.

Hebdige, Dick. *Subculture: The Meaning of Style*. Routledge, 1981.

Husser, Nate. "Catherine" *YouTube*, uploaded by Nate Husser, 4 October 2017, https://www.youtube.com/watch?v=d8ixm4609Xk. Accessed 10 March 2024.

Jacobs, Carol. "Dusting Antigone." *MLN*, vol. 111, no. 5, December 1996, pp. 889–917.

Kilbourn, Russell J.A. "The 'Fast Runner' Trilogy, Inuit Cultural Memory and Knowledge (Re-) Production." *Indigenous Knowledges in North America*, special issue of *Zeitschrift für Anglistik und Amerikanistik: A Quarterly of Language, Literature and Culture*, edited by Kerstin Knopf and Birgit Dawes, vol. 68, no. 2, 2020, pp. 191–208.

The Passion of Joan of Arc. Directed by Carl Theodor Dreyer, Société générale des films, 1928.

Plate, Liedeke, and Anneke Smelik, eds. *Performing Memory in Art and Popular Culture*. Routledge, 2013.

Rancière, Jacques. *The Emancipated Spectator*. Translated by Gregory Elliott, Verso Books, 2009.

Rothberg, Michael. *Multidirectional Memory: Remembering the Holocaust in the Age of Decolonization*. Stanford University Press, 2009.

Sophocles. *The Three Theban Plays: Antigone, Oedipus the King, Oedipus at Colonus.* Edited by Bernard Knox, translated by Robert Fagles, Penguin, 1982.

Stevenson, Seana. 2020. "*Antigone* Interview: Sophie Deraspe." *Muff Blog*, 8 January 2020, https://medium.com/the-muff-society/antigone-interview-sophie-deraspe-a8446e2e213e. Accessed 12 May 2021.

Terdiman, Richard. *Present Past: Modernity and the Memory Crisis.* Cornell University Press, 1993.

7

"YOU ARE NOT ONE THING"

NARRATIVE AND MEMORY IN ZALIKA REID-BENTA'S *FRYING PLANTAIN*

UCHECHUKWU PETER UMEZURIKE

THE LAST FIVE YEARS have witnessed the efflorescence of a generation of young Black Canadian women writers such as Eternity Martis, Djamila Ibrahim, Téa Mutonji, Rebecca Fisseha, Francesca Ekwuyasi, Jane Igharo, and Zalika Reid-Benta.[1] Their work exemplifies Black diasporic writing in Canada. This chapter focuses on Reid-Benta, whose debut short story collection, *Frying Plantain*, interrogates what it means to be Black and Jamaican in white-dominated Canada. Reid-Benta is based in Toronto, holds an MFA in fiction from Columbia University, and has been hailed as "a writer to watch" by eminent Canadian writer, poet, and critic George Elliott Clarke.[2] Since Reid-Benta published her book in 2019 with House of Anansi Press, the literary community has also hailed her as a writer whom it cannot ignore. She depicts intergenerational maternal dynamics in a subtle and understated tone, and there is nuance in her depiction of the dialectics of (hyphenated) identity (Jamaican and Canadian)—or what she labels "a third culture" in one of her interviews ("Zalika Reid-Benta"). *Frying Plantain* narrates the experiences of Black Canadians, revealing slippages in the metanarrative of citizenship that Paul Barrett describes as "the trap of multicultural hyphenation that marks black Canadians as belonging elsewhere" (6). This marking of Black Canadians is part of what Rinaldo Walcott considers in *Black Like Who?*, where he argues that "In Canada, Black identities must be rooted elsewhere and that elsewhere is always outside Canada. Black subjects become knowable objects through a simple, uncomplicated story of origins" (105). Reid-Benta dramatizes Walcott's observation on Black identities, countering the hegemonic discourse that (re)locates Blackness outside of the Canadian nation.

In this chapter, I examine selected studio interviews with Zalika Reid-Benta to underscore the links between memory, narrative, and media. My approach is to "listen to" her recollections, how she re-presents the past and relays it throughout her interviews with the media, thus disseminating the contestations around identity and legibility. Although I listened to and watched the interviews posted online, I did not read for verbal or facial cues—tones, pauses, expressions, and gestures—but limited myself to speech only. In doing so, I argue here for listening as a critical mode of reading the digital archive in order to understand how interviewers and interviewees generate memory across digital topographies. Studio interviews afford Reid-Benta a space to perform memory and re-enact her struggles as a Canadian-born Jamaican. Through her creative expression, she resists Eurocentric narratives of Blackness as a homogenous category, as well as urges to reify Blackness and to root Black culture in essentialism.[3] Similarly, for Reid-Benta, interviews instantiate an "ongoing reiteration of the self" (Cover 60 qtd. in Poletti and Rak). In thinking about memory, textuality, and digital media, I draw on ideas by theorists in memory studies and Black cultural studies. Liedeke Plate and Anneke Smelik, for instance, urge us to consider how we act and do memory, how memory *happens*, its process, and the practices constituting it as embodied acts of remembering. They remark that memory is a performance of the past in the present; therefore, memory is performative (14). Shifting to consider the relationship between memory and acts of remembrance, Holocaust historian Michael Rothberg writes that "memory nonetheless captures simultaneously the individual, embodied, and lived side *and* the collective, social, and constructed side of our relations to the past" (4). Reid-Benta's fiction shows the connection between individual and collective memory, specifically, how a Black Jamaican and Canadian woman's memory is interwoven with her social relations, collective, institutional, and national memories, and cultural practices.

My methodology encompasses analyses of Reid-Benta's book and her responses in various interviews with mainstream Canadian and Caribbean news media posted on digital platforms. I bring the textual, audial, and digital into conversation as I contemplate the work of memory. First, I give an overview of *Frying Plantain* to contextualize and enhance our appreciation of Reid-Benta's responses and how they relay personal and collective memory. Her studio interviews operate as channels that can mediate and remediate memory, making it relatable and legible for audiences. They also function as a circuit of memory: as I will show in subsequent sections, Reid-Benta's responses activate a circuit of remembering between her and her interviewers, delineating how memories can be routed and shared among people and even across virtual communities. In their study of internet culture, social media, and identity production, Anna Poletti and Julie Rak write that affordances show the ideological elements behind the production of online identities and communities (5). I suggest that we could read recorded video interviews archived in the digital environment as part of technological affordances since they enunciate representational practices and identity presentation.

Media affordances such as studio interviews provide Reid-Benta with a space to recall and elucidate her art while revealing how memory informs imaginative fiction and how fiction can provoke instances of remembering. I juxtapose my analysis of selected responses with passages from *Frying Plantain* to illustrate how she illuminates the struggles with which second-generation Black Canadians—or "third culture kids," as she puts it—contend in Canada. I argue that Reid-Benta disavows Blackness as an "uncontested signifier of identity" (Tettey and Puplampu 6); instead, she represents identity as contingent and riddled with ambivalences.[4] Finally, I demonstrate the ways in which Reid-Benta operationalizes fiction as a mode of mediating and re-presenting memory. Throughout her interviews, she reiterates that fiction can help to "commemorate" community, demonstrating that she, in the words of Paul Ricœur, is "struggling against forgetting" (30). For Ricœur, the intellectual labour necessary for recall and the duty of memory "consists essentially of a duty not to forget" (30). Reid-Benta uses fiction to remember the Toronto that she knew while growing up in the early 2000s. Her experiences shaped and sharpened her sensibilities as a creative writer, especially since she is a child of two cultures, born and raised in a predominantly non-white community. Therefore, this chapter contributes to scholarship on memory, Black and diaspora literatures, media studies, and digital humanities, as well as ongoing discussions about Black, Caribbean, and Canadian subjectivities.

MEMORY AND NARRATIVE

Astrid Erll et al. underline the multifarious character of the concept of cultural memory and how people tend to use it "in an ambiguous and vague way" (1); yet Plate and Smelik note that we can appreciate cultural memory "as a process of dealing with the past in the present that is embodied and mediated, linking a present to a past and to a future" (12). Furthermore, while Mieke Bal et al. understand cultural memory as a phenomenon that can be both individual and social (vii), Jan Assmann defines it as "a kind of institution" that "may be transferred from one situation to another and transmitted from one generation to another" (qtd. in Erll 110–11). For his part, Mordechai Neiger applies the term *collective memory*[5] rather than cultural memory, describing it as the "relations between the individual and the community to which [her or] she belongs and enables the community to bestow meaning upon its existence" (4). He underscores how mass media can operate as the most prevalent channel for the (re)construction of the past in the present. Newspapers, radio, and television thus play a vital role in the shaping and transmitting of collective memory.[6] Their function is even more evident when considering how the modern state (liberal or authoritarian) constructs its narratives and myths around national identity and citizenship.

Similarly, a narrative can function as a cultural mediator and a channel for writers to reconstruct their memory of what is forgotten and re-enact the past in the present. Ron Eyerman explains memory in terms of the work that it does by providing a "mobile" narrative. As he expounds, "The narrative can travel, as individuals travel, and it can be embodied, written down, painted, represented, communicated and received in distant places by isolated individuals, who can then, through them, be remembered and reunited with the collective" (161). Memory, therefore, operates through a medium (Plate and Smelike 2). Erll, for instance, remarks that cultural memory is always mediated, describing how literature serves as a medium in the creation and transmission of cultural memory (144). She also includes religious texts, historical paintings, and documentaries as memory media (389). Relatedly, Richard Terdiman declares that novels can participate in the process of memory, showing how writers reconstruct their relation to, or even reimagine, the past (25). Literature and art are thus not only "objects of memory" or "memory objects" but also "media" of cultural memory and "carriers of memory" (Assmann 111). *Frying Plantain* provides Reid-Benta with a medium to represent some aspects of her lived experiences and those of her community. As a memory object, her book circulates narratives of remembering among its readers; additionally, it helps them to reimagine what the past might have been for others and recall events that they might have experienced some time ago.

BLACK DIASPORIC LIFE IN CANADA

Frying Plantain contains twelve interlinked stories about Kara Davis, a Canadian girl of Jamaican descent who lives with her single mother, Eloise, in a predominantly Caribbean neighbourhood in Toronto. Other memorable characters are Kara's grandparents, Verna and George. While Kara is a second-generation Canadian and Eloise a first-generation Canadian, Verna and George are immigrants from Jamaica. Reid-Benta dramatizes the contradictions underlying cultural and individual identities within immigrant and diasporic communities in Canada, and in this book, she employs the trope of the mother-daughter relationship to interrogate home, heritage, race, transnationalism, hybridity, and liminality. She narrates the story from Kara's girlhood in high school to her womanhood in university, chronicling her negotiations of maternal and peer pressures, among a multitude of other personal struggles. Reid-Benta tells a nonchronological coming-of-age story set in the Eglinton West and Marlee neighbourhood of Little Jamaica, Toronto. She writes in a social realist mode, with many of the actions, reflective of Black diasporic experiences, occurring on the streets of Toronto—though that part of the city is also undergoing gentrification, a fact that she recounts in an interview with Desirée Seebaran ("Home and Away").[7] John C. Walsh and James William Opp comment that writers can "assert the significance of place as a site made meaningful by memory and commemorative practices" and that "*placing* is critical to memory's making and to its social, cultural, and political power" (4). Similarly, in her review of *Frying Plantain*, Zuri H. Scrivens reiterates this connection between spatiality and memory, underlining how Reid-Benta's "repeated use of place names celebrates and memorializes a distinctly Jamaican Canadian geography, mapping it so that it may endure, even in the face of change" (n.p.). Scrivens adds that "*Frying Plantain* does more than reference Marlee Avenue and Belgravia Avenue; it insists that readers remember this place and its people. In the face of gentrification and potential erasure, Reid-Benta offers an undeniable testament to those who have called—and will continue to call—this Little Jamaica home" (n.p.). However, what gentrification fails to erase is the memory associated with the habitation of the Caribbean people, which is what Reid-Benta attempts to memorialize through fiction.[8]

In this attempt at memorialization, Reid-Benta illustrates how memory is "closely aligned with identity" (Rothberg 4). This alignment of memory and identity manifests in the responses that she gives in the media, especially in how she describes her book as a story of Jamaican diaspora in Canada. In *Blackening Canada,* Paul Barrett examines how Dionne Brand, Tessa McWatt, and Austin Clarke mobilize their diasporic consciousness to rethink multiculturalism, thus subverting the normative paradigms of citizenship in Canada. Barrett argues that for these writers, "citizenship and community have been tenuous accomplishments at best, and unfulfilled aspirations at worst, often resulting in a hyphenated and interstitial relationship with Canada" (5). Likewise, Reid-Benta devotes little attention to the nation but critiques the social dynamics of belonging in the micro-spaces of schools and neighbourhoods. Her interest is to portray the private or the ordinary life as the basis of human relationships;[9] therefore, the family and its community provide a lens through which she can critique the Canadian nation and its politics of belonging.

Frying Plantain opens with an unsettling image of a pig's head in the eponymous story "Pig Head" and ends with a scene of affection between grandmother and granddaughter in "Frying Plantain." The two titles reference Jamaican gastronomy. While the first story shows Kara at the age of ten, the last story portrays her as an undergraduate student. In "Pig Head," Kara is with her mother in Jamaica for a brief holiday when her aunt tells her to get some beverages from the icebox. Upon pulling up the icebox lid, she sees, much to her horror, "a pig's severed head" among the bottles (Reid-Benta 3). The story foreshadows themes such as the tensions between Canadian, Jamaican, and female identities, posturing, and belonging that define the collection. In this opening story, Kara's cousins expect her to be as knowledgeable about and familiar with elements of nature as any "rough" Jamaican child, who can strangle chickens, throw stones at alligators, or simply climb trees. But she is "too afraid to join in" their games, so they treat her "with a new-found

Uchechukwu Peter Umezurike

delicacy" (4). In their eyes, she is "a soft one," and her "softness" shows when she squeals upon seeing her cousin Rodney—the same age as her— effortlessly wring a chicken's neck. Although they taunt Kara for her softness, she feels "grateful for the inclusion" (5). Her cousins, therefore, perceive her as *different*, as if her being Canadian makes her *different* and delicate. Her interactions with them imply that Canada is composed of sensitive people and that it is a place that could make any child soft and delicate. Unlike Canada, Jamaica is figured as a place of toughness and wildness that hardens children, a place where her cousins could only invite Kara to "games they thought Canadian girls could stomach" (5). The imagery of sensitivity is herein evoked.

The foregoing passage implies that Canada is a site of deficiency, as evident in the question that Rodney poses to Kara: "Yuh no cook soup in Canada?" (4). Kara will carry this feeling of deficiency back home to Toronto, which she describes as "the great misfortune of being Canadian-born" (14). The discourse of civility—in which Canada is projected as a civilized nation—is referenced in a fighting scene between mother and daughter. When Auntie sees Kara's mother and her grandmother fight-ing, she declares: "Mi thought Canada was supposed fi be a civilized place, how yuh two fight like the dogs them? Cha" (6). The scene is para-doxical because it problematizes the presentation of Canada as civilized, since both fighting women reside in Canada and are Canadians, even though they are of Jamaican descent. That they could clash with each other typifies how "wildness" or canine ferocity, "like the dogs," is not limited to a particular location, such as Jamaica. Nonetheless, this story is relevant to how we begin to understand Kara's sense of difference and cultural estrangement, her identity struggles as a citizen of two national-ities (Jamaica and Canada), and her attempts, even if futile and point-less, to fit into the cultures of both nations.

For instance, there is an emphasis in the text on familial affec-tions and tropes around food, especially with the figure of the grand-mother looming in the opening and concluding stories and emphasizing the tenacity of Jamaican culture. This tenacity materializes in the paint-ing on the wall that catches Kara's eye as she exits the apartment, "a colourful print of a Jamaican marketplace by the coast, slightly, almost barely, torn" (252). On *Cityline Book Club,* Reid-Benta tells Tracy Moore that "[food] is definitely a way that my family shows affection, and I think that kind of naturally came, came out." She mentions how for Verna, food serves as a "love language" and a way for her to show affection to her granddaughter. In the final story, "Frying Plantain," Verna insists that Kara must eat or drink something before she leaves. Kara vacillates but only long enough for her grandmother to hand her a bag of food to share with her mother at home. Verna's pride in preparing Jamaican food demonstrates that it remains a means for her to connect with her family and to emphasize connections to her Jamaican culture.

NARRATIVIZING MEMORY

Reid-Benta's interview responses and sample passages from her book illustrate the mimetic character of art and its relationship with memory. She demonstrates that literature can serve as a medium that builds and observes memory (Erll 391). Some common themes suture her inter-view responses and the passages, including cultural identity, aesthetics, authenticity, and childhood. Most interviewers ask Reid-Benta whether *Frying Plantain* reflects her personal experiences. In a pre-launch inter-view of the book on *In the Now,* Reid-Benta tells Simone Smith that

> Some of it is me in terms of Kara loves plantain. I love plantain...But, like, I live in the same neighbourhood that she lived in, in terms of stuff like that...So, like, a lot of the locations are based on locations that I have been in...a story that takes place in a specific fast food place called like New Orleans Donut, Vaughan and Oakwood, was not there anymore...[Reid-Benta clarifies that] what happened in that restaurant didn't actually happen to me...[but she decided to] write something just that takes place like that.

The unnamed story that she cites in the interview is "Snow Day." Reid-Benta's incorporation of her childhood memories of landmarks demonstrates the extent to which art can imitate life and fiction can represent personal memories. Assmann argues that "[t]hings do not 'have' a memory of their own, but they may remind us, may trigger our memory, because they carry memories which we have invested into them" (111). Memory plays a crucial role in Reid-Benta's representation of the pig's head she saw during her visit to Jamaica. When Smith asks about "Pig Head," Reid-Benta explains, "[when] I was in Jamaica, I didn't see an actual pig head, I just saw the blood on, like, the thing, and I was like, where did this blood come from, and then that was when one of my cousins was like, 'the pig head,' and I was like, 'what?'" Reid-Benta gives a similar response to Moore of *Cityline Book Club* when she is asked about "Pig Head," revealing that she wanted to narrate experiences to which she could relate while growing up as a child. Fiction thus functions as a medium for Reid-Benta to remember the pig's head that she saw in Jamaica; furthermore, the interviews helped her to re-memorialize it.

Walcott writes that "[to] be black and at home in Canada is both to belong and not belong" (148). Smith broaches this issue of identity struggle, expressing how second-generation Jamaicans usually feel that "sometimes we are stuck," and wondering "what are we." Reid-Benta responds that

> I really wanted to write about third culture kids, I really wanted to write about kids in the diaspora, or like growing up in the diaspora, and how you are not one thing, but you are not the other thing, so does that make you something else, and you relate to one culture, in this case, she relates to her Jamaican culture more than her Canadian culture, but she is still not exactly Jamaican. And so, and like, that was something my friend and I contended with a lot, growing up, especially in Toronto. And I really wanted to capture that experience.

Reid-Benta further reflects that "[w]hen I was in Eglinton West and Marlee, when I lived around there, when I went to school around here, being Canadian was like the worst thing. You didn't want to be Canadian, you wanted to be something else. So, I really wanted to get that, em, get that in this book." Her recollection of her teenage experience encourages Smith to also recollect her own struggles over identity: "Because it is an experience. You are not accepted by Jamaicans. You are not Jamaican, you're Canadian. You are not accepted fully by Canadians because they ask you stupid questions, like, you are Jamaicans, and do all Jamaicans smoke weed? It is so weird because it's like, it is true, it's like this limbo that you live in." On the *Your Morning* show, Reid-Benta discloses that she intended for Kara to be a character who "learns to be okay with herself throughout her journey. Because, you know, there is [a] different set of tensions around what it means to be because there is a different set of tensions around what it means to be Canadian...what it means to be soft or what it means to be, like, sort of hardened. I think she just kind of come to terms with her personality." These tensions echo Clarke's observation that "the constant challenges to African-Canadian identity create fissures and disjunctures in the culture that makes it what it is—as fraught with indefinition as Canada itself" (34). As Reid-Benta recalls to Moore on *Cityline Book Club*, she wanted to capture these "cultural-like fissures" in her writing because it was something that she dealt with while growing up: that feeling of not quite belonging, of not being Jamaican or Canadian enough.

Though these interviews take place in digital spaces, they activate collective memory, inspiring and fostering a virtual community of recallers, especially those who identify as Black Canadians. When they watch videos of and listen to how Reid-Benta and her interviewer discuss *Frying Plantain*, they likewise relive their respective identity struggles and fraught relationships with the Canadian nation while interrogating the promises of multiculturalism. Conversely, when white literary enthusiasts watch and listen to those interviews, they realize that Canada appears antagonistic to the flourishing of Black lives and perhaps recognize their privileges and complicity with a system that underwrites such antagonism. The interviews not only amplify Reid-Benta's voice but also the visibility of her book, circulating its thematic concerns online, across time and space even long before such readers eventually get a copy to read. These instances all speak to how the digital space can make memory and relationship "mobile" among people in disparate places.

On *Home and Away*, Reid-Benta reveals to Seebaran that she grappled with her hyphenated (Caribbean/Canadian) identity while she was growing up: "From the perspective of the Canadian girl...It was just this kind of thing. When I was growing up, in the schools that I attended, and among my friends, you didn't want to be Canadian, there was just something about being Canadian. You just wanted to represent other islands where your parents were from." She recollects that the Toronto of her childhood informed her characterization of Kara and the representation of third culture in communities. Many Caribbean girls growing up in Toronto at the time experienced an identity crisis exemplified by the feeling of never being Canadian enough and not even being accepted by their peers. It is important to point out that there was another Black Canadian in that interview on *Cityline Book Club*, Tracy Peart, who tells both women that she "grew up in the exact neighbourhood" depicted in *Frying Plantain*. Her neighbourhood, Peart recalls, "was very Caribbean but very Jamaican particularly." However, she explains that she is a fourth-generation Black Canadian, recalling what Walcott labels the "rhizomatic character of Blackness in the Canadian context" (101). Peart elaborates that "I am not Jamaican. I am not Caribbean. My ancestors came through the Underground Railroad and settled in Nova Scotia." Whenever fellow Black Caribbean Canadians see her, they assume that she is Caribbean, placing her Blackness as Caribbean while ignoring the fact that she is Black Canadian, not Caribbean, and not African Canadian. Her perspective on Blackness challenges how being Black in Canada is easily associated with (migrant) Caribbean or African identity. As such, Peart problematizes the notion of a monolithic Blackness, affirming the plurality of Blackness in Canada. This negotiation—and its attendant contestation—of Blackness and Canadianness is a theme that Reid-Benta dramatizes in *Frying Plantain*.

Although "Snow Day" also deals with hyphenated identity, it portrays accent as an additional identity marker. As a linguistic feature, it can be used by some people to question, define, or authenticate a person's identity, belonging, and kinship. One's accent can "place" or even "displace" someone within a community since it constellates around belonging and affiliations. Indeed, it is what makes one "real" or legible among Canadian and Caribbean communities. The story begins on a morning with a heavy snowfall that results in the principal announcing that the school will be closing early. Students are therefore expected to go home, although Kara remains at her desk because "she had nowhere to hurry to." Finally, as she heads out of the classroom, her friend Rochelle invites her and their friends "to hang out at her place for the rest of the day" (Reid-Benta 29). As Kara desires to fit into this clique—comprising Rochelle, Jordan, Aishani, and Anita—she begins to feel an immense amount of anxiety. In "Pig Head," it becomes clear that Kara's anxiety stems from her feeling like an "outsider," even though she is technically part of the clique (10). This feeling arises anytime she is among these girls because she finds herself struggling with the "need to twist [herself] into a new identity" (22). Though she cares little about their "insults," she longs for "the kind of inclusion [she'd] had and lost with [her] cousins" (10). Therefore, on this day, she feels again the pressure to belong, to authenticate her Jamaican identity and to perform Jamaicanness. Anita, who appears to enjoy taunting Kara, retorts, "Nuh fret it, Chelle, you know she's not gonna come. She too 'fraid of Mummy. Got her on lockdown and shit, she canna even run 'cross di street fi buy a patty at lunch" (29). This passage recalls how Kara's cousins conceive of her as "soft" in "Pig Head." Kara remembers that her mother has threatened to enrol her in "her old school downtown on Ferndale Avenue if she got into any sort of trouble" (30). She, however, accepts Rochelle's invitation and goes along with the girls. On their way, Anita taunts her again and Kara counters, "Quiet, Anita. Yuh run yuh mouth too much," but Anita does not relent: "What's this? Miss Canada gwine fi bust out the patois? Yuh need to stop Ja-fakin' it, Kara" (32). Kara stops herself from responding because she knows that "[trouble] usually followed whenever they spoke in that stance" and she has "the weakest accent out of all the Canadian-borns" (33). By branding her "Miss Canada," Anita seems to suggest that there is nothing "real" about Kara's Jamaican identity—it is all a performance. Richard Schechner notes that "performances mark identities" (10), and this observation corresponds with the implication of Kara, being perceived by Anita, as "representing" Canadianness. Implicitly, Kara can only perform—or in this case, fake—Jamaicanness. Her peers hardly doubt her Canadianness, only her Jamaicanness. Therefore, if Kara attempts to assert any semblance of her Jamaican identity, it will come off as posturing—a performance—to her peers.

Throughout *Frying Plantain*, Kara struggles with patois, a language that marks an individual as authentic among Jamaican Canadians. The person who speaks patois well gains esteem among their peers. This reality is part of the pressure that Kara faces because "their accent was better" than hers. She feels that her patois is not "real" since it sounds like "something she had to put on" (32). Ironically, Kara's eloquence in Canadian English does not mark her as "real"; instead, it brands her as other, reminding her of "the great misfortune of being Canadian-born" (14). Because Kara speaks patois haltingly, unconvincingly, Anita reprimands her to "stop Ja-fakin." It is not enough to be Jamaican unless one speaks patois fluently, and it is therefore nativity in Jamaica rather than in Canada that confers realness. Realness is thus associated with Jamaicanness, while otherness indexes Canadianness. The Indian girl in the group, Aishani, finds herself in the same situation—she was born in Canada and "could not put on the accent," and her clique mocks her for this lack (32). It is telling that Aishani also fakes her nationality, claiming to be from Trinidad if "any boy swaggered up to her" (32). Reid-Benta comments on this notion of performance, or faking—"posturing," as she describes it—on *Kobo in Conversation*: "When you are a third culture kid, especially in a predominantly Caribbean-Jamaican neighbourhood, there is a certain level of am I Caribbean? Am I Jamaican? And that's something [Kara] and her friends definitely grapple with and go through." Reid-Benta suggests that identity is a form of posturing or "trying to put up a persona."

"Pig Head" and "Snow Day" thus present Kara and Aishani as posturing and performing identity.

Yet it is not accent alone that defines Jamaican identity—the shape of a girl's body does, too. "Inspection" examines questions about appearance, behaviour, and Kara's performance of femininity. The theme of posturing—how a girl must construct the *proper* persona—also figures in this brisk, humorous story. Schechner points out that performing is "an ongoing, never-ending activity or set of activities" (5) and that it "takes place both in doing and showing doing...In everyday life, performing is underlining an action, showing off" (4). "Inspection" illustrates an instance of performance as gender enactment, a mode of self-fashioning, respectability, and desire for social mobility. Traditional and popular gender discourses construe propriety as a feminine virtue and therefore associate it with womanhood. In this story, Kara is fourteen and set to visit her old neighbourhood of Eglinton West and Marlee, which she last visited three weeks earlier. Her mother preens her for this implicitly significant visit. Here Reid-Benta shows that self-presentation or performing the right persona is crucial to how a community—specifically the Caribbean community—identifies and appraises its members. Because Eloise is concerned with appearance and behaviour, she inspects her daughter's "body for an imperfection to catch and correct" (Reid-Benta 104). Kara is made to take a second shower, use expensive body wash, coat her legs in lotion three times or even more, all so she can smell like rose petals (99–100). Finally, she is made to wear "an outfit dressy enough for people to know she has standards, that her mother taught her well and her grandmother before her" (101). As the "Miss Canadian" that she is, she "prefers jeans, even shorts," but she must please her mother because appearance is critical in performances of propriety in patriarchal culture. Kara hates the dress because it "falls on her like it's a sheet," but she hates it even more because it "accentuates her lack of breasts, lack of curves, lack of voluptuous beauty that makes her aunts and cousins laugh behind their hands and say, Yuh sure yuh be a Jamaican gyal?" (101). Kara's apparent skinniness marks her as more Canadian than Jamaican, causing her relatives to doubt her

Jamaicanness. Embodiment thus becomes a visible marker of identity, illustrating how a culture recognizes and evaluates its members *somatically*. Fleshiness is to Jamaicans as thinness is to Canadians; therefore, fleshiness, or rather, voluptuousness, orchestrates a discourse of (Jamaican) sexuality.

"Inspection" also dramatizes what Reid-Benta recalls to Moore on *Cityline Book Club* about Eloise being "intensely protective of Kara." As a single parent struggling to live above the poverty line, Eloise does not want her daughter to repeat the mistake she thought that she had made as a teenager. She wants a different standard for Kara, so she inspects her daughter to ensure that that standard is intact. Kara is aware of her mother's fears and so she wants to dress well and properly so that "[no] cars will slow down for her, no church ladies will whisper 'slack' when they see her dress" (Reid-Benta 104). Consider here how Eloise's "inspection" constitutes an approximation of Foucauldian self-technologies:

> If you see someone we know, make sure to say ma'am.
> I will.
> And if you see someone from our family, don't talk our business.
> I won't.
> If your fast friends start talking to some boys, leave and meet them somewhere when they're done.
> Of course. (104)

The inspection does not immediately end once Eloise has recited these imperatives: as Kara "heads for the door," she tells us that her mother "is running through a list in her head, making sure she hasn't missed any instruction or overlooked any direction" (104–05).

However, beyond her mother's anxiety about appearance and behaviour dramatized in that passage, there is the spectre of danger lurking on the street personified by "fast friends" and "some boys," who can threaten not only her daughter's body but her future, as well. In

Michel Foucault and the Games of Truth, Herman Nilson remarks that "[in] an ethics of existence, in which care of the self had central place, attention to the body's regimen began with the external and internal dangers which threatened it" (49). We could thus read this group of youth as "external dangers" that threaten Kara's "body's regimen." Eloise's anxiety and apprehension are justifiable, considering that she got "pregnant at seventeen" (Reid-Benta 240). Reid-Benta explains to Moore on *Cityline Book Club* that Eloise is only protective of Kara because she knows "What Canada is like" for Blacks, and she "knows what systemic racism is like." All of these personal memories, infused with past experiences and regret, cause Eloise to be "intensely protective" of Kara. Reid-Benta hints that her own mother was also intensely protective of her as a child, so "the whole idea of protection [as affection] was something she wanted to get at" in her writing. Protection can operate as a mode of control in two ways, as seen in Eloise's list: first, it constrains Kara's self-autonomy, what she can and cannot do, how and in what form she must present herself; second, it manages *in anticipation* the danger that might befall Kara, warding off persons who threaten her bodily autonomy.

"Drunk" portrays another incident where Kara's friends cast doubt on her Jamaicanness. In the story, she accompanies her high school friends, Justin and Hannah, to another friend's home. While they are lounging in the living room, Ryan offers her "his freshly rolled joint" and looks surprised when Kara declines: "Really?" He kept his arm outstretched. "Aren't you, like, Jamaican or something?" Before Kara can respond, Hannah intervenes promptly, "Kara's Canadian anyway" (Reid-Benta 211). Ryan's speech is steeped in a stereotype that frames marijuana as integral to Jamaican culture and Jamaicans as conventional hemp smokers. He begins to sputter only because he cannot understand how Kara does not "[t]oke," not because he realizes that his statement was problematic. Hannah's response is fraught with implications, though, as well. First, she erases Kara's Jamaican identity, subsuming her under her Canadian counterparts. Second, Hannah implies that even as she herself shares a joint with Ryan, Kara is a *different* Canadian. Lastly, and even more remarkably, Hannah indirectly uncovers the idea that one could be both Jamaican and Canadian, so being Canadian is not limited to whiteness. Her response negates the ideology of racial purity espoused by white nationalists, demonstrating that whiteness is not intrinsic to Canada and enunciating the multicultural ideal to which the modern Canadian nation aspires.

Verna re-emphasizes Kara's Canadian identity in the last story "Frying Plantain." The story revolves around a dream that Verna had the night before; she then phones Kara's mother to share the dream with her, but Eloise sends her daughter instead to find out about it. Kara explains that dreams are part of Jamaican culture and "aren't something to be messed around with. If a family member has one of another member, it's their duty to report it—not to do so would be spiteful" (225). Nonetheless, she is hesitant to listen "to Nana's ramblings on the prophetic powers of vivid dreams" (224–25). When she finally arrives at her grandmother's home, Verna offers to cook for her and eventually serves her a plate of fried plantain and eggs. While eating, Kara asks about the dream, but her grandmother replies, "You nuh care about dream. You are a *Canadian* girl" (244, original emphasis). Verna's accentuation of Kara's Canadianness implies that her granddaughter is not true to her Jamaican culture, for she thinks that dreams are trivial and have no place in Western capitalist society. Verna suspects that Kara would "make light of such things" (245), but Kara knows that some dreams carry omens. At last, Verna divulges the dream and Kara recognizes that "Losing dream teeth, I know, is a bad sign" (245). She recognizes this dream and its cultural significance, especially among her people, and therefore appreciates her Jamaican heritage even more. The story ends with Kara going home with a bag of food. Heading to the door, she smiles as she remembers all the leftovers Verna had given her throughout the years.

Reid-Benta's fiction attempts to excavate the memory behind the reconstruction of her city. Throughout her interviews, she affirms her intentionality about remembering Little Jamaica, her childhood neighbourhood, in her fiction. Erll comments that "every conscious remembering of past events and experience—individual and collective—is accompanied by strategies which are also fundamental for literary narrative" (146). Therefore, when Seebaran ("Home and Away") asks Reid-Benta how fiction can deal with memory, she replies that she did not initially set the stories in Toronto but located them in "an amorphous city" that could be anywhere. Then she says that every time she came back to Toronto, she noticed that it

> was changing very fast and all of the landmarks that I grew up with were being stripped and being turned into condos and especially Eglinton West and Marlee neighbourhood. And now it is, like, under total construction and barely recognized. And now that really hurt just because there were so many memories...like, I attach so many memories and so many feelings to that neighbourhood...And so I ended up putting that Toronto in my story, and all of my different stories, and I was just kind of, like, I kind of want to commemorate this place...a neighbourhood that I feel is no longer around.

Reid-Benta establishes the entanglement between memory and narrative, revealing how literature and cultural memory "exist within a shared space of topoi, tropes, images, references, echoes" (Irimia et al. 6). *Frying Plantain* thus exemplifies how a writer can commemorate "versions of the past," helping its readers to appreciate the significance of a temporal event or a given culture.

CONCLUSION

This chapter has examined selected online interviews of Zalika Reid-Benta and passages from her book to unravel the connections between memory, narrative, and media. She used her media interviews to relay childhood experiences and recollect cultural ambivalence around hyphenated identities. In several interviews, she narrated her attempts to fictionalize the "past," reliving the "Toronto" that she used to know. As such, *Frying Plantain* is an example of Black diasporic writing that reconstructs the identity struggles of second-generation Canadians living in a predominantly white culture. Blackness is a site of cultural (cum racial) contestation. On *CTV Your Morning*, Reid-Benta affirms to her host that "[you] can individually define what being Canadian is," demonstrating that identity is equally about how people choose to present themselves. Significantly, she shows that the past "lives" in the present and that our relations to the past are never severed.

NOTES

1. See Ibrahim's *Things Are Good Now*; Igharo's *Ties That Tether*; Fisseha's *Daughters of Silence*; Martis's *They Said This Would Be Fun*; Mutonji's *Shut Up, You're Pretty*; Ekwuyasi's *Butter Honey Pig Bread*.
2. Clarke's words: "Zalika Reid-Benta is prophecy to be fulfilled. She has grown up within the context of an immigrant Caribbean community thrusting firm roots into Canadian soil, and she is attuned to all the nuances of that transplantation, the difficulties of maintaining connections to soul and spirit in a cold climate and in a society that did not (and still does not) welcome immigrants de couleur with open arms."
3. Stuart Hall critiques the politics of representation, especially in popular culture, stating that the signifier "Black" is not "a category of essence" (111). See "What Is This 'Black' in Black Popular Culture?"
4. In "The Fiction of Belonging: On Second-Generation Black Writing in Canada," novelist David Chariandy addresses these ambivalences and how they inflect the subjectivities of second-generation Blacks in Canada (820).
5. French philosopher and sociologist Maurice Halbwachs introduced the concept of collective memory in 1925. He views it as the memory of "a coherent group of people" (48). See *On Collective Memory*.
6. See Bak et al., *Politics and Cultures of Liberation*.
7. Scrivens explains that "[i]ndeed, the real Little Jamaica of today is a place of transformation. An expansion to Toronto's transit system, set to open in 2021, includes nineteen kilometres of light rail running through the neighbourhood. Planners say the Eglinton Crosstown will reduce commute times and reinvigorate the community...there are growing concerns within

Little Jamaica: will this distinct cultural enclave survive such a change?" See "In Little Jamaica," *Literary Review of Canada.*

8. Janet Donohoe writes that "[a]lthough landscapes can be transformed with new buildings or destruction of old buildings or natural areas, it is virtually impossible to completely erase a city's history and traditions in so doing. We cannot begin with a clean slate because memory and tradition are written on the landscape itself. One glance around a city convinces us of the many layers of sedimented history captured there" (13). See *Remembering Places.*

9. South African novelist and scholar Njabulo Ndebele conceives of "the ordinary" for us to appreciate contemporary fiction by South African writers. Though he argues that these new writers are more interested in representing the lives and struggles of ordinary South Africans, his ideas can further illuminate how we read Reid-Benta's interests in depicting the "ordinary concerns of [Black Canadian] people" (156). See Ndebele, "The Rediscovery of the Ordinary: Some New Writings in South Africa." French philosopher Sandra Laugier also discusses "the ordinary" in "The Will to See" and "Politics of Vulnerability and Responsibility."

WORKS CITED

Assmann, Jan. "Communicative and Cultural Memory." *Cultural Memory Studies: An International and Interdisciplinary Handbook,* edited by Astrid Erll et al., De Gruyter, 2008, pp. 109–18.

Bak, Hans, et al. *Politics and Cultures of Liberation: Media, Memory, and Projections of Democracy.* Brill, 2018.

Barrett, Paul. *Blackening Canada: Diaspora, Race, Multiculturalism.* University of Toronto Press, 2015.

Chariandy, David. "'The Fiction of Belonging': On Second-Generation Black Writing in Canada." *Callaloo,* vol. 30, no. 3, 2007, pp. 818–29.

"Cityline Book Club: *Frying Plantain* Chat." *Cityline Book Club,* 11 December 2019, https://www.facebook.com/Cityline/videos/cityline-book-club-frying-plantain-chat/2869437623087889/

Clarke, George Elliott. *Odysseys Home: Mapping African-Canadian Literature.* University of Toronto Press, 2002.

Cover, Rob. "Becoming and Belonging: Performativity, Subjectivity, and the Cultural Purposes of Social Networking." *Identity Technologies: Constructing the Self Online,* edited by Anna Poletti and Julie Rak. University of Wisconsin Press, 2013, pp. 55–69.

Donohoe, Janet. *Remembering Places: A Phenomenological Study of the Relationship Between Memory and Place*. Lexington Books, 2014.

Ekwuyasi, Francesca. *Butter Honey Pig Bread*. Arsenal Pulp Press, 2020.

Erll, Astrid. *Memory in Culture*. Translated by Sara B. Young, Palgrave Macmillan, 2011.

Erll, Astrid, et al. *Cultural Memory Studies: An International and Interdisciplinary Handbook*. De Gruyter, 2008.

Eyerman, Ron. "The Past in the Present: Culture and the Transmission of Memory." *Acta Sociologica*, vol. 47, no. 2, 2004, pp. 159–69.

Fisseha, Rebecca. *Daughters of Silence*. Goose Lane Editions, 2019.

Halbwachs, Maurice. *On Collective Memory*. Edited and translated by Lewis A. Coser, University of Chicago Press, 1992.

Hall, Stuart. "What Is This 'Black' in Black Popular Culture?" *Social Justice*, vol. 20, no. 1/2, 1993, pp. 104–14.

"Home and Away: New Fiction by Zalika Reid-Benta and Elizabeth Walcott-Hackshaw." *Home and Away*, 2 October 2020, https://www.youtube.com/watch?v=mza9N3I7ofw&ab_channel=NGCBocasLitFest. Accessed 12 March 2024.

Ibrahim, Djamila. *Things Are Good Now*. House of Anansi Press, 2018.

Igharo, Jane. *Ties That Tether*. Jove, 2020.

Laugier, Sandra. "Politics of Vulnerability and Responsibility for Ordinary Others." *Critical Horizons*, vol. 17, no. 2, 2016, pp. 207–23.

Laugier, Sandra. "The Will to See: Ethics and Moral Perception of Sense." *Graduate Faculty Philosophical Journal*, vol. 34, no. 2, 2013, pp. 263–81.

Martis, Eternity. *They Said This Would Be Fun: Race, Campus Life, and Growing Up*. McClelland & Stewart, 2020.

Mutonji, Téa. *Shut Up, You're Pretty*. VS. Books, 2019.

Ndebele, Njabulo S. "The Rediscovery of the Ordinary: Some New Writings in South Africa." *Journal of Southern African Studies*, vol. 12, no. 2, 1986, pp. 143–57.

Neiger, Mordechai. *On Media Memory: Collective Memory in a New Media Age*. Palgrave Macmillan, 2011.

Nilson, Herman. *Michel Foucault and the Games of Truth*. St. Martin's Press, 1998.

Plate, Liedeke, and Anneke Smelik. *Performing Memory in Art and Popular Culture*. Taylor and Francis, 2013.

Poletti, Anna, and Julie Rak. *Identity Technologies: Constructing the Self Online*. University of Wisconsin Press, 2013.

Reid-Benta, Zalika. *Frying Plantain*. Astoria, 2019.

Reid-Benta, Zalika. "Zalika Reid-Benta." *Internet Archive*. https://web.
archive.org/web/20210621134135/http://www.newcollege.utoronto.ca/
academics/new-college-academic-programs/caribbean-studies/alumni/
zalika-reid-benta/.

Ricœur, Paul. *Memory, History, Forgetting*. University of Chicago Press, 2004.

Rothberg, Michael. *Multidirectional Memory: Remembering the Holocaust in
the Age of Decolonization*. Stanford University Press, 2009.

Schechner, Richard. *Performance Studies: An Introduction*. 4th ed.,
Routledge, 2020.

Scrivens, Zuri H. "In Little Canada: Stories from a Changing Neighbourhood."
Literary Review of Canada, July–August 2019, http://reviewcanada.ca/
magazine/2019/07/in-little-jamaica/. Accessed 12 March 2024.

TCNTV. "In the Now Relaunch: Special Guest Zalika Reid-Benta." *YouTube*,
31 May 2019, https://www.youtube.com/watch?v=F43FW7NXkEo.
Accessed 10 March 2024.

Terdiman, Richard. *Present Past: Modernity and the Memory Crisis*. Cornell
University Press, 1993.

Tettey, Wisdom, and Korbla P. Puplampu. *The African Diaspora in Canada:
Negotiating Identity and Belonging*. University of Calgary Press, 2005.

Walcott, Rinaldo. *Black Like Who?: Writing Black Canada*. 2nd ed.,
Insomniac Press, 2003.

Walsh, John C., and James William Opp. *Placing Memory and Remembering
Place in Canada*. University of British Columbia Press, 2010.

Your Morning, CTV. "*Frying Plantain* Captures the Experience of Growing
up in Two Cultures." *YouTube*, 3 June 2019, https://www.youtube.com/
watch?v=liDdfvtZ2p0. Accessed 10 March 2024.

"Zalika Reid-Benta, author of Frying Plantain." *Kobo in Conversation*,
8 September 2020, https://www.youtube.com/watch?v=Jni7CeP4acE&ab_
channel=Kobo. Accessed 10 March 2024.

8

TOWARD A LITERARY MÉTIS HOMELAND

A DIGITAL ANALYSIS OF GREGORY SCOFIELD'S *LOUIS: THE HERETIC POEMS* AND MARILYN DUMONT'S *THE PEMMICAN EATERS*

MATTHEW TÉTREAULT
AND STEPHEN WEBB

DWELLING ON THE CIRCULATION of historical Métis narratives, we consider, through methods of digital analysis, the function of literature in re-storying the Métis homeland and complex Métis kinscapes. Digitally analyzing a pair of collections by two major Métis poets—Gregory Scofield's *Louis: The Heretic Poems*, and Marilyn Dumont's *The Pemmican Eaters*—we examine not only how these works resume and re-story narratives of Métis resistance, but also how they illustrate broader cultural underpinnings that inform Métis identities. In their evocation of expansive connections between people, places, and other-than-human beings, Scofield and Dumont simultaneously draw upon and amplify Métis historical, national, and cultural memories. Considering how these works might chart a literary homeland and, in some ways, the intersection between national history, narrative, and memory, we begin to trace, map out, and compare the geographies of not only the territories, but the *relations* between people and place in both collections; in other words, a mapping of the collective memory that undergirds the national and historical narratives that Scofield and Dumont re-story. The irony of mapping literary texts dealing largely with Métis nationalist resistances sparked by Canadian settler-colonial surveying of Métis lands is not lost on us; rather, it informs our critical approach. That historic moment in which "Louis [Riel] planted his beaded moccasin on the survey chain" (Dumont 18) in Red River in 1869 thus impels us to foreground Métis culture and historical contexts in our literary analysis. As Métis scholar Adam Gaudry notes in the *Indigenous Peoples Atlas of Canada*, "re-mapping (and perhaps also de-mapping) the places now claimed by Canada allows [Indigenous people] to assert ongoing Indigenous presence in our homelands" (n.p.). Although digital tools hold promise for illustrating Indigenous peoples' ongoing presence in their homelands—and our project participates in the digitization of Métis experiences and memory, through their literary expressions, in order to better apprehend the breadth of their analogue resonances—we recognize that Indigenous literatures challenge these mapping projects through the ways that evocations of kinship and relations with land are not always wholly represented. We caution that while digital tools can reveal and enlighten, without due care and attention to Indigenous epistemologies and cosmologies, they can also easily obscure and elide.

In this chapter, we first situate our mapping project against a brief history of other Métis maps, territorial claims, and articulations of experience and connection to specific geographies—from the recent map issued by the Métis National Council to Louis Riel's literary evocations—as we consider how such contemporary claims are entangled with broader questions of identity and sovereignty.[1] With an awareness of contemporary Métis literature's aesthetic, produced in part by its impulse toward the "re-collection of scattered parts" (LaRocque 134), from remembering and re-storying personal stories to collective histories, we re-examine our own methodological approach in translating poetry to data visualization. We then analyze our mapping visualizations, beginning with geographically situated heatmaps, contrasting the "literary homelands" of either collection, before turning to the "networks" produced by the relationships between persons and other beings.

ON HISTORY, CONTEXT, AND MÉTIS TERRITORIALITY

What might a Métis literary homeland look like? This question arose for us in the wake of the Métis National Council's release of a map of the Métis homeland in November 2018; this map centres on the northern half of North America and displays settler-colonial (national and provincial) boundaries. Overlaying these boundaries are Métis territorial claims: an amorphous swathe that encompasses most of the prairie provinces, portions of northwestern Ontario, northeastern British Columbia, some southwestern sections of the Northwest Territories, as well as northernmost parts of Minnesota, North Dakota, and Montana. The map is imperfect: it adheres oddly to settler-colonial borders in some places, such as the Manitoba/Ontario border, has been criticized for appearing to lay claim to other Indigenous territories, such as Blackfoot territory in southern Alberta (Monkman), fails to acknowledge or demonstrate the complex kinship networks that link Métis and other Indigenous peoples, and regrettably elides other Indigenous nations whose homelands overlap—Cree, Saulteaux, Assiniboine, and Dakota, among others. However, as Will Goodon, minister of housing for the Manitoba Métis Federation, hints, the map constitutes a form of nationalist resistance that is "not meant to...lay claim to territory [and] to the lands outlined, but rather to help Métis governments decide who their members are" (Monkman n.p.). More than a delineation of territory, it is a manifestation of historical memory: the map functions as a reminder that Métis peoplehood and nationhood are historically located, or rooted, in these specific places.

Although this map itself is new, the articulations of relationships with these areas are not. As Métis scholar Darren O'Toole points out in his recent discussion of the Métis homeland, when Louis Riel "sang the praises...of *le peuple Métis canadien-français*...the areas and peoples [Riel] mentions—the Indians of Minnesota, the Dakota tribes, the mountains and prairies of the Northwest, Regina, Montana, Manitoba—all fall within what is today termed the Métis homeland" (O'Toole; italics in original).[2] Aside from underscoring significant historical geographic references, O'Toole also alludes, through his brief synopsis of Riel's poem, to the literary resonances of these territorial claims. Penned in 1883 following a journey to Red River from Montana, where he attended his sister's wedding, Riel's Ode, "Le peuple Métis-canadien-français," is a fascinating reflection on Métis national history and identity that not only maps out the geographic boundaries of the Métis homeland, but also interweaves these references through human geography and the relationships between the Métis and other Indigenous peoples of the plains (both antagonistic and sympathetic), as well as with Europeans such as the French and the English.[3] In many ways, the poem exemplifies Pascale Casanova's concept of "combative literatures," as a text which arises from a small literature and is largely preoccupied, through its enumeration of the Métis' "brillants succès" (Riel 4: 319), with "claims to a national existence" (Casanova 129). In his Ode, Riel demonstrates how the Métis are a post-contact Indigenous people, emerging in the late eighteenth and early nineteenth centuries from the multiple encounters between First Nations and European fur traders. Through a complex web of kinship networks, cultural practices, and economic activities spread across the North-West—but importantly also centred on specific places such as Red River, in what becomes Manitoba—the Métis developed their own language, laws, and customs.[4]

A similar impetus marks Métis literature up to the present: an abiding concern with history, territory, language, and culture. Métis scholar Emma LaRocque notes, for instance, how "contemporary Metis Nation resistance discourse [which informs and constitutes an important segment of Métis literature] relies on its own resistance history" (134). This abiding concern is intrinsically tied to the history of settler colonialism, and even Métis national dissolution, in the decades after the military defeat at Batoche in 1885. What followed were the "forgotten years," when—dispossessed of land, shamed, discriminated against, and marginalized in the developing settler society—many Métis lost their national and cultural identities, not to mention suffered from a lack of economic security and physical well-being. Although Métis political re-organization gained traction in the second half of the twentieth century, with leaders securing recognition in the 1982 Canadian Constitution as an Indigenous people and forming the Métis National Council in 1983, the struggle for recovery (of land, language, and culture) is far from complete.

The work toward recovery and re-affirmation of identity is in part a process of memory: the remembering of language and culture, re-knitting connections, and retelling stories as well as histories; or, as LaRocque describes it, the "re-collection of scattered parts, both personal and communal" (134). In terms of Métis literature, LaRocque argues that "re-collection" produces an "aesthetic [that] is marked by mixing, transgression, and a reinvention of genres, languages, tropes, and techniques" and that through this interplay of form and content, it becomes a form of "discursive resistance" (134). That is, in its collective efforts to re-story Métis narratives, Métis literature often confronts settler narratives that have historically sought to erase Métis political and cultural traditions. One particular area of discursive resistance is in the re-storying of the resistances, and in these efforts, Scofield and Dumont are not alone; rather, they are part of a broader tradition that extends beyond "literary" arts. As Hannah Roth Cooley demonstrates in her survey of the historical narratives published in *New Breed Magazine* between 1969 and 1979, a publication by the Association of Métis Non and Status Indians of Saskatchewan, "[h]istorical memory was a tool of activism that *New Breed*'s editors and contributors employed to reinforce bonds of community, promote Indigenous political activity, and offer the Métis community a greater voice in Canadian media" (Cooley 112).[5] As such, what Scofield and Dumont articulate in their collections is part of a longer reframing of the story (or history) of the resistances—a story that is not simply of individual experiences, but one of a people. As with the community of Métis writers and readers of *New Breed*, so too are Scofield and Dumont part of an active tradition of reshaping and enriching Métis historical, cultural, and national memories.

METHODOLOGICAL CONSIDERATIONS

This chapter seeks to demonstrate how Métis literature is rooted in specific peoples and places. While there may be expected persons and places that emerge from a consideration of two texts that in large part narrate Métis nationalist resistances (Louis Riel and Gabriel Dumont, Red River and Batoche), an account of the accumulated references and allusions provides insight into their significance to the narrative. We contend that their frequency lends increased weight to those persons and places in the literary imaginary; as Scofield and Dumont's texts are literary works, not histories, we also argue that such concerted references gesture not only toward the efforts of contemporary Métis writers to assert narrative authority over such histories, but that they also bolster and enrich the memory of said figures, spaces, and experiences. Digital mapping offers a way to underscore what these stories emphasize and to also consider what is de-emphasized or forgotten in that retelling. Thus, we undertook the task of producing our own digital objects of study, which are examined complementarily to the texts from which they derive. Moreover, we acknowledge the obligations that our digital assets possess toward their non-digital sources.

Our methodology is premised on a resistance to datafication of Indigenous knowledge while still allowing for the possibility of producing interpretable visualizations. As Dumont's poem "To a Fair Country" refrains its own impossible desire "to forget [the] orderly ledgers / lists, records / and deceptively even-handed calculations" (58–59) of the scrip commissioners, land surveyors, and other agents of settler colonialism that dispossessed the Métis of their lands, we too must exercise caution with respect to the extractive impulses of data collection so as to not divorce the data from the poems or their contexts. Rather than automating the process of data collection, we manually entered each element of the project into a dense database with extra fields that allowed for contextual and descriptive detail.[6] This process required constant recursive questioning of our assumptions and examination of any implications that specific categorizations might produce. Instead of the extractive connotations of text mining as well as of distant reading to produce big data, ours was a process of intimate reading that attempted to produce robustly datafied constellations that might still cohere to the cosmologies of the texts and culture.

Drawing out references to persons and places from both texts to trace and map their presence led to methodological and interpretative challenges. Working with printed copies, we manually parsed the texts line by line, creating a database of geographic locations and persons, contextualizing the data as we went along. We noted geographic features—a river, territory, or settlement—as well as geographic coordinates; for persons, we attempted to list their nationalities, noting if they were Indigenous or not, and whether they were contemporary to Riel and Dumont or Biblical, apocryphal, or historical figures. Some subtle allusions were difficult to disambiguate: for instance, powerful evocations of prairie landscapes in Dumont's text proved impossible to map precisely; and shifts in the poetic voice, focalization, ambiguous allusions and pronouns as well as an occasional blurring between historical and fictional figures also troubled our disambiguation of persons. Our methodology also proved unable to wholly account for specific Cree-Métis lifeways. We were unable to adequately represent the expansive kinship networks alluded to in Dumont's text: from the suggestion of *wahkohtowin*,[7] or kinships and obligations between human as well as other-than-human beings, as evidenced through the evocation of kinship between Gabriel Dumont and the buffalo in Dumont's poem "Notre Frères" (10), or the blurring between beading, berries, animals, landscapes, and human kin in Dumont's bead poems, or Gabriel's intimate familiarity of prairie landscapes around Batoche, where "not a single blade / of grass will renounce you / your life depending on the coulees, leaves, limbs, and blades of / buffalo grass" (24). Despite such challenges, we generated data visualizations that provide some insight into the central narratives that these collections mobilize.

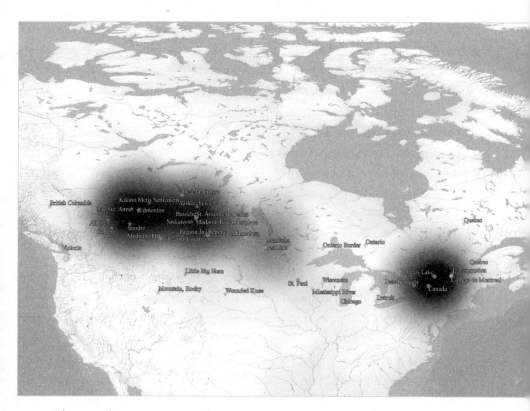

FIGURE 8.1.
Scofield (diamonds) vs. Dumont (stars) heatmap of place mentions.

MAPPING A LITERARY HOMELAND

In creating these maps,[8] we made a conscious decision to avoid settler-colonial borders and boundaries. Instead, the aim was to emphasize the geographical elements that feature so prominently in the poetry. Using monochromatic relief raster data for a basemap that would provide recognizable elevation features, we added lakes and waterways to provide further contextual clues for place. While the data was in the form of singular locations for the named places in the texts, the desire to avoid imposing rigid borders led to the utilization of heatmaps. These visualizations work by calculating the relative density of points and presenting them as varying levels of colour intensity on the map with a gradual fading effect at the edges. This liminality seemed appropriate not only to elude settler-colonial borders so ubiquitous to mapping, but also in the ways that it encourages a different reading, one largely relying on the relationality of waterways to locate place.

In Figure 8.1, Scofield's mentions of place have been represented with diamond nodes, while Dumont's have been represented with star nodes. A greyscale heat map has been added to show the density of their combined references and allusions to territory, with repeated mentions significantly darkening the heat map. Unsurprisingly, there is a marked density of points in what is currently Alberta and Saskatchewan, corresponding with significant references and allusions to traditional Métis settlements such as Batoche, Lac St. Anne, and areas around Edmonton, as well as geographic references such as the North and South Saskatchewan Rivers. There is much less emphasis on Red River, or Manitoba, in comparison to points further west, which would seem to reflect a focus on the second of the armed resistances and the consequences of the Métis' defeat. Notably, there is a dense cluster centred on eastern Canada as well, which functions to reference Riel's attachments to Montreal, where he had family, obtained much of his formal education, and also spent time once exiled from Red River. This cluster also alludes to the looming presence of Ottawa and the federal government in the lives of the Métis in the late nineteenth century.

With Scofield in Figure 8.2 and Dumont in Figure 8.3, the authors have been separately mapped. We added point location nodes to further emphasize the location of the places that they mention. As with the heatmap layer, the nodes also contain gradient hue intensities linked with increasing numbers of mentions in each text. Differentiating between Scofield and Dumont, we observe meaningfully contrasting visualizations of Métis literary geography: eastern Canada and Batoche dominate Scofield's heatmap, which suggests that his narrative focus rests on the antagonistic conflict between the Métis and "Ottawa" and, temporally,

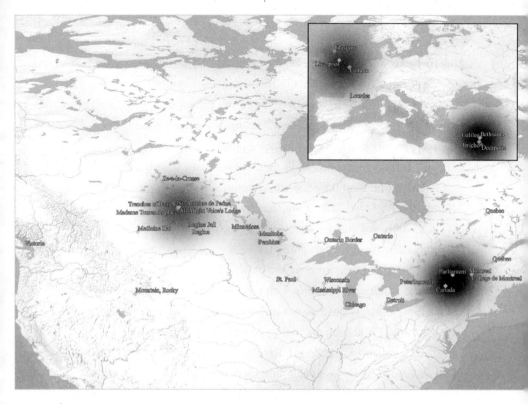

FIGURE 8.2.
Scofield heatmap with coordinate datapoints (overseas in top right inset).

on the second of the resistances; meanwhile, the Red River Settlement is much less prominent. Waypoints between the Prairies and the east are also quite evident, as Scofield includes poems of travel in his work; Riel's childhood journey to Montreal, for example, and settlers migrating westward from Europe. Dumont's heatmap, in contrast, prominently features a broader Métis geography. Although she also makes reference to eastern Canada, she relies less on an antagonistic juxtaposition than Scofield. Dumont's heatmap also reveals a Métis geography absent from Scofield's text: whereas she similarly references Red River and Batoche, she also includes numerous references to Edmonton and the Lac Ste. Anne region

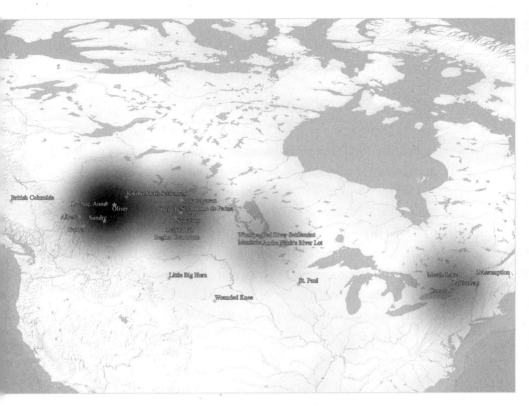

FIGURE 8.3.
Dumont heatmap with coordinate datapoints.

as well as other areas in what is now Alberta, such as the Kikino Métis Settlement and the town of Sundre. Through such references, Dumont's heatmap gestures to her more contextual approach in re-storying the North-West Resistance, relying less on narrativizing the battles or the conflict of personalities between Riel and Macdonald, which become coded geographically as Batoche and Ottawa. She instead fleshes out the people and communities that these conflicts affect.

Even as they provide insights into the individual collections' narrative focuses and show points of convergence and divergence between them, these geovisualizations only reveal so much in and of themselves and require close readings of the texts to interpret the unique ways that broader re-storied narratives are mapped. As Sally Bushell points out, "digital mapping of literary place and space is problematic primarily because the represented place and space of the literary work of art (and many of the characteristics that make it literary) so significantly exceed in richness, complexity and depth the attempt to generate maps from them" (137). Part of the issue that Bushell identifies is a result of the static nature of maps and their inability to adequately demonstrate movement across both time and space: Riel's childhood journey to a pre-Confederation Montreal becomes blurred with post-Confederation, settler-colonial Ottawa; the data points representing Métis settlements in the west obscure their large, seasonal hunts for "Li Bufloo" (Dumont 11), as well as their freighting, transportation, and other economic and social activities. In Dumont's poem "Not a Single Blade," for instance, both Batoche and the South Saskatchewan River are referenced twice, yet mapping these references does not quite capture how Dumont also evokes "the coulees, leaves, limbs, and blades of / buffalo grass" (24) that populate this space, nor Gabriel Dumont's particular experiences, "hiding in the bluffs / concealed in the coulees / crouched in the willows" (25) of that space as he stalks Canadian soldiers following the Métis defeat at Batoche. While mapping geographic references makes visible the places undergirding Dumont's poetic narrative, it is the *experience* of these spaces that Dumont's text presents. Literature provides not a "mere representation of place," Bushell argues, "but the possibility of a shared experience that is not at *one step removed* from how we experience place in the world but a more sophisticated articulation of that experience into which we enter and by which our own sense of place can be changed" (Bushell 131; italics in original). Again, in her survey of *New Breed*, Cooley also shows how Batoche "served as what Pierre Nora describes as a *lieu de mémoire*—a site that provided the material, symbolic, and functional power to connect memories with the present" (119; italics in original). Dumont's envisioning of Gabriel Dumont's relationship with the "coulees, leaves, limbs, and blades / of buffalo grass" (25) seems then to shift the emphasis of the "*lieu de mémoire*" from the human-made settlement to the natural world, the particular geography upon which that settlement was established. Thinking through Cooley's citation of Nora, we might argue that Marilyn Dumont demonstrates, through Gabriel Dumont's memory—and which the heatmap fails to capture—*how* Métis lived *with* the territory around Batoche.

In terms of the second heatmap (Figure 8.2), Scofield's many allusions and references to Biblical, historical, and apocryphal figures, such as "the blind man in Bethsaida" or "the paralytic of Capernaum" (25), multiple references to "David" and "Goliath" (39), and references to "Glasgow...Liverpool...[and] London" (51), generate a dense concentration of data points in the Middle East and Great Britain (Figure 8.2 inset) that are not entirely contemporary to Louis Riel. Yet despite the temporal flattening of the map, the overseas data points demonstrate the extent to which such places occupy space in Riel's thoughts, as represented by Scofield. Moreover, they suggest that Scofield's re-storying of the North-West Resistance is concerned with notions of state (the Crown) and religion (Catholicism). However, despite the apparent narrative weight suggested by a mapping density that rivals points over Batoche or eastern Canada, the points over the Middle East and Great Britain are somewhat misleading. That is, while these references betray their overall frequency in the collection as a whole, they do not reveal the infrequency of references from poem to poem, or concentration in certain poems. The Biblical and apocryphal figures are largely located in two poems, "Infinity of Maybe" and "The Interview," while references to cities in Great Britain are mostly drawn from "A Settler's Almanac." Also, the map does not show the great temporal divide between the two, as those of Great Britain are directly associated with European settlement of Rupert's Land and the North-West Territories.

The idea of "deep maps" would seem to offer a path to better contextualize these initial figures, and perhaps unflatten the maps. As David Bodenhamer explains, "A deep map is a finely detailed, multimedia depiction of a place and the people, animals and objects that exist within it and are thus inseparable from the contours and rhythms of everyday life" (212). Elaborating, he argues that deep maps are not confined to the tangible or material, but include the discursive and ideological dimensions of place (the dreams, hopes, imaginations and fears of residents); they are, in short, positioned between matter and meaning. They are also topological and relational, revealing the ties that places have with each other and tracing their embeddedness in networks that span scales and range from the local to the global. (212)

In a sense, Dumont and Scofield's collections of poetry are already somewhat akin to deep maps in the ways that they gesture toward and evoke broader relationality between people, places, and other-than-human entities. As alternatives to deep maps, or perhaps in conjunction with them, cartograms and anamorphic projections might offer some further abstraction of space to align with the Métis literary homeland that the poetry charts. As all map projections rely on a degree of abstraction, and as this has traditionally been biased toward colonial powers, it may be worth experimenting with further abstractions that emphasize and focalize Métis presence and place. In sum, the challenges in mapping these evocations require a depth of consideration and representation toward which our demonstrations can only gesture; our work digitizing such representations is only the beginning of any such undertaking and the concomitant discussions of how to do justice to poetry with cartographic visualization.

NETWORK GRAPHS:
TOWARD A MÉTIS LITERARY KINSCAPE?

Network graphs offer the opportunity to consider affinities and connections between entities. As a literary project, it was crucial to keep the textual elements explicit while creating this web of interaction.[9] The database graphs as an ego-centred network, with the two authors as hubs from which textual affiliations of the poems are the first-degree nodes,

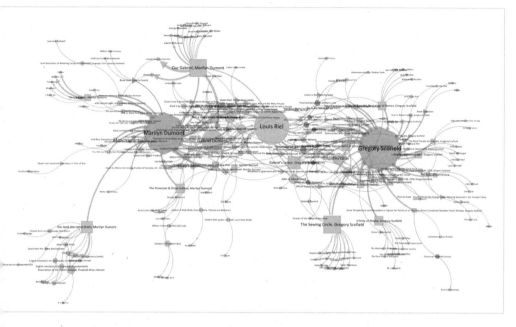

FIGURE 8.4.
Scofield-Dumont literary network, full extent.

and then persons and paratext are at further degrees of remove from the centre (Newman 45, 58). Entities are coloured by types, with authors, persons, poems, and paratextual containers differentiated.[10] Nodes are enlarged in the network based on their frequency in the texts, and the edges between nodes thicken and darken with increased interactions. The nodes' actual positions on the abstract plane adhere to an algorithm based on a basic repulsion mitigated by the strength of the ties.[11]

The Scofield-Dumont literary network, as visualized in Figure 8.4, exhibits the full extent to which poetry and paratext mediate the relationship between the authors and the persons and entities that they name. Louis Riel occupies a central position between the two authors, with a gravity well of footnotes and endnotes surrounding them, denoting how each author chose to refer to historical records and scholarly citations to further flesh out their depictions. The second most prominent individual aside from the authors and Riel is Gabriel Dumont, who orbits closer to Marilyn Dumont and reflects her particular focus in narrating her own family's journey in the "acknowledgement of [their] blood connection to Gabriel Dumont" (5). In this way, the relative proximity of Gabriel Dumont to Marilyn Dumont in the network representation is not just one of narrative focus, but one of kinship connection as well.

The noise contained in the expansive representation renders the static images sometimes unwieldy for detailed interpretation. In considering how we might curtail this expansiveness, attempting to reduce the noise, and in keeping with the re-storying impetus of the texts themselves, we filtered the network to draw out an Indigenous-exclusive representation. While the resulting network of such a selection might seem to correspond to a kinscape, the assumption of an equivalence between the two is problematic. Even as Macdougall uses "kinscapes" to discuss "Métis relationality across expansive distances and identity beyond reductive notions of blood" (Justice 262), our network graph tends to flatten such connections. Although the network graph might gesture toward a Métis kinscape, its lack of genealogical and cultural detail, and more crucially, its inability to contextualize relationships, curtails its representational capacity.[12] Instead, we offer a new term to describe this network more accurately: a kithscape. While its modern use has been reduced to its combination with the more intimate term *kin*, *kith* has older connotations that correspond with the network we map. Kith offers the conjoining definitions of "persons who are known or familiar, taken collectively; one's friends, fellow-countrymen, or neighbours"; "country or place that is known or familiar; one's native land, home"; and "[k]nowledge how to behave; rules of etiquette" (*OED*). In short, *kith* describes the complexity of connections derived from our databasing of these poetics through their relationships to persons and place. Reapplying the force-directed layout to the network, filtered to retain only Indigenous entities, produces this important cultural configuration: a kithscape (see Figure 8.5).

With just the poetry and Indigenous individuals connected by their associations, the kithscape graph shows both the drawing closer of

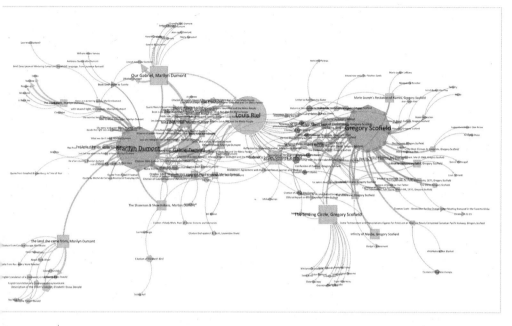

FIGURE 8.5.
Scofield-Dumont literary network, Indigenous filtered kithscape.

certain poems to their authors, as well as a number of poems that cascade out to distinct groups of Métis persons. This reconfiguration brings into sharp focus Riel's movement away from Scofield's authorship node, despite Riel being Scofield's eponymous figure for the poetry collection. A methodological decision was made early in this project to not create linkages between Scofield's poems and Riel for moments where the author took on the voice of Riel. The rationale was to abide by explicit mentions of persons or entities, and often a narrator's invocation of pronouns can be subject to ambiguity. Moreover, as Riel looms so large over Métis history and literature already, this decision was an attempt to see how he might be decentred by only accounting for explicit mentions of his name. The result, as the full network (Figure 8.4) and kithscape network (Figure 8.5) demonstrate, is that Riel continues to occupy a pronounced

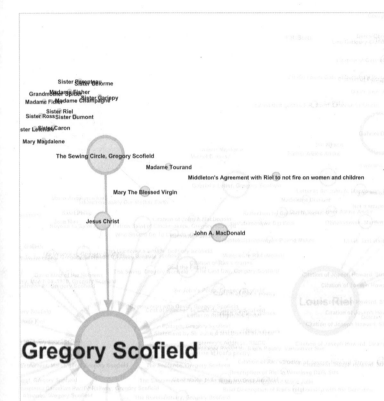

FIGURE 8.6.
Scofield-Dumont literary network, "The Sewing Circle."

position despite these decisions. Furthermore, the links between authors and individuals are positioned based on intermediary nodes representing their poetry, so Riel's position between the two authors is significant and in many ways makes him the apparent ego-centre of the network. The Riel node occupies that place between the authors because the bonds of their poetry equally draw from and re-story his memory. This not only resonates with what Cooley observes as to how, "rather than simply lamenting the injustices of the past, Riel's memory could serve to bolter activism going forward" (137); it demonstrates how Scofield and Dumont are working within a broader tradition, but it also gestures to the struggle over Riel as a symbolic figure. Re-storying Riel's memory becomes a way to partially detach him from an exclusively symbolic signification and to re-humanize him, re-claim him, and re-position him as a person within the kinscape, story, and memory of the Métis Nation.

Considering the full network again, how the poetic pieces are positioned in relation to the authors and the individuals and entities they name can be interpreted to provide some insight. While Dumont's "Otipemisiwak" and Scofield's "Gabriel's Letter" each represent a bridging work between the authors, some other poems still hold near centrality in this visualization of a Métis literary kithscape when singular and obscure mentions might otherwise push clusters to the periphery. In the case of "The Sewing Circle" (Figure 8.6), these references gesture to the network of Métis women, and particularly to those who sought shelter during the battle of Batoche. Notably, in this visualization, the non-Indigenous individuals demonstrate the embeddedness of the antagonisms that the poems depict. In addition to the connections between women are also supplications to Jesus, the Virgin Mary, and even the mention of Mary Magdalene. John A. Macdonald's node occupies a central position as a bridging concern between many of the poems of each author. This antagonism, in fact, both through the naming of Macdonald and the appeal to Biblical and/or spiritual figures, also draws the poem itself into a more central position in the network. Interestingly, the poem's many links to the network are also influenced by significant contextual references contained in a paratextual epigraph of an excerpt of a letter from General Middleton to Louis Riel, sent on the third day of the resistance at Batoche, which exhorts him to place the women and children in a safe place, where they would not be fired upon.

Scofield's poem, "Gabriel's Letter," highlighted in its first-order connections in Figure 8.7, raises interesting questions about its relative position. In some ways, the poem's connections are somewhat scattered. This may in part be evidence of Scofield's focalization of Riel—that is, of his embodiment of Riel's voice: thus, even as, graphically, Biblical

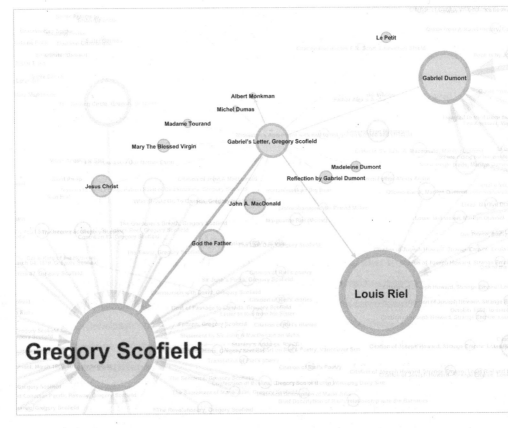

FIGURE 8.7.
Scofield-Dumont literary network, "Gabriel's Letter."

figures seem drawn to Scofield's authorial node while the Riel node remains somewhat detached from these references and drifts instead between Scofield and Dumont, textually, the link is much more direct, as it is Scofield's focalized Riel that invokes and appeals to God and Jesus. Undoubtedly, the positions of nodes of God and Jesus closer to Scofield reflect his representation of Riel's Catholicism, but, notably, Riel himself seems to gravitate towards Marilyn Dumont, particularly as shown in Figure 8.5. We might contend that, comparatively, Dumont seems to draw Riel out from his Catholicism—which is one of the central ways by

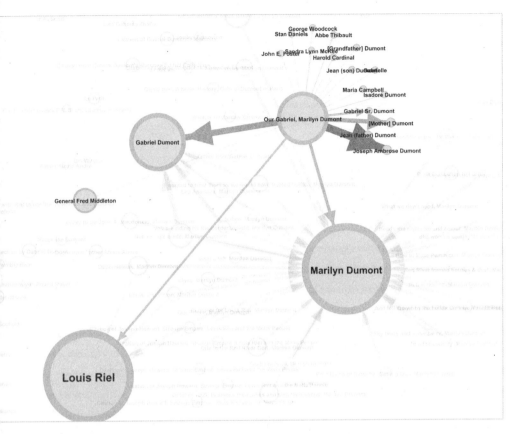

FIGURE 8.8.
Scofield-Dumont literary network, "Our Gabriel."

which Scofield characterizes him—as she instead primarily characterizes Riel through nationalist narratives rather than religious ones.

Dumont's prose poem, "Our Gabriel" (Figure 8.8), provides another intriguing case in the graphic network. While structured similarly to Scofield's "The Sewing Circle," as a plethora of persons fan out from the poem node, Dumont's poem occupies a much more intimate position in the network, almost nestled (though perhaps pushed to the side by its size) between Dumont's authorial node and Gabriel Dumont's node. Though the poems share some poetic similarities in the ways

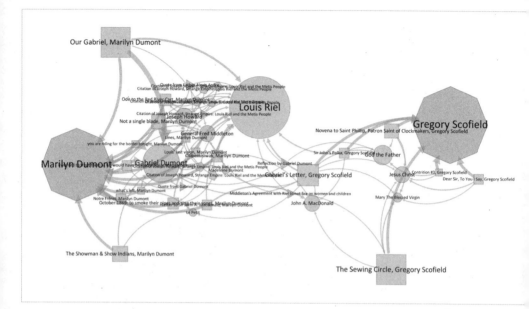

FIGURE 8.9.

Scofield-Dumont literary network, filtered for centrality (k-core 3).

that they touch on broader kinship networks, "Our Gabriel" gestures toward the larger network of the Dumont Clan and traces their relationship with their famous kinsman. While "The Sewing Circle" seems separated from the network centrality, even as it hints at the kinscapes of Batoche's women, with "Our Gabriel," the network graph draws the poem closer to the centre by accounting for the poem's recursive references to Gabriel Dumont.

Lastly, touching upon the network's central features, the final graph (Figure 8.9) presents a narrower focus by using an iterative process of filtering out peripheral nodes.[13] The core of the Scofield-Dumont network is striking. Following the iterative filtering, an uneven number of poems remain from each author. Whereas Dumont's side of the network presents about twelve poems, Scofield's side retains only six poems. Additionally, on Dumont's side, numerous paratextual elements remain, while these almost all disappear from Scofield's. Although this last point might also gesture at their contrasting writing styles in the use of intertextual sources to inform and supplement their poetic oeuvres, it largely represents the texts' *acknowledgement* of these sources; that Joseph Howard—author of *Strange Empire*, an important early text on Riel and the Métis—remains nestled amid paratextual nodes seems to suggest that Dumont takes a more consistent citational approach than Scofield. Finally, turning to the nodes of persons and other entities, we see, much like the earlier discussions of the heatmaps and the poem "The Sewing Circle" pointed out, how Scofield's focus narrows upon concerns of religion and state: aside from Riel, Scofield's remaining entity nodes are God the Father, Jesus Christ, Mary the Blessed Virgin, and John A. Macdonald. He shares with Marilyn Dumont references to Gabriel Dumont, his wife Madeleine Dumont, and his famous rifle, "Le Petit," as well as General Fred Middleton. That Middleton, the Dumonts, and the rifle are drawn closer to Marilyn Dumont's authorial node suggests that they occupy a more central concern for her text than Scofield's. What the graph fails to distinguish, however, is the temporal differences between figures and the interactions between figures. Those persons/entity references drawn closer to Marilyn Dumont's authorial node are narratively linked to the re-storying of the North-West Resistance in 1885, while for Scofield, references to religious figures as well as to Macdonald, although also linked to events in 1885, reflect a broader temporal influence: the church's near-constant presence in Riel's life, from his early childhood to his execution, and the decade and a half of antagonism between Riel and Macdonald, from the Red River to the North-West Resistances. In their unique approaches to re-storying Métis historical events, both Scofield and Dumont demonstrate certain breadth and depth; however, for all of its temporal depth, Scofield's text, as suggested by the k-core network (Figure 8.9), retains a more narrow, predictable focus than Dumont's text. The plethora of poems, paratextual references, and contemporary (to the resistance period) figures that orbit Dumont's authorial node not only reveal how these are enmeshed in complex networks of relationships but perhaps also contain textual traces of *wahkohtowin*.

Although these graphical representations evoke a Métis literary kinscape (or kithscape, for Figure 8.5), they are largely limited, partial, and incomplete. Drawing from only two texts out of the authors' bodies of work, they ignore not only their wider oeuvres, but the works of other Métis writers such as Katherena Vermette, Chelsea Vowel, and Conor Kerr, or earlier writers such as Maria Campbell and Beatrice Mosionier. Not to mention, aside from notable exceptions such as "God The Father," and Gabriel Dumont's rifle "Le Petit," the network did not adequately account for references to other-than-human entities, animals, plants, and other beings. We are left to imagine the significance of a buffalo node, or the graphical representation of connections between various authors who reference the rougarou. The graph also fails to capture linguistic concerns, demonstrating neither how nêhiyawak (Cree) was the lingua franca of the North-West in the nineteenth century, nor how the leadership of the resistances drew significantly from francophone Métis communities. However, such lacunae are not entirely due to our methodological approach in reconstituting these literary works as digital objects of study (although they are partially so); they also reflect the consequences of settler colonialism, policies of assimilation, as well as significant cultural and linguistic ruptures that mark Indigenous literatures. Nevertheless, these graphical networks not only provide an intriguing glimpse into a Métis literary imaginary, they also demonstrate how that literary imaginary is rooted in particular places, people, stories, and relationships. Although this study is perhaps too limited to confidently declare how remembrance and the re-storying of historical, nationalist narratives of Indigenous resistance to settler colonialism shapes both historical and contemporary Métis literatures, it certainly indicates how memory continues to play a significant role in Métis literature, akin to LaRocque's "re-collection" (134). This study shows some of the ways in which Métis writers remember, and reshape, historical narratives, focusing on certain aspects (Scofield's persistent focus on the antagonism between Riel and Macdonald, for instance) while also greatly expanding on what have been underrepresented aspects (such as Dumont's contextual broadening of the North-West Resistance or Scofield's representation of the women at Batoche). Kristina Fagan Bidwell argues that remembering the resistances largely "forms the core of [the Red River Métis's] claim[s] to Metis identity" (125), but what this core actually encompasses is "the history, events, leaders, territories, language, and culture associated with the growth of the buffalo hunting and trading Métis of the northern Plains" (Andersen 24). Remembering the resistances offers a way to examine broader issues of Métis nationhood and peoplehood and not only link historical and contemporary communities, but alongside recent court cases and decisions,[14] literary re-storying also provides insight into how such legacies continue to influence and shape Métis communities as well as the ongoing relationship between the Métis and Canada beyond the literary.

NOTES

1. Other notable Métis mapping and digitally informed projects include Evelyn Peters et al.'s *Rooster Town*, which traces the history of an urban Métis community (Winnipeg) through the twentieth century; Frank Tough's work on Métis scrip (https://www.ualberta.ca/native-studies/research/map-lab.html); and Kisha Supernant's report for the Rupertsland Centre for Métis Research at the University of Alberta in which she maps historical Métis families' movements across the homeland.
2. O'Toole notes that these locations also "more or less [correspond] to the waterways of the Lake Winnipeg drainage basin."
3. Though penned in 1883, "Le peuple Métis-canadien-français" was published a decade and a half later, on 23 June 1898, in *L'Echo du Manitoba*, a French-language newspaper.
4. For more on Métis identity, nationhood, and people, see: *Contours of a People: Métis Family, Mobility, and History* (St-Onge, Podruchny, and Macdougall); *Métis: Race, Recognition, and the Struggle for Indigenous Peoplehood* (Andersen); or *The North-West is Our Mother: The Story of Louis Riel's People, the Métis Nation* (Teillet).
5. Cooley broadly identifies three main themes in her survey: the significance of Batoche as a site that "ground[s] memory in space"; reflections on historical economies such as the fur trade and bison hunts, which demonstrate how "modern issues [such as corporate industrialization are]

continuations of earlier colonial processes"; and the "adopt[ion] of Riel as an icon of the Métis struggle" (117–18).

6. The relational database was created using the MySQL server version of phpMyAdmin from the Wampserver 3.1.7 suite of tools.

7. Métis scholar Brenda Macdougall defines *wahkootowin* as more than a "worldview" (8); it is a value system that emphasizes not only a "sense of relatedness with all beings" (3), such as "between human and non-humans, the living and the dead, and humans and the natural environment" (8), which "conveys an idea about the virtues that an individual should personify...such as reciprocity, mutual support, decency, and order" (8).

8. The map visualizations were created using QGIS 3.16 Hannover, with Natural Earth vector data (Gray Earth with Shaded Relief, Hypsography, Ocean Bottom, and Drainages) and raster data (lakes and rivers).

9. The network diagrams were created using Gephi 0.9.2.

10. Each work used a different approach when it came to notation, Scofield using footnotes while Dumont chose endnotes. Furthermore, we went so far as to include the dedications and prefaces in our consideration of paratextual containers, which in turn would have references to persons.

11. This model uses Gephi's "Yifan Hu" force-directed layout, which is then slightly adjusted by the "Noverlap" layout to make it more human readable.

12. There are traces of genealogy in both collections: Scofield's "Marie-Joseph's Recitation of Names" (13–14), which situates Riel within the North-West, linking him to ancestral relations at Île-à-la-Crosse; and Dumont's "Our Gabriel" (1–5), which relates her family's unearthing of their kinship ties to Gabriel Dumont.

13. This process uses the Gephi filter for k-core degree distribution, to a degree of k-core three (for degree distribution calculation, see Newman 314).

14. In 2013, the Supreme Court of Canada found that "[t]he federal Crown failed to implement the land grant provision set out in s. 31 of the *Manitoba Act, 1870* in accordance with the honour of the Crown" (Supreme Court 691).

WORKS CITED

Andersen, Chris. *"Métis": Race, Recognition, and the Struggle for Indigenous Peoplehood.* UBC Press, 2014.

Bidwell, Kristina Fagan. "Metis Identity and Literature." *The Oxford*

Handbook of Indigenous American Literature, edited by James H. Cox and Daniel Heath Justice, Oxford University Press, 2014, pp. 118–36.

Bodenhammer, David J. "Making the Invisible Visible: Place, Spatial Stories and Deep Maps." *Literary Mapping in the Digital Age*, edited by David Cooper et al., Routledge, 2016, pp. 207–20.

Bushell, Sally. "Mapping Fiction: Spatialising the Literary." *Literary Mapping in the Digital Age*, edited by David Cooper et al., Routledge, 2016, pp. 125–46.

Casanova, Pascale. "Combative Literatures," *New Left Review*, no. 72, 2011, pp. 123–34, https://newleftreview.org/issues/II72/articles/pascale-casanova-combative-literatures. Accessed 6 May 2019.

Cooley, Hannah Roth. "Historical Memory and Métis Political Resurgence in *New Breed* Magazine, 1969–1979." *Canadian Journal of History*, vol. 54, no. 1–2, 2019, pp. 111–39.

Dumont, Marilyn. *The Pemmican Eaters*. ECW Press, 2015.

Gaudry, Adam. Foreword. "Maps: De-Indigenizing and Re-Indigenizing Our Territory." *Indigenous Peoples Atlas of Canada*, https://indigenouspeoplesatlasofcanada.ca/forewords/maps/. Accessed 16 December 2020.

Justice, Daniel Heath. *Why Indigenous Literatures Matter*. Wilfrid Laurier University Press, 2018.

LaRocque, Emma. "Contemporary Metis Literature: Resistance, Roots, Innovation." *The Oxford Handbook of Canadian Literature*, edited by Cynthia Sugars, Oxford University Press, 2016, pp. 129–49.

Macdougall, Brenda. *One of the Family: Metis Culture in Nineteenth-Century Northwestern Saskatchewan*. UBC Press, 2010.

Monkman, Lenard. "Map Showing Métis Homeland Boundaries Sparks Online Conversation." *CBC*, 1 December 2018, www.cbc.ca/news/indigenous/map-showing-m%C3%A9tis-homeland-boundaries-sparks-online-conversation-1.4928401. Accessed 15 December 2020.

Newman, Mark. *Networks*. 2nd ed., Oxford University Press, 2018.

O'Toole, Darren. "Toward a Métis Homeland." *Canadian Geographic*, 10 November 2017, www.canadiangeographic.ca/article/toward-metis-homeland, Accessed 15 December 2020.

Oxford English Dictionary Online, "kith, n." Oxford University Press, December 2020, www.oed.com/view/Entry/103759. Accessed 30 December 2020.

Peters, Evelyn J., et al. *Rooster Town: The History of an Urban Métis Community, 1901–1961*. University of Manitoba Press, 2018.

Riel, Louis. "Le peuple Métis-Canadien-français." *The Collected Writings of Louis Riel / Les Écrits complets de Louis Riel*, vol. 4, edited by Glen Campbell and George F.G. Stanley, University of Alberta Press, 1985, pp. 319–25.

Scofield, Gregory. *Louis: The Heretic Poems*. Nightwood Editions, in collaboration with the Gabriel Dumont Institute of Native Studies and Applied Research, 2011.

St-Onge, Nicole, et al. *Contours of a People: Metis Family, Mobility, and History*. University of Oklahoma Press, 2012.

Supernant, Kisha. "Nodes, Networks, and Names: Narrative Report for Rupertsland Centre for Métis Research Fellowship, 2017–2018." *Rupertsland Centre for Métis Research*, 2020, https://www.ualberta. ca/native-studies/media-library/rcmr/publications/rcmr-fellowship-narrative-report-supernant.pdf. Accessed 4 April 2024.

Supreme Court of Canada. *Manitoba Metis Federation Inc. v. Canada (Attorney General)*, 2013 SCC 14 (2013), 1 S.C.R. pp. 623–738. https://scc-csc.lexum.com/scc-csc/scc-csc/en/item/12888/index.do. Accessed 6 August 2020.

Teillet, Jean. *The North-West is Our Mother: The Story of Louis Riel's People, The Métis Nation*. Patrick Crean Editions, 2019.

Tough, Frank. "Métis Archival Project (MAP) Research Lab." *Faculty of Native Studies*, University of Alberta, www.ualberta.ca/native-studies/research/map-lab.html. Accessed 4 April 2024.

9

BEYOND THE BORDERS OF THE CITY AND THE DIGITAL SPACE

QUEER (UN)BELONGING AND MEMORY WORK IN DIONNE BRAND'S *THIRSTY*

ANNA KOZAK

"FROM TIME TO TIME...frequently, always / there is the arcing wail of a siren, as seas / hidden in the ordinariness of the city" (Brand 63)—these are the words with which Dionne Brand begins the final page of her long poetry book, *Thirsty* (2002). "In a siren," she explains, you can hear "the individual muscles of a life collapsing" (63). If this siren signifies the loss of life, then the question is: does it come in the form of a life-saving ambulance, or is it the police siren that signifies the stolen life of another innocent Black person? At the heart of *Thirsty* is the murder of Jamaican immigrant Albert Johnson, who was shot and killed by police during a domestic call in 1979 (Sanders xiii). The remainder of the poem stems from this act of police brutality as *Thirsty* assumes the form of collage, intertwining multiple voices together and linking them through memories of endless past, present, and future acts of racialized city violence. The sound of the siren thus

203

evokes generational trauma as well as memories of ongoing violence for the African-Caribbean subject. Through *Thirsty*, Brand—an African-Caribbean queer woman and prominent Canadian poet—depicts the experiences of life in the city of Toronto for intersectional subjects with interwoven lives.

Focusing on the interactions between Brand's queer African-Caribbean subjects and the city, I will discuss Brand's poetry through Johanna Garvey's conceptualization of queer (un)belonging. Through the subversive capacity of such (un)belonging, *Thirsty* emphasizes the productive (im)possibility of belonging in Toronto for the queer subject whose identity is also shaped by the African-Caribbean diaspora. While a literal examination of the term "diaspora" tends to prioritize movement across national borders, queer (un)belonging suggests that queerness itself is diasporic as it denies modernity's heteronormative narrative formation processes. Brand's work challenges the established perception of diaspora as being chiefly concerned with peoples and borders, calling for a redefinition of the term to encompass queerness as a disruption of not only heteronormativity, but also of nation building, which is predicated upon linear and normative constructions of heterosexuality, time, and space. Brand's representation of the racialized queer subject in the city disrupts heteronormative notions of belonging and works through the tensions between assigned identities—which encompass the intersections among race, gender, sexuality, and class—and the desire for more fluid identities. As Brand highlights these tensions between assigned intersectional identities and fluid, fragmented, or self-assigned identities, she situates the notion of queer (un)belonging within the realm of identity formation, which is intrinsically linked to memory work. Thus, I am interested in examining how the concept of memory informs Brand's focus on identity formation in her poetry and extends into how Brand's work and narratives about her work circulate in digital spaces. The first part of my chapter will focus on the spatial as well as an identity- and memory-based conception of queer (un)belonging in Brand's poetry, which builds towards a discussion in the second section of how *Thirsty* operates across digital mediums. I argue that through the transposition of *Thirsty* into digital spaces, Brand highlights the specific experiences of city life for subjects with particular intersectional identities and positionalities while also opening up dialogue on how memory work functions beyond the physical space of the city and in the digital realm.

As Brand's poem emanates from an act of police brutality on the streets of Toronto, it assumes the non-linear form of collage as Brand intertwines multiple voices. This collective poetic voice highlights not only the inherent instability of the autonomous subject but also the spatial and temporal fragmentation and alienation that city inhabitants experience, especially if they are queer, Black, and diasporic. Queer and racial violence in the city strengthens feelings of queer (un)belonging for queer African-Caribbean diasporic subjects, functioning as the re-enactment and evolution of ongoing colonial oppression. Yet the queer diasporic figure also challenges such linear, (re)productive forms of nation building in the city space, working within fluidity and fragmentation to destabilize their identities and surroundings. *Thirsty* queers the notion of diaspora, becoming what Omise'eke Natasha Tinsley refers to as a "praxis of resistance," a "disruption to the violence of normative order" (199). Brand's text calls for a redefinition of diaspora to encompass queerness as a disruption to heteronormative national projects, which is a function of memory work. As stories are created through acts of memory, they have the ability to challenge normative narratives pertaining to sexuality and the nation. This chapter ultimately focuses on the capacity of fluid diasporic identities and the notion of (un)belonging to disrupt heteronormative national projects that manifest in the microcosm of the city as well as the theorization of diaspora as existing beyond spatial and digital borders.

Branching out from the context of the poetic page, the second part of my chapter will examine the extension of *Thirsty* into digital spaces, specifically that of YouTube. Through the act of sharing and digitally rereading excerpts from Brand's poetry book in online spaces, the notion of queer (un)belonging can be examined on the digital stage as it proliferates as a cultural memory agent, transcends physical and digital borders, and contributes to a renewed understanding of diaspora.

I will use the YouTube video "Walking Cities: Toronto" as a case study for the collective growth and extension of *Thirsty* into the digital sphere: in the video, as Brand walks through the city of Toronto with Trinidadian-Scottish poet Vahni Capildeo, she gives her a "tour" of the city while simultaneously discussing the embeddedness of colonial memories within its structure and architecture. The video ends with Brand's brief recitation of an excerpt from *Thirsty*; this excerpt, along with the "tour" itself, underscore the relationship between physical spaces, like the city, and memory work in the digital sphere. The "tour guide" (in this case, Brand) mixes her memories of Toronto with broader colonial memories that circulate within national narratives, while the "tourist" (Capildeo) absorbs them. Yet, Capildeo is not merely absorbing—she simultaneously recalls her own colonial, and even literary, memories of Toronto that had familiarized her with the city prior to her visit. This digital adaptation of *Thirsty* thus engages in memory work that demonstrates how queer (un)belonging can be used to envision a queer diaspora beyond not only geographical and identity-based borders but also digital ones.

THIRSTY IN THE CITY SPACE

Queerness, diaspora, and memory intersect in various ways, and these intersections manifest meaningfully in the city space for the queer diasporic subjects of *Thirsty*. Diaspora studies are continuously expanding to encompass more than simply research on movement across borders: historically, "the term [diaspora] is often limited to population categories that have experienced 'forceful or violent expulsion' processes (classically used about the Jews)"; however, more recent scholarship suggests that diaspora "may also denote a *social condition*, entailing a particular form of 'consciousness', which is particularly compatible with postmodernity and globalisation" (emphasis in original; Anthias 560). An example of this type of diasporic consciousness, one that connects with memory and does not necessarily entail movement across borders, lies with the Indigenous people of Turtle Island (North America) in the face of the historical and ongoing effects of colonialism. Indigenous people have undergone and continue to undergo dislocation and displacement within their own land. This is but one example of the possibility of experiencing a complex diasporic consciousness that exists beyond strict definitions of national borders, lodging itself deep within and influencing a collective, cultural memory. Furthermore, contrarily to how the traditional diasporic subject experiences alienation due to movement across space, Indigenous dislocation and displacement results from decreased mobility, confinement to reserves, and disconnection from ancestral land.

Modernity and mobility are also connected to diaspora and memory more specifically. Many scholars (Walter Benjamin; Roland Barthes; Susan Sontag) see modernity as the time in which memory gained prominence in popular culture through technological means such as photography, for example, and argue that the introduction of these technologies led to a heightened focus on memory and identity in moments of crisis. These scholars suggest that the invention of technologies like the camera and news media enabled people to document and circulate stories about trauma and identity in ways that were not as accessible previously. Other aspects of modernity that are more closely tied to mobility—including the rise of transnational immigration and the construction of rural and commuter highways, urban streets, and alleyways—often produce the opposite of their intended effect: reduced mobility. Modern ideologies of acceleration harm the environment, create and sustain distance between people, and disenfranchise social groups that are already vulnerable, including women, LGBTQ+ communities, migrants, and Indigenous populations. Although advancements in mobility have led to a more hyper-connected, globalized world, an increase of international movement paradoxically creates a tightening rather than a loosening of national borders (Glick Schiller 24–25). Thus, modernity and its accompanying technologies actually produce contradictory and often detrimental consequences for mobility.

Queer (un)belonging in *Thirsty* falls in line with this broader definition of diaspora, depicting alienation and displacement across subnational spaces—such as that of the city—and identities—particularly the intersectional identity of the queer African-Caribbean diasporic subject—rather than exclusively across national borders. Moreover, complicating traditional notions of diaspora as merely a process of relocation is essential since, as Garvey notes, "relocation primarily means dislocation, displacement, and the home becomes not here and no where [*sic*]" (760). To add to her conceptualization of the term, I suggest that relocation must not necessarily refer to concrete locations or to the movement of bodies from one geographical space to another; diaspora can also refer to fluid and perspectival shifts within the self that are often accomplished through memory work. By privileging the "point of 'origin' in constructing identity and solidarity," diaspora studies also "does not adequately pay attention to differences of gender and class" (Anthias 558). In other words, intersectional identities become obscured by the focus on national borders and origins. Thus, I turn from diaspora studies to queer (un)belonging through a focus on memory studies. Queer (un)belonging is powerful precisely because in queering the diasporic subject, we can shift the focus from a specific homeland or point of origin to the realm of fluid memory and identity. Although the queer African-Caribbean diasporic subjects of Brand's poetry come from specific homelands and find themselves in the urban space of Toronto, they also experience profound dislocation and displacement that can be understood more comprehensively through a focus on their identities and memories.

It is also important to emphasize the connection between one's intersectional identity and one's experience of (un)belonging to a nation. The link between nation building and sexuality has long been discussed by scholars (Mary Louise Pratt; Doris Sommer) in examining how "national projects [are] coupled with productive heterosexual desire" (Sommer 2). If the (re)productive heterosexual subject becomes indispensable to the nation by virtue of their normative sexuality, then the queer subject becomes disposable. In turn, if national belonging is predicated on this heterosexual paradigm, then the queer subject thus experiences (un)belonging. That being said, Garvey's conceptualization of "queer (un)belonging" (758) can be a particularly dynamic concept as it focuses on the ways in which the queer subject can disrupt linear, (re)productive national formations by becoming (un)productive in a countercultural sense. Queerness exposes and "demonstrates that even the formulation of sexual orientation...is interwoven with and produced out of colonial matrices" (McCullough 579). These "colonial matrices" permeate the mind, accumulating through memories and influencing one's process of identity formation; they are the points at which memory and intersectional identities connect with nationhood. By stressing the relationship between heterosexuality and colonialism in nation-building projects, queer (un)belonging reinforces the disruptive power of the queer diasporic figure.

For instance, in the first passage from *Thirsty*, Brand opens with a speaker whom I interpret as assuming the role of a queer African-Caribbean immigrant who recently moves to Toronto. "The poet/narrator," or the speaker, according to Leslie C. Sanders, embodies "the poetic eye and voice," which is "painterly, descriptive, observant, unjudgemental, tender and full of love for the city and its inhabitants who have come from all over the world, thirsty" for belonging (xiii). This passage depicts the relationship between the individual and the city of Toronto in tension with her connection to other city dwellers. I use the pronoun "her" in accordance with Sanders' pronoun use, which I argue suggests that Brand's voice enters the poem as a metafictional poet figure. Like Sanders, Garvey also refers to the speaker as the "narrative 'I'," adding that the speaker "engages in a queer romance with the city" (762). It is through this queer romance that the speaker begins to unravel the national and colonial myths of the city.

Brand begins *Thirsty* with the poetic eye ("I"), which absorbs the city's aesthetics while acknowledging the alienation and danger inherent in city life. She opens the poem with the following passage:

> This city is beauty
> unbreakable and amorous as eyelids,
> in the streets, pressed with fierce departures,
> submerged landings,
> I am innocent as thresholds

and smashed night birds, lovesick,

as empty elevators. (1)

At first, the speaker describes the city through romantic, aesthetically charged language, using words like "beauty," "unbreakable," and "amorous" to implicate the city as her lover. Yet the speaker also draws attention to the increasing disconnection that she feels from her actual human relationships. While the speaker initially describes herself as "innocent" and these loaded words focus on Toronto's superficial qualities in the form of its aesthetic appeal, amid this emotive imagery, the speaker foreshadows her own impending disillusionment by contesting the term "unbreakable" and recalling "*smashed* night birds" (emphasis mine). In this context, the term "smashed" has two meanings: that of being intoxicated and that of being broken. The first definition furthers the notion of the speaker's naivety to the reality of city violence in her focus on the city's aesthetics, likening her perception to alcohol-induced oblivion. The second definition contradicts the speaker's initial description of the city as "unbreakable," instead depicting its inhabitants as broken. The ambiguous term "smashed" thus creates a tension between the queer diasporic figure's naive desire to enjoy life in a new city and the reality of the broken relationships, the alienation, and the violence towards queer and racialized people that city life entails. This tension exposes how cities like Toronto, which are often praised for their ostensible inclusivity of queerness and diversity through misguided understandings of multiculturalism, offer "paradoxical safety" (Garvey 760). Toronto remains a place where gender non-conformity is possible—especially in queer spaces—but, in a sense, non-conforming gender expression must conform to whiteness and capitalism; in other words, individuals with particular intersectional identities are nevertheless in constant danger there of street harassment as well as queerphobic and racial violence.

With the speaker's growing knowledge of the violence of the normative order in the city, the speaker continues to deconstruct her initial perception of the city as a beautiful, romantic place. This deconstruction enables her to arrive at a more nuanced conclusion about city life by the end of the second stanza of the poem:

> let me declare doorways,
> corners, pursuit, let me stay
> standing here in eyelashes, in
> invisible breasts, in the shrinking lake
> in the tiny shops of untrue recollections,
> the brittle, gnawed life we live,
> I am held, and held. (1)

With statements such as "the brittle, gnawed life we live," the narrator demonstrates her increasing disillusionment with city life as she begins to experience the alienation and the violence that this life entails. This depiction of life as "brittle" rather than "unbreakable"—as the speaker describes it in the previous stanza—prompts us to consider the city's fragmentation, compression of geographical space (i.e., high-density housing), and fast-moving temporality (i.e., the "hustle and bustle" of city life). The planning of the city discourages human connection in its promotion of economic production; thus, this fragmentation and compression of time and space in the city increases disconnection and alienation. Nonetheless, the speaker simultaneously speculates about the disruption of the normative linear constructions that contribute to the dominant heterosexist and nationalist frameworks involved in nation building, and her initial experience of the city and her focus on its aesthetic qualities shifts to a deeper understanding of the dangers of city life for the queer diasporic subject as she gradually becomes more entrenched in it.

As the narrator becomes increasingly knowledgeable about the queer and racial violence of the city, her feelings of queer (un)belonging strengthen, and she begins to acknowledge how memory mediates her experiences and identity formation process. At the core of *Thirsty* is the 1979 murder of Albert Johnson, and this moment of violence becomes a symbol for the ongoing widespread issue of police brutality in urban centres. Throughout the text, Brand evokes Albert Johnson through the character named "Alan," whom she first mentions in Section IV on page 7 of *Thirsty*. Switching between speakers in each section of her poetry book, Brand intersperses Alan's story with other voices to highlight the lingering quality of city violence. The poem's fragmented, non-linear narrative branches out of this memory of racialized violence, condensing past, present, and future traumas together. The speaker's memories and identity are intertwined with colonial memories, which resurface with every traumatic experience that she endures or witnesses. *Thirsty* invokes institutional racism and the legacies of slavery and colonialism, which contribute to generational trauma and violence for the African-Caribbean diasporic subject. As Garvey argues, the poem demonstrates how "desire, loss, and longing rooted in migration and its concomitant traumas structures the [narrative]" (757). Brand places these experiences of violence and trauma alongside "a meditation on the role of aesthetics in addressing contemporary urban experience" (757). The speaker's connection with the city through aesthetics is not separate from her recognition of colonial memories and the generational trauma and violence that inform these memories. Rather, the city's aesthetics—its structures, technologies, and architecture—are all constant reminders of its colonial past, present, and future.

Thirsty further unravels as the speaker continually collides with these memories and continues to experience realizations regarding the city's paradoxical safety and superficial feelings of belonging. As she explains,

> the touch of everything blushes me,
> pigeons and wrecked boys,
> half-dead hours, blind musicians,
> inconclusive women in bruised dresses
> even the habitual grey-suited men with terrible
> briefcases, how come, how come
> I anticipate nothing as intimate as history. (1)

When the speaker states that "the touch of everything blushes" her, she uses the term "everything" rather than "everyone" to signify that her interactions with the city encompass objects or even animals, such as pigeons, in addition to—and sometimes rather than—people. It is the "dresses" that are "bruised" rather than the "inconclusive women," and it is the "briefcases" of the "habitual grey-suited men" that are "terrible." Moreover, the term "blushes" evokes not only the romantic redness of the speaker's cheeks, but also the concept of blemished innocence, signalling her increasing realization of the city's violence and alienation. If the speaker anticipates "nothing as intimate as history," perhaps it is her turn to personal history in the form of memory that can provide her with intimacy and respite from the alienation of city life. But, the question is, can history and memory also shield her from violence?

The following stanza provides us with the answer as it is the first specific reference to the police brutality that resulted in Albert's death. The narrator describes

> iridescent veins, ecstatic bullets, small cracks
> in the brain, how would I know these particular facts,
> how a phrase scars a cheek, how water
> dries love out, this, a thought as casual
> as any second eviscerates a breath. (1)

As the narrator ponders how she knows the "particular facts" of Albert's murder, she also acknowledges how "a phrase scars a cheek" and how a "thought as casual as any second" has the power to take away one's breath or life. These words have a dual function: on the one hand, they demonstrate how dominant racial ideologies circulate and permeate a particular encounter, such as the one between Albert and the police, which caused a thought this "casual" to turn into a murder; on the other hand, they signal how the narrator's knowledge of the specific facts of Albert's death and her broader memories of the racial and colonial violence have the ability to bring her harm too. The narrator's increased recognition of these traumatic memories that resurface during her experiences of urban life contributes to her loss of innocence regarding the city's paradoxical safety. As Diana Brydon points out, "As an early twenty-first-century citizen, Brand's persona is bombarded by media recording violence near and far, so that the traces deposited within her being reach inward and outward, embracing the specific history of black diaspora along with the specific complicities of anyone now living in North America" (995). As the media records and circulates violence, bombarding the speaker with these acts, it demonstrates how cultural memory causes an individual to reach "inward and outward" to understand where they are situated within this longer chain of generational trauma and violence. As the speaker continues to become more mentally involved in her new life in Toronto, she must reorient her identity as a queer diasporic African-Caribbean individual who is now living in Canada, a place with its own histories of colonial and racial violence that are tied to those of the Caribbean.

The city's fragmentation of time and space and the pressure to conform to the capitalist, heteronormative expectations of (re)productive citizenship further contribute to the speaker's accumulating experiences of psychological dislocation and displacement. She is initially unaware of the ways in which the constant work that is required of her to maintain her life in the city as well as the subsequent alienation that she experiences tear apart her relationships with other people. The speaker discusses the fleeting interactions between herself and her love interests. "We meet at careless intervals" (2), she states, signalling how little time there is in the city for interpersonal intimacy. When people do communicate, it is through "prosthetic / conversations" (2) that no longer feel meaningful. The words, like prosthetics, simply fill an emotional void but do not restore the sensation of the lost limb—the intimacy itself. The more the speaker becomes engulfed in her relationship with the city, the more her contact with other people slips away, amplifying her experiences of queer (un)belonging. These moments of realization open up crucial discussions on the disruptive potential of queer (un)belonging as the queer diasporic individual is positioned as an outsider to nation building.

Thirsty offers a raw depiction of the fragmentation and alienation that Brand's queer African-Caribbean poetic subjects experience in the city. While the speaker begins as a naive, diasporic figure that enters the city space, her increasing knowledge about the disconnection and the violence that is specifically directed at queer and racialized individuals leads to an accumulation of personal memories that unravel the broader collective and cultural memories of racialized, colonial violence. As the speaker's initial feelings of being "unbreakable" disintegrate, her acknowledgement of how memory work creates the space for a fragmented, fluid identity and experience of city life signifies the disruptive potential of queer (un)belonging.

THIRSTY IN THE DIGITAL SPACE

Through the process of sharing and digitally rereading excerpts from Brand's poetry book in digital spaces, such as the YouTube video, the notion of queer (un)belonging opens up further levels of inquiry. This digital adaptation of *Thirsty* in the "Walking Cities: Toronto" video demonstrates how queer (un)belonging envisions a queer diaspora beyond technological borders. In this video, the digital space enables a closer examination of a physical space—the city of Toronto—by forming connections across time and space as well as across mediums, shifting from the physical to the virtual sphere. This video is part of the larger "Walking Cities" project, which has so far covered the Canadian cities of Vancouver, Winnipeg, Toronto, and Montreal. According to the official website, it is a "literature program [that] connects contemporary voices from Canada and the UK to exchange on ideas related to identities, places and territories" (British Council). This website description elicits similar themes to those of *Thirsty*, from evoking the relationship between the physical space of the city, including its structure and architectural design, to its ongoing colonial and national history, which builds into contemporary cultural or collective memory. The "Walking Cities" program makes explicit the colonial connection between Canada and the UK, which (along with the United States) influences the structure, design, and organization of Canadian cities. As Brand and Capildeo walk across Bloor Street West ("the Annex"), a prominent part of the city, they discuss this embeddedness of colonial memories within the city structure, prompting an analysis of how digital spaces can act as further extensions of memory work. This video opens up the space for dialogue on how colonial memories manifest across not only literary or poetic media but also digital. As such, the video itself becomes a digital memory agent, acting as a site in which cultural or collective memory not only gets stored but also builds upon the colonial memories evoked by physical spaces, such as that of the city of Toronto.

The video opens on the streets of the Annex, lined with cars, construction, and the now-gone Honest Ed's, a landmark historical bargain store that used to occupy a significant portion of the street (the block from Bloor and Bathurst to Markham Street). Although Honest Ed's permanently closed on 31 December 2016, the city only removed the store's massive iconic sign from the building itself on 23 May 2017. In the video, Brand begins her conversation with Capildeo with a direct reference to Honest Ed's: "So, this is Bloor Street. And that...used to be a sort of massive emporium. I'm not sure how many years old, but certainly when I came to this city it was there already, and that was, like, forty-seven years ago...But only recently it's been shut down." Since the Honest Ed's sign appears in the video and Brand explains that the store had only recently been shut down, this situates the filming process as having occurred between a year prior to the video's release date (which, according to YouTube, is 10 December 2017) and the date that the sign was taken down. Not only does this remind us that the video's release date is removed in time and space from its original filming date, which causes it to function as a memory fragment, but it also testifies to the lingering quality of national and colonial memories. Honest Ed's is a relic of Canadian capitalism, and like the CN Tower, it is an iconic symbol of Toronto's cosmopolitanism: it is the city's connection between nationalism and globalization as well as its link to memories of colonialism and earlier stages of capitalism. As a discount store, Honest Ed's originally appealed to new immigrants and lower-income families, and its destruction for the purpose of building more condominiums is a classic case of gentrification. The iconic Honest Ed's sign will also be repurposed and attached to the Ed Mirvish Theatre, another Toronto landmark, demonstrating how the city retains its memories through the shifting and repurposing of its architecture.[1] The landmark will also be immortalized in the historical records of the city as well as through various artistic, educational, and technological mediums, including this video itself.[2]

Although Brand and Capildeo begin their discussion with references to the city's links to nationalism, capitalism, and colonial memories through their focus on Honest Ed's, they then shift to a conversation about the distribution of city space in relation to languages and cultures in Toronto, describing their own versions of prevalent multiculturalism myths. Looking at Bloor Street, Capildeo asks Brand, "If you walk along here, you hear a lot of languages too, right?" Signalling to the west, Brand responds,

> So, down that way a bit you hear Korean. And then you
> go further down, you'll hear Hindi. And then you go
> further down and you'll hear Spanish. And then you
> go way down this street and you'll hear Ukrainian,
> and so on. So, I have this friend who says that, 'you
> know, wouldn't it be wonderful if, as you walked into a
> language, you could actually speak it? You could kind of
> ingest it and speak it also.' And this is a kind of perfect
> city for thinking about that as an idea.

Brand and her friend's conceptualization of the city space as a series of compartmentalized streets based on languages and cultures is fascinating; yet I would argue that the city space is more fluid than Brand initially seems to suggest. The people that move across the streets of Toronto fill it with more languages than can be held by traditional understandings of "neighbourhoods" or even Brand's conceptualization of blocks of different languages. Brand's friend's idea of ingesting languages could almost theoretically work if the city streets were truly as compartmentalized as Brand suggests. In reality, however, the city space is much more convoluted and less structured. At any particular moment, the crowds that would normally fill the streets would stimulate the ingestion of multiple languages at once rather than one language per street or neighbourhood. Nevertheless, even though these spatial divisions are more porous than they initially appear, Brand's compartmentalization of the city space is a compulsion that evokes Anne Anlin Cheng's theory of racialized melancholy. Adapting Freud's early writing on melancholia, Cheng argues that melancholia is a kind of consumption and "condition of endless self-impoverishment" that is also "nurturing" (8). The narrative that Toronto—like the rest of Canada—is an inclusive space is a myth that mostly dissolves in the face of attentive scrutiny. Nonetheless, this inclusivity myth attempts to sustain itself by inviting racialized and sexualized others into the city space to maintain a "national topography of centrality and marginality" in which the other is positioned as "lost to the heart of the nation" (10). Although the other is not at the heart of the nation, they must be positioned somewhere at its extremities as a function of queer (un)belonging. As Cheng argues, although "racism is mostly thought of as a kind of violent rejection, racist institutions in fact often do not want to fully expel the racial other; instead, they wish to maintain that other within existing structures...the racial question is an issue of *place*" (12; emphasis in original). If these racist institutions can convince the other to incorporate themselves into the city space—albeit incompletely, since the other can never experience full incorporation or belonging—then they can successfully sustain the myth of inclusivity while maintaining the hierarchical structures that marginalize the other in the first place. Thus, Brand and her friend's desire to ingest multiple languages in the city space reflects the perception of Canada as a cultural mosaic and perpetuates neocolonial notions of multiculturalism, demonstrating the pervasiveness of these kinds of national narratives within our cultural memory.

Capildeo expands on Brand's theorization of the compartmentalized city space, furthering the inclusivity myth that is infused with racialized melancholy. She explains that "it's very interesting, because that also means that it's not only 'or, or, or,' but 'and, and, and'...So, a corner is cumulative space. By the time you've arrived here, you have so many different musics. And for us, as writers, to be in a corner like this is incredibly exciting, because it means you can access the multiple musics." Capildeo's conceptualization of the city space as cumulative is in many ways reflective of Brand's idea, but it also acknowledges the messiness of accumulation. I would argue that the city space is more like the "ands" are piled up on top of each other within the same space rather than divided into separate streets or neighbourhoods. Although one might be more likely to hear a particular language being spoken in a certain neighbourhood, the city space is still more fluid and heterogeneous than more rural locations. While it appears that Brand and Capildeo romanticize the city for its inclusion of "multiple musics," which are inspiring for poets and artists, they also turn to the issues that arise within it, mirroring the conceptual arc of *Thirsty*: in the poem, the subject begins her life in the city as hopeful but becomes increasingly disillusioned with it. Although the speaker in *Thirsty* is primarily frustrated with the alienation and violence inherent in city life, Brand and Capildeo emphasize the connection between city space and national or colonial memories in their conversation. Through the video's paralleling of the poem's narrative arc we see how this digital memory work makes room for not only the repetition of Brand's ideas from her poetry, but also a variation on her discussion of life in Toronto.

Brand and Capildeo's deeper examination of these less-than-idealistic components of the city begins with its architecture, which in many ways combines the focus on aesthetics with an acknowledgement of the issues with city life. Capildeo comments on how, in the Annex, "everything is at a human level, because everything is very low- to mid-rise," suggesting that "elsewhere in Toronto where I've been they're very high rises, where you can look down on fellow human beings and see them like tiny robots. But here, nearly everyone, you can meet their eyes, or you can imagine meeting their eyes." Capildeo emphasizes the city's aesthetics, suggesting that its architectural design is indicative of varying levels of human connection. Brand responds, "Yes, for the moment," and explains,

> [b]ecause we're being kind of overtaken by a certain logic of capitalism that might push these buildings much, much higher. That brings me to the thing about disappearances. So, I think that the corner is kind of significant of both appearances and disappearances... Like, appearances of populations of people as well as their disappearance, because of the way that we kind of live in capital and everything disappears and it's always regurgitated and comes back again, in a way.

Brand's discussion of the "logic of capitalism" that pushes buildings higher into the sky signals the increasing alienation and disconnection from other people in the city. This logic of capitalism is also the reason for gentrification and the destruction of buildings like Honest Ed's, which were once significant historical landmarks but are now being repurposed or, to use Brand's terminology, "regurgitated" into condominiums. If the logic of capitalism neglects the cultural and historical memories of the city due to its emphasis on upward mobility, it is the work of poetry and art as well as digital mediums to preserve these memories in new and interesting ways.

Brand and Capildeo's discussion then shifts towards examining the ways in which cultural memories are disseminated, demonstrating how people can become familiarized with a place before ever actually visiting it in person. Brand states:

> Now, I find it very interesting along this street to see, for example, different patterns of brickwork and different sizes of building lot, which suggests to me a very layered history...Okay, there are cities that I know because of colonialism. Right? Because of the way the British built cities everywhere. So that, when I went to, as I said

BEYOND THE BORDERS OF THE CITY AND THE DIGITAL SPACE

before, when I went to London, then I knew I'm standing somewhere and I think, 'Oh! I think I know where
to go. I should go around that corner and down that
way.' And I'll be right. And that has nothing to do with
me ever having been in London before; it had to do with
that structure. The architecture in the brain, which is,
you know, layered on that knowledge, that knowledge
of what that British Empire brought. How it brought its
architecture and sat it down. But I think the other ways
that I know cities, come to know cities, is books.

Brand discusses Toronto's "very layered history," which consists of its
colonial heritage shaping the design of the buildings and structures that
we see within it today. Her notion of "architecture in the brain" depicts
the ways in which people subconsciously absorb a city's architectural
or structural knowledge and apply it during their travels to other cities.
This cannot be possible without the colonial expansion of the British
Empire through the physical acts of building new cities with traditional
blueprints on colonized land as well as the dissemination of knowledge
through literature and art. Astrid Erll's notion of cultural memory
provides useful context here, as she discusses the "interplay of present
and past in sociocultural contexts" (2). Erll's theory defines culture
through a three-dimensional framework, comprising "social (people,
social relations, institutions), material (artifacts and media), and mental
aspects (culturally defined ways of thinking, mentalities)" (4). Brand's
knowledge of the city intertwines these social, material, and mental
aspects of cultural memory as she uses her discussions with other people
(social), information from books, art, and digital media (material), and
her own memories of other cities as well as her cultural awareness of how
colonialism influenced the development city spaces (mental) to envision
other cities.

The conversation between Brand and Capildeo ends with a
direct reference to *Thirsty*. Brand explains that her poem "is about this
city, and about the kind of complexity...I wanted to get into all of the kind

of craziness, the brittleness of that." She then reads an excerpt from her poetry book as she continues to walk with Capildeo through the streets of Toronto. This is the same excerpt from the beginning of the poem that I reference earlier:

> This city is beauty
> unbreakable and amorous as eyelids,
> in the streets, pressed with fierce departures,
> submerged landings,
> I am innocent as thresholds
> and smashed night birds, lovesick,
> as empty elevators. (1)

This first stanza of this poem encapsulates Brand's ongoing ambivalence about Toronto. The oral aspect of Brand reciting her poetry breathes new life into it as the poem mobilizes the digital space to expand its reach even as it permeates the cityscape. The dialogic, relational qualities of the video expand on *Thirsty* as they emphasize the interplay between the ideas of the two poets, Brand and Capildeo, as well as the city space, including its other inhabitants and architectural design. Ultimately, through the YouTube video, which acts as a digital memory agent, Brand's intricate conversation with Capildeo about how the city's architecture reflects national and colonial memories builds upon her observations in *Thirsty* and reflects them in digital form.

CONCLUSION

Through *Thirsty* and, later, the digital medium of YouTube, Brand examines how colonial and national memories intersect with the architecture and structure of the city as well as the thoughts and identities of the people who dwell within the city space. The city, according to Brand, is simultaneously able to encompass multiple languages and cultures alongside alienation and violence. Through transposing *Thirsty* into a digital space, Brand theorizes a diaspora that transcends geographic borders. Her literary and digital depictions of the city furthermore offer insight into the life experiences of queer African-Caribbean diasporic subjects, including their intersectional identities and experiences of queer (un)belonging, and demonstrate how such (un)belonging evokes national and colonial memories and contains the power to disrupt heteronormative national projects.

NOTES

1. More information about the Honest Ed's sign and its new location can be found in this article from the *Toronto Star*: https://www.thestar.com/news/gta/2017/05/23/honest-eds-sign-to-get-a-new-home-over-mirvish-theatre.html.
2. Another example is a 2020 documentary about Honest Ed's, *There's No Place Like This Place, Anyplace*: https://gem.cbc.ca/media/cbc-docs-pov/season-4/episode-8/38e815a-0135009eb91.

WORKS CITED

Anthias, Floya. "Evaluating 'Diaspora': Beyond Ethnicity?" *Sociology*, vol. 32, no. 3, 1998, pp. 557–80.

Barthes, Roland. *Camera Lucida: Reflections on Photography.* Translated by Richard Howard, Hill and Wang, 1981.

Benjamin, Walter. "The Work of Art in the Age of Its Technological Reproducibility." *Walter Benjamin: Selected Writings, 3: 1935–1938*, edited by Marcus Bullock and Michael W. Jennings, Harvard University Press, 2006, pp. 101–33.

Brand, Dionne. *Thirsty.* McClelland & Stewart, 2002.

Brand, Dionne, and Leslie Catherine Sanders. *Fierce Departures: The Poetry of Dionne Brand.* Wilfrid Laurier University Press, 2009.

British Council Canada. "Walking Cities: Toronto." *YouTube*, filmmakers Adrian Smith and Jason Hopfner and post-production by Productions Spectrum, 10 December 2017, https://youtube.com/watch?v=SwjseXkKAO4&ab_channel=BritishCouncilCanada. Accessed 11 March 2024.

Brydon, Diana. "Dionne Brand's Global Intimacies: Practising Affective Citizenship." *University of Toronto Quarterly*, vol. 76, no. 3, 2007, pp. 990–1006.

Cheng, Anne Anlin. *The Melancholia of Race: Psychoanalysis, Assimilation, and Hidden Grief.* Oxford University Press, 2000.

Erll, Astrid. "Cultural Memory Studies: An Introduction." *Cultural Memory Studies: An International and Interdisciplinary Handbook,* edited by Astrid Erll et al., De Gruyter, 2008, pp. 1–15.

Garvey, Johanna. "Spaces of Violence, Desire, and Queer (Un)belonging: Dionne Brand's Urban Diasporas." *Textual Practice*, vol. 25, no. 4, 2011, pp. 757–77.

Glick Schiller, Nina. "Transnationality, Migrants and Cities: A Comparative Approach." *Beyond Methodological Nationalism: Research Methodologies for Cross-Border Studies*, edited by Anna Amelina et al., Routledge, 2012, pp. 23–40.

McCullough, Kate. "'Marked by Genetics and Exile': Narrativizing Transcultural Sexualities in Memory Mambo." *GLQ: A Journal of Lesbian and Gay Studies*, vol. 6, no. 4, 2000, pp. 577–607.

Pratt, Mary Louise. *Imperial Eyes: Travel Writing and Transculturation.* Routledge, 1992.

Sommer, Doris. *Foundational Fictions: The National Romances of Latin America.* University of California Press, 1991.

Sontag, Susan. *On Photography.* Anchor Doubleday, 1989.

Tinsley, Omise'eke Natasha. "Black Atlantic, Queer Atlantic: Queer Imaginings of the Middle Passage." *GLQ: A Journal of Lesbian and Gay Studies*, vol. 14, no. 2, 2008, pp. 191–215.

10

THROUGH THE DIGITAL PRISM OF ACADIAN IDENTITY

AESTHETICS, POLITICS, AND COUNTERCULTURE

MATTHEW CORMIER

ACADIE AS A GEOGRAPHICAL AREA has no official status, either national or otherwise, but most Acadians generally consider it to occupy parts of Canada's Maritime provinces, with eastern New Brunswick often considered a hub. Its tangled sociolinguistic history and minor standing make it and its aesthetic productions, especially literature and visual art, fascinating areas of study in terms of memory studies, and even more so in the digital age and its associated memory agents who perform and influence Acadian culture. French colonizers settled the area at the outset of the seventeenth century, before the British deported them in 1755; therefore, Acadie has a complex past, having become a postcolonial culture but with colonial roots. Henceforth, and particularly since the development of its institutions and literature from the turn of the twentieth century onward, critics have chiefly read Acadian literature and identity as part of a minor culture caught between the francophone epicentres of Quebec and France as well as dominated by the anglophone majority on Canada's east coast. Acadian institutionalization began with the inauguration of St. Joseph College (1864) and newspaper *Le Moniteur Acadien* (1867), to be followed by the adoption of a national holiday (1881) and national flag (1884); later came the Université de Moncton (1963) and publishing press Éditions d'Acadie (1972), to be replaced by the current monopoly, Éditions Perce-Neige (1980).[1]

While these last institutions were particularly fundamental to Acadie's independence in constructing its cultural memory and representations of itself, they might now be gatekeeping artistic expressions of Acadian identity, whether deliberately or not; put otherwise, they in several ways prescribe Acadian cultural memory through the curation and choice promotion of its cultural artifacts. In the age of social media and digital performance online, however, a certain counterculture—if such a movement is even possible within a minority—has risen with some resistance to force a dialogue and to reveal tensions as to the consistency of Acadian literary and cultural productions in terms of representation and memory. This chapter examines several online platforms that intersect print culture and identity formation, from Perce-Neige's promotional material to book reviews of their publications on the webzine *Astheure* to pieces from the *Fragile: autres regards sur l'identité acadienne* art exhibit (2019), in an effort to demonstrate the power dynamics at work in trying to maintain a certain image of Acadian cultural memory and identity.

ACADIAN CULTURAL MEMORY AND INSTITUTIONS

Scholars have studied Acadian identity and its myriad representations in art through the prism of cultural collectivity, veering off in critical directions that include nationalism, postcolonialism, history, community, linguistics, ethnography, minority, and periphery, among others. As I have argued elsewhere as a critique of nationalist readings of Acadian literary productions in particular, perhaps memory studies—due to its inclusive nature and in light of Acadie's intricately convoluted history— stands as the most malleable point of entry into Acadie's artistic representations of identity, particularly via the notion of cultural memory.[2] I see the key to reading Acadie and its multitude of aesthetic performances as a meeting of cultural memory constructs that take place, ideology, relativity, and subjectivity into account. Since Acadie is so difficult to define as a collective, therefore, the now well-established work of Homi K. Bhabha remains useful, especially in understanding Acadie in terms of what he, harking back to Benedict Anderson's "imagined community," calls a "locality of culture":

> This locality is more *around* temporality than *about* historicity; a form of living that is more complex than "community"; more symbolic than "society"; more connotative than "country"; less patriotic than *patrie*, more rhetorical than the reason of state; more mytho- logical than ideology; less homogenous than hegemony; less centred than the citizen; more collective than "the subject"; more psychic than civility, more hybrid in the articulation of cultural differences and identifications. (292; Bhabha's emphasis)

Bhabha's locality of culture is unstable, nuanced, and in flux, and it is thus more illustrative of Acadie than many other direct or simplistic approaches to studying the subject's complexities. Moreover, it lends itself well to the epistemological analysis that memory studies allows and that Acadie necessitates.

Max Saunders points out that memory is more agential than history in terms of its contemporaneity because it "is necessarily a transformation of the remembered event or experience" (323). To consider cultural memory as a supplement to history, therefore, has the potential to be much more generative for studies on layered identities because memory offers greater agency, or at least a central presence, to

Matthew Cormier

the culture in question: as critic Astrid Erll explains, cultural memory in particular encompasses the "interplay of the present and past in sociocultural contexts" (2), insofar as culture is a three-dimensional concept consisting of "social (people, social relations, institutions), material (artifacts and media), and mental aspects (cultural defined ways of thinking, mentalities)" (4). These memory agents—the social, material, and mental—represent the pillars of memory, and one can see the similarities between these pillars and the affective dynamics at work in Bhabha's locality of culture; yet they are perhaps better described as resting on a lift that oscillates between the levels of the individual and the collective (5). Memories are mediated and remediated, cropped and edited with added or subtracted filters from one level to the other in an inseparable back and forth, bringing us to what Erll describes as "modes of memory," or *how* the past is remembered (7). She gives the loaded example of remembering war, but in the case of Acadians, no better example persists in the cultural imaginary than the Deportation. The violent episode expunged Acadie's own colonial past from its cultural memory, effectively leaving mostly representations of a peaceful, victimized people that was cruelly deported from its lands for refusing to obey the laws of British rule. Relatedly, and especially in the modern era of Acadian cultural representations from the latter half of the twentieth century onward, it is helpful to see cultural memory, in the words of Jan Assmann, as "a kind of institution. It is exteriorized, objectified, and stored away in symbolic forms that...are stable and situation-transcendent: [t]hey may be transferred from one situation to another and transmitted from one generation to another" (110–11). The objectified cultural memory, as Michael Rothberg deems, is "multidirectional: as subject to ongoing negotiation, cross-referencing, and borrowing; as productive and not privative" (3). As a result, cultural memory frames identity, since its affective agents both prefigure and recirculate its conscious, self-reflexive performances and representations.

Certain institutions in Acadie at present, as symbolic containers of its cultural memory, end up monopolizing these affective agents by their very nature and circumstances; they effectively shape representations and perceptions of Acadian identity, especially as these have centred the French language. This monopolization incrementally began to solidify with the establishment of the francophone Université de Moncton and Éditions d'Acadie during the 1960s and 1970s that occurred alongside the election of the first Acadian premier of New Brunswick, Louis J. Robichaud, and his implementation of the Language Rights Act in 1969, making it the first and only officially bilingual province in Canada. Acadians at this time thus began to gain autonomy and assertiveness with greater access to education and equal opportunities in addition to self-sufficient means of publishing literary works in French that contributed to contemporary cultural formation. This Acadian renaissance carries a great deal of weight in the culture's memory due to the political, neonationalist thrust of its younger generation, who protested the anglophone domination of Acadians at the Université de Moncton in 1968:

> The wave of protests is the result of the exasperation felt by the younger generation of Acadians at the traditions of their forefathers, especially at what is perceived to be their submission to Anglophone domination. It thus speaks to a generational gap tied in particular to the minority position of Acadians, but also to a disagreement with the previous generation's nationalist strategy. (Belliveau 18–19)[3]

Several factors thus contributed to these protests, which anticipated the early militant publications of the newly founded Éditions d'Acadie: from writers such as Raymond Guy Leblanc, Herménégilde Chiasson, and Guy Arsenault, the Acadian press published politically charged poetry that expressed and informed the cultural shift at the time against traditional articulations of Acadie and anglophone oppression. So while the memory of the Deportation, one such traditional referent, persists in the Acadian imaginary, it no longer offered concrete inspiration to the emerging Acadian poetry of the era nor to the institutions that endorsed it; instead, the sense of "exile" originally tied to the Deportation lingered affectively in Acadian cultural memory.

This sense of exile took on different forms—whether socioeconomic, linguistic, or geographical—yet remained a dominant force in Acadian cultural memory and its evolving representations of identity.[4] It morphed into an almost survivalist attitude that appears to have infiltrated Acadie's institutions in subsequent years; often manifesting as resistance or anger, this attitude has defined the literary movements that have come since the latter half of the twentieth century. Moreover, this atmosphere of resistance, born from these feelings of exile and exclusion, prompted the further development of Acadie's institutions into new iterations and created space for writers from diverse backgrounds and with different styles and goals. Publishing was thus particularly important to the growth of Acadie's poetry and, in turn, its cultural identity, as it advanced Acadie's causes for collective unity, autonomy, and innovation. Éditions d'Acadie, for instance, bolstered the feminist writers of 1980s, including Hélène Harbec, Rose Després, Dyane Léger, and France Daigle. Simultaneously, Gérald Leblanc, with the Association of Acadian Writers, inaugurated a second Acadian press in Éditions Perce-Neige, which has since become the chief literary venue in the region; Leblanc himself would become a significant contributor to Acadie's cultural memory with his exploration of urbanity and Americanism in his poetry and acclaimed novel, *Moncton Mantra* (1997). These writers and institutions grew alongside one another into the turn of the millennium, concentrating an Acadian cultural memory that spanned roughly fifty years and created certain prerequisites for future aesthetic productions of identity.

Yet although the concretization of this minoritized cultural memory, centralized around a sense of militant, francophone nationalism, was critical to Acadie's survival, it also became determinative, leaving some of its people to feel alienated from its institutionally backed identity. In particular, those who chose to write about topics that were not typified as "Acadian" according to this neonationalist wave, as well as those who would write in English or even "Chiac," a French dialect that includes English words and its own unique grammar and syntax, have at times been met with resistance by those occupying the majority within the minority. While acknowledging the numerous authors who, with some success, broke from these cultural expectations at the turn of the twentieth century is essential—including Jean Babineau, Éric Cormier, Jonathan Roy, Marie-Claire Dugas, and France Daigle—the dilemma remains that institutions in Acadie continue in some ways to monopolize and market this brand of "minor" ideology based on exile, survival, anger, and the French language as a cultural currency, even while some in Acadie show that it has perhaps moved beyond these concerns.

MOVING ONLINE: INSTITUTIONAL GATEKEEPING

With the turn of the twenty-first century and the digital age came the closing of Éditions d'Acadie and the continued rise of Perce-Neige as Acadie's chief press. Perce-Neige—which, as it rightfully claims on its website, has been "at the heart of Acadian literature since 1980" (n.p.; my translation)—has become Acadie's sole major press and is thus integral to the ongoing production of Acadian texts as cultural artifacts. Namely because of its influential status as *the* Acadian literary institution, representation with Perce-Neige often becomes a rite of passage for young Acadian writers and a major step toward recognition and opportunity. Yet while the success of this institution in some ways ensures a future for Acadian literature as a stable cultural backdrop, it also determines the literary artifacts that shape Acadian cultural memory and representations of identity; in a way, then, and perhaps only consequentially, Perce-Neige acts as an institutional gatekeeper of Acadian culture by default.

The concept of publishers as potential gatekeepers more broadly is not new: back in 1975, and in the American context, Lewis A. Coser made the case that "[relations] between producers of ideas and their consuming publics or audiences are typically mediated through social mechanisms that provide institutional channels for the flow of ideas. These channels, in turn, are controlled by organizations or persons who operate the sluicegates; they are gatekeepers of ideas inasmuch as they are empowered to make decisions as to what is let 'in' and what is kept 'out'" (15). He then elaborated on this thought, which still holds today, by pointing to the fact that "[even] though one could argue that, in the age of modern electronic media, publishing no longer occupies the near-monopolistic position in the realm of culture that it once enjoyed, it seems obvious...that the men and women who control access to the medium that Gutenberg invented are still in a position to channel the flow of ideas and control a central, though by no means the only, medium for ideas" (15). Coser based his analysis of the American publishing industry on three major structural conditions: the decentralization of the industry, the unpredictability of its market, and its internal organization (15–16). Of course, in this case, Perce-Neige, as Acadie's major press, is decidedly *not* decentralized, nor is its market that unpredictable since it dictates much of it by mere virtue of its imposing status; moreover, its internal organization appears to be small, suggesting a limit to the diversity of perspectives as to what is "in" and what is "out." As Coser argues in reference to such cases, "understanding the function of gatekeeping and analyzing the factors that determine the gatekeepers' decisions will hence give major cultural clues about the ways in which cultural products are selected for distribution" (15).

On Perce-Neige's website—which promotes a vision of Acadie both in terms of its cultural memory and its future direction, with considerable reach as an online presence—certain indications reveal the underlying but conceivably totalizing stakes of the press as the only major publishing option in Acadie, especially for emerging writers. For example, Perce-Neige's mission statement on their website's homepage reads as such:

> A non-profit organization, Perce-Neige publishes literary works that speak to the continuity and renewal of contemporary Acadian literature. The purpose of the press is to publish the driving forces of Francophone literature in Acadie, to privilege emerging writers who

represent its continuation, and to contribute to the development of this literature in Canada's Maritime provinces, all the while preserving the Acadian literary heritage. (n.p.)[5]

With respect to its standing as a key institutional container of Acadian cultural memory, this statement reads as Perce-Neige's inclusive acknowledgement of the multiple voices that comprise Acadie's literature. It accurately and fairly emphasizes its non-profit status as a press that endeavours to publish works that speak to the evolution of Acadian literature in French, prioritizing rising writers who will build the press's list while preserving Acadian literary heritage. And yet, while maintaining its commitment to a multiplicity of voices, the publisher by nature of its singularity as a cultural curator, in addition to other mitigating factors, still incurs the risk of pigeonholing literary expressions of Acadian identity.

One detail to consider, for instance, even within the greater tapestry of other influential cultural institutions in Acadie, is that Perce-Neige claims to not accept unsolicited works. While this facet might not have the same repercussions in other contexts, it is extremely significant for an Acadian minor culture whose aspiring writers, more often than not, rely heavily on this press to publish and circulate their literary works. Whether deliberately or not, then, Perce-Neige's institutional status as *the* legitimizing means of publication in Acadie, coupled with its policy of not accepting unsolicited works, squarely situates it as a major gatekeeper of Acadian cultural memory and its written representations—the great filter. Simply enough, the facts of the matter make it so. Not so simple, however, are the implications for emerging writers, especially those who might not fit into the press's cultural vision. How does an emerging writer in Acadie gain "solicited" status? What if they diverge from the publisher's mission? Some younger authors have been able to break through to publish with Perce-Neige: these rising writers include poets Joannie Thomas, Monica Bolduc, Sébastien Bérubé, and Gabriel Robichaud, among notable others. Bérubé and Robichaud, in particular, have found success in recent years, with each having published multiple collections with the Acadian press. While Bérubé has apparently not yet been able to shed the "emerging" descriptor, Robichaud appears to have transcended it, and viewers of Perce-Neige's online catalogue can find his works alongside those of other seasoned poets.

Robichaud's latest collection of poetry, *Acadie Road*, published in 2018, is an especially compelling case in the context of Acadie's institutional machine and its digital cogs. On the book's page in Perce-Neige's catalogue, one can find a link to a video of the book launch as well as a review of the book, an addition that stands out since as most other books do not feature such material. While the inclusion of a review seems promotional, the write-up is lukewarm: for the digital publication *Le mouton noir*, critic Clara Lagacé categorizes *Acadie Road* as a "classic wandering narrative made popular in America: a road trip in search of identity, but this time in Acadie" (n.p.). She goes on to deem the collection a success, but one that repeats the work of others:

> While Robichaud's method is not new, and in fact several other Acadian writers before him have sought to name their territory to affirm their existence and survival, he fully takes ownership of it. Thanks to numerous verses with biting humour that act as counterweights to those poems that are more dithyrambic, such as the admirable "Manifeste diasporeux," co-written with Jean-Philippe Raîche, this collection by the poet from Moncton succeeds in stabilizing the precarious balance between banality and wonderment. (n.p.)[6]

According to Lagacé, a strength of the collection appears to be its ability to balance mundanity with fascination, even though its method has nothing original and the poem that they single out in this conclusion as particularly poignant is the only piece in the collection that is co-written with another author. The insertion of this review as a promotional bit on Perce-Neige's website might seem odd, considering the reviewer's lack of conviction about *Acadie Road*; however, in reconsidering the press's mission statement, such advertisement is perfectly logical: not only does the text feature the "road trip" popularized in America and that had a significant impact on Acadian cultural memory because of its incorporation by Gérald Leblanc and others as part of a continued effort of naming the Acadian territory, but in doing so, according to Lagacé, it also takes up a strategy used by past Acadian writers while appropriating it for a new generation. As a result, *Acadie Road* performs Perce-Neige's vision of promoting emerging voices while preserving a certain Acadian literary heritage, a vision that continues to inform Acadian cultural memory and related representations of identity.

The institutional influence of the press in Acadian culture also extends to other organizations, especially in the digital sphere. For instance, it has a consistent promotional outlet in the form of the Acadian webzine *Astheure*, which includes a section for Acadian scholars to impart literary reviews, many of which are dedicated to Perce-Neige's new releases. Once these emerging writers secure their status by publishing with the press, their works can then circulate digitally as cultural currency, contributing to a particular brand of Acadian memory and culture; soon after publication, each of the aforementioned poets had a critique written about their collections in *Astheure*'s reviews section. That being said, the reviews were not always overwhelmingly positive: Acadian literature expert Benoit Doyon-Gosselin claims that reading Bolduc's first collection, *Dead End*, is important, even if readers should hope that her next collection—if she publishes one—will be more daring and take new creative directions ("Loin d'être un cul-de-sac!" n.p.); the same reviewer assessed Thomas's *Quatre pattes Catherine* as containing all the issues of an incomplete first work ("Je m'ennuie de Josée Yvon" n.p.). Meanwhile, another scholar, Isabelle Kirouac Massicotte, argues that Bérubé's *Là où les chemins de terre finissent* is more of a social project than a literary one due to its lack of formal command, redundancies, and sense of incompletion. Kirouac Massicotte also criticizes Robichaud's *Acadie Road* as "road trip writing" devoid of adventure, as the author does not leave on a quest in search of any novelty or to engage the "other" (n.p.). So while *Astheure* certainly does not always praise the directions taken by the literary institution, as a digital memory agent in itself, it participates in circulating Perce-Neige's vision of Acadian culture in a popular discourse that is continuously recirculated as it shapes its Acadian consumers.

The press's influence also reaches other significant containers of Acadian cultural memory, including representative events that have come to embody contemporary Acadian identity in the performances that they headline. Many of its published writers, for example, feature in the week-long Acadie Rock cultural festival that takes place each year in Moncton, New Brunswick and is focalized around Acadie's "national" holiday on 15 August; the festival is highly publicized online and has a significant social media presence both before and during events, since many incorporate various types of live streams. In this context, two years removed from its publication, Robichaud's critically contested *Acadie Road* became a focal point of the COVID-19 pandemic-ridden 2020 Acadie Rock festival, meriting its own event of music and poetry on the night of the national holiday itself titled "Acadie Road : un road trip musical et poétique" (n.p.). Featuring only a few short descriptive passages about the event and a listing of the performers who would appear there, an entire paragraph is dedicated to promoting the book of poetry on the festival's website:

> It is therefore time (if you wish to do so!) to (re)read
> Gabriel Robichaud's book of poetry, *Acadie Road*, in
> order to impregnate yourselves with his magnificent
> and impactful words since these will guide you in this
> road trip unlike any other. [This was followed by options
> to purchase the book from various retailers.] (n.p.)[7]

Once again, the promotional description of the collection as comprising "magnificent and impactful" words is somewhat at odds with some of its scholarly reception: established Acadian critic Mathieu Wade's 2019 review of the book, again published on *Astheure*, instead calls these same words narrow, embarrassingly juvenile at times, and the pure commercial product of an Acadie that does all it can to please the masses, to recycle an established Acadian cultural memory (n.p.). And while Wade never goes so far as to explicitly single out Perce-Neige itself in his critique, with this latest promotional move to sell copies of *Acadie Road* at the festival, it is difficult to ignore the publisher's effort to circulate a brand of Acadie and as a forceful memory agent now thriving in the digital landscape.

In fact, Wade's assessment of Robichaud himself as a recognizable Acadian writer appears to indict the press more than its authors. As Wade claims,

> Poetry is a particular genre in Acadie. Only music surpasses it in its capacity to market Acadie, to brand Acadianism. Among current literary representatives of the commercial brand *Acadie*™, Gabriel Robichaud is imposing himself as a central figure. He is the archetype of the "Acadian and Francophone succession" and one of the most institutionalized subsidiaries of *Acadie*™. On the verge of his thirties, he has already published three collections of poetry and a play, [landed] several roles as an actor, and has found a way to carve out a privileged space for himself in the official French-Canadian ecosystem; he is the literal flag-bearer of New Brunswick's Acadie in French-Canadian and global circuits. (n.p.)[8]

What Wade is discussing here—and this is interesting in the context of Perce-Neige's aforementioned vision—is the commodification of a particular performance of Acadian cultural memory, one that Robichaud and his works represent as perfect archetypes. While this result might be completely unintentional on the publisher's part, since it has no "real" competition in terms of publication venues with different views, the institutional press, even by mere circumstance, continues to fortify a specific kind or brand of Acadian cultural memory, one that circulates and informs popular discourse and identity. In Wade's words, this reinforcement of *Acadie Road* as a "true" Acadian artifact to behold results in a stereotyped and static Acadie (n.p.), one that becomes impenetrable even to Acadians if they do not identify with the cultural memory pillars that support it.

COUNTERCULTURE PROJECTS

If—whether by circumstance or with purpose—the representative publishing press of the Acadian people, as a key institution and container of artistic expression, has monopolized and gatekept the community's cultural memory in terms of literary productions while proliferating and marketing it tangibly and through cyberspace, so too have other voices and projects attempted to join the dialogue and counterhegemonic representations of Acadie. One such example is the *Fragile: autres regards sur l'identité acadienne* art exhibition, which was put on in Moncton, New Brunswick, by Galerie Sans Nom (GSN) as part of the National Acadian Congress in 2019.

According to the GSN website, the exhibition features "new, dynamic, innovative and critical works to highlight historical, cultural and linguistic issues which define the Acadian zeitgeist…created in collaboration with artists from multiple disciplines" (n.p.), including Marc Chamberlain, Céleste Godin, Xavier Gould, Geneviève Violette, and Becka Viau. These artists were asked "to deconstruct the symbols and conventions associated with Acadian culture in order to present them in a contemporary context" (n.p.). This context, as the title of the exhibition suggests, "refers to the fragility felt when an identity is not confirmed or affirmed fully. The exhibition is a destabilizing experience where one has to reflect on one's cultural identity and what that culture means for oneself and one's community" (n.p.).

Each participating artist thus addresses the fragility of Acadian identity by challenging elements of its homogenous cultural memory;

FIGURE 10.1.
Xavier Gould's "iel c'est moi, mais yelle c'est mon hook" from the *Fragile* exposition at the Galerie Sans Nom.
(Photo courtesy of Mathieu Léger.)

by doing so, they also circulate their own memory agents and engage different mediums and spaces, both physical and virtual. Xavier Gould's multimedia sculpture, for instance, criticizes prevalent Acadian heteronormativity, sexism, homophobia, and transphobia; for Gould, the sculpture, as queer art, represents imaginary escapes that must be built from leftovers, from nothing, and yet which ceases to be queer once it is made tangible (GSN n.p.) (Figure 10.1). Gould's work speaks to the impermeability of cultural memory generally and Acadie's in particular, along with how some of its representations are widely accepted, while others, like queer positionalities, cannot discernably cross into this collective sphere. Perhaps unrelatedly but still interestingly, Gould's piece is also the only one that does not come with an English translation of its description, and so it sets itself apart from the authors on its linguistic level as well. For her part, Geneviève Violette's piece comprises a photographic triptych that show sinister hands covering the eyes and mouths of their subjects. "In Acadie," Violette contests, "we rapidly take on ourselves the role of the victim. By looking at my series, we come to the realization that it is the characters that are censoring themselves" (GSN n.p.). Violette, therefore, appears to be advocating for less complacency and more resistance against the monopolizing forces that act as conservators of Acadian cultural memory, going on to state that: "Fragility is synonymous with vulnerability. In order to reconstruct a solid cultural oneness, we need to allow ourselves to be vulnerable and enjoy the freedom of expression even if we fear judgment by our society. To be strong, we have to become fragile." These two projects seem to imply that even in the margins of the minority, differences persist in Acadie, as one artist favours a turn toward vulnerability, while another opens up about the difficulties or impossibilities of even *living* vulnerability. Becka Viau's piece adds to these differences by evoking Acadian history: the work consists of a looped video of a white flag blowing in the wind, overlooking a cliff and the horizon. As Viau describes it, her piece features "a handmade white flag, the type of flag flown by many Acadians during the 100 + years before the expulsion. The white flag was and remains a symbol of neutrality or resistance, a symbol of individual humbleness bustled up with national pride or identity" (GSN n.p.). The work thus encapsulates one prevailing self-representation in Acadie opposite the British colonials; however, it also—as many other Acadian artistic creations do—whitewashes Acadie's settler history and colonial occupation in the Maritimes.

Perhaps the two most intriguing pieces from *Fragile* that attempt to capture digital memory agents in Acadie are Céleste Godin's "Le Confessionnal" and Marc Chamberlain's "tl;dr:acadie." "Le Confessionnal" (Figure 10.2), is based on Godin's online work with a Facebook page entitled "Confessions Acadiennes," which urged users "to write a confession, completely anonymously" (GSN n.p.).

FIGURE 10.2.
Céleste Godin's "Le Confessional" from the *Fragile* exposition at the Galerie Sans Nom.
(Photo courtesy of Mathieu Léger.)

Stemming from the idea of the Catholic confession, a familiar process in Acadie due to its people's close ties to the Church, Godin's project is meant to simulate the experience through anonymous online disclosure on topics such as "new discussions about the impostor syndrome linked to the Acadian identity, the desire for a #metoo movement to denounce Acadian aggressors, and the heartbreaking difficulties that sometimes accompany exogamous couples" (GSN n.p.). The way in which Godin sees her piece linking concepts such as confession and anonymity as they relate to Acadie is particularly revealing in terms of the concerns that some Acadians feel with respect to being perceived as "other" in the face of popular conceptions of Acadian cultural memory. In promising that confessions will be heard without "punishment or guilt" (GSN n.p.), Godin suggests that these repercussions exist for Acadians who speak out against the status quo, and especially for those who are identifiable. Although the need for such a platform in an exclusive ecosphere is in and of itself a public statement, the project also encourages the passive consumption of other Acadian perspectives, raising awareness while maintaining anonymity and security. In a sense, too, the piece reclaims some of anonymity's agency from its digital counterpart, since permanently scrubbing one's identity from a digital medium such as Facebook is a difficult task.

Relatedly, and as Chamberlain's piece shows, Facebook is also a virtual forum that fosters opinions and discussions, though these are not always generous and especially when the topic is one of the most contested in Acadie: language. Chamberlain's installation shows the Facebook discussion incited after a user posted a produced video of Chamberlain discussing his aesthetic perspectives, alongside the actual video playing on a loop. There was also space for participants to add to the discussion online; these participants "navigate both in and out of these fragile gaps so as to demonstrate a cultural moment that becomes increasingly fragmented despite its efforts towards unification" (GSN n.p.) (Figures 10.3 and 10.4).

Chamberlain effectively gets to the elitist stakes at hand for those Acadians whose beliefs align with Acadie's constructed cultural memory versus those whose do not:

> Following the release of a video montage produced by La fabrique culturelle documenting my artistic practice, a member of the Facebook group "L'incubateur de l'esprit critique en Acadie" ignited a discussion of my work after having posted a link to the video in question. Soon after, my practice and the manner in which I expressed myself were both subjected to various delegitimizing efforts within the comment section. A comment left by a certain "Jasmin Cyr," in particular, appears to underline the fragility which often frames nationalist perspectives

FIGURE 10.3.
Marc Chamberlain's "tl;dr:acadie" from the *Fragile* exposition at the Galerie Sans Nom.
(Photo courtesy of Mathieu Léger.)

on one's cultural identity: "The problem is that, within minorities such as l'Acadie, the consequence lies in the destruction of one for the benefit of the other. Language (in this case, chiac) maintains a social impact which exceeds a mere book" (Chamberlain's translation). Such extreme polarization with respect to the space occupied by Francophones vis-à-vis Anglophones within a city such as Moncton, as well as the damning conceptualization of Chiac's role in the survival of one linguistic group over another, exemplify a problematic tendency to anchor dichotomic ideology within a nationalist framework, wherein They always exists at the detriment of Us. From such tendencies, feelings of anxiety arise when faced with a polyphony of voices echoing from the extreme frontiers of nationalism and its counterpoints. (GSN n.p.)

Here Chamberlain underscores an inner conflict that persists in a number of minor cultures, especially those having complex ties to ideas of nationalism. The conflict—representative of a fragility—lies in this case with the tensions and contradictions between Acadie's colonial and postcolonial histories, leaving gaps that demand to be filled by a cohesive cultural memory.

As the Facebook thread shows, many Acadians buy into the certainty and homogeneity promised cultural institutions that valorize a nationalist Acadie and the French language. The following passages, for example, reveal the fear of the cultural and linguistic "other"—those Acadians who write in English or Chiac and about topics other than Acadie.

In the first comment, the same Jasmin Cyr worries that Chamberlain's approach of mixing English and French to write works that are not necessarily about Acadie will extend to others and begin a new movement. Another, Jean-Guy Dugay, asks if Chamberlain's work means that Acadians are finally committing genocide on themselves, to which Cyr responds that the issue is that the divide is too great between Acadians who value their language (French) and those who do not, and thus he equates Acadie to a "poor society." Rachelle Landry, who has apparently been following Chamberlain's work since 2014, given that she cites him from an interview given that year, argues that the more Acadians cede their linguistic territory to anglophones, the higher the chances that they become artisans of their own death. Not only are these comments made unironically, given Acadie's colonial history, but they also reveal the potency and pervasiveness of this nationalist cultural memory based chiefly on language and Acadie's institutions—not only Perce-Neige but also the Université de Moncton, for instance—as they swarm Chamberlain's perspective in the digital space, compellingly named "the incubator of the critical spirit in Acadie" (n.p.).

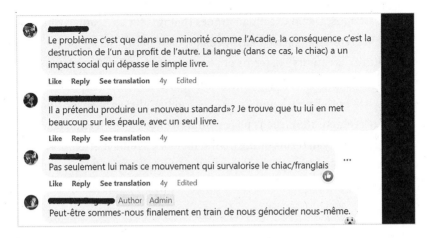

FIGURE 10.4.
Section of the Facebook conversation featured in Marc Chamberlain's "tl;dr:acadie" from the *Fragile* exposition at the Galerie Sans Nom. (Photo courtesy of Mathieu Léger.)

This fear of extinction or fragility of existence thus appears to go so far as to suppress alternative voices in Acadie that do not conform to its core, institutionally endorsed cultural memory, creating fragmentation among marginalized people even online. Curiously enough, this narrative has ensured that the opposite view be held of Acadian literature and culture in certain critical circles. For instance, the recently published *New Brunswick at the Crossroads: Literary Ferment and Social Change in the East* (2017), a collection of essays edited by Tony Tremblay, features several comments on the strength of Acadie's literary and cultural presence in the province. In his introduction to the text, Tremblay claims that "Acadians are much more advanced than their English neighbours in cultural and critical enterprise" (3). Additionally, he observes that Acadie "comfortably accepts the contradictions and negotiations of current artists and citizens alike, and functions as a model of pluralism for not only New Brunswick but also a multicultural Canada" (14). Relatedly, in the afterword to *New Brunswick at the Crossroads*, David Creelman argues that insofar as Acadian Chiac represents "the emergence of blended language [and] as a signal of the culture's creativity" in terms of identity construction (Boudreau and Gammel qtd. in Creelman 166), "[in a sense], all literature in New Brunswick, both English and French, is and has always been written Chiac" (Creelman 166). Yet as pieces from the *Fragile* collection demonstrate, especially in terms of the digital memory agents it attempts to capture, countercultural narratives in Acadie continue to face overwhelming opposition from the core cultural memory narrative.

CONCLUSION

If the situation in Acadie can offer some kind of lesson, it must be to recognize the prismatic power of cultural memory in minor cultures that define themselves by various iterations and derivatives of "survival," and even more so the ways in which this memory can be complicated in the digital age. Even in a minority—niche, some might call it—imaginary such as Acadie, identity politics are angled and intensified: the monopolization of artifacts such as literary texts; the hegemonic work of institutions; the countercultural narratives and their deterrents; the outside perspectives of the cultural memory in question. Within this virtual microcosm, one can read the struggle to control, preserve, or even shatter the Acadian cultural memory and its hold both within and without. What appears to be certain with efforts such as the *Fragile* exhibition is that the resistance to the current status quo will continue to press on and demand changes, especially as the arena moves into the digital, a sphere with which the younger generations are quite comfortable—comfortable enough to engage for their own exposure, but also to reveal the attitudes of those in power. With the advent and solidification of digital memory agents in Acadie, its third renaissance is perhaps not too far to follow.

NOTES

1. For detailed summary and analysis of these historical events, see Lonergan (2013) and Belliveau (2014).

2. See Cormier with respect to my case for memory studies instead of nationalist history as a means of studying Acadian literary movements.

3. My translation; French original: "La vague de manifestations est présentée comme le résultat d'un ras-le-bol chez la jeunesse acadienne des traditions de ses pères et, surtout, de ce qui est perçu comme leur soumission à la domination anglophone. Il s'agirait donc d'un choc entre les générations, mais d'un choc bien particulier, lié avant tout à la situation minoritaire des Acadiens et d'un désaccord sur le type de stratégie nationaliste à favoriser" (18–19).

4. In what could now be considered a significant memory studies analysis of Acadie, Patrick D. Clarke tackles the theme of exile from what he calls an anthropological perspective.

5. My translation; French original: "Organisme sans but lucratif, Les Éditions Perce-Neige publient des œuvres littéraires qui témoignent de la continuité et du renouvèlement de la littérature acadienne contemporaine. La raison d'être de la maison est d'éditer les forces vives de la littérature de langue française en Acadie, de privilégier les auteurs émergents qui en sont le prolongement et de contribuer au développement de cette littérature dans les Provinces maritimes du Canada, tout en préservant le patrimoine littéraire acadien."

6. My translation; French originals: "classique déambulation à l'américaine : un road trip identitaire, mais cette fois, en Acadie"; "Si la démarche de Robichaud n'a rien de nouveau, en effet plusieurs auteurs acadiens avant lui ont cherché à nommer le territoire pour affirmer leur existence et leur survivance, il se l'approprie pleinement. Grâce aux nombreux vers à l'humour cinglant qui agissent à titre de contrepoids aux textes plus dithyrambiques, comme l'admirable "Manifeste diasporeux," coécrit avec Jean-Philippe Raîche, le recueil du poète originaire de Moncton réussit à tenir l'équilibre précaire entre banalité et émerveillement."

7. My translation; French original: "Il est donc temps (si vous le souhaiter!) de (re)lire le recueil de poésie *Acadie Road* de Gabriel Robichaud afin de vous imprégner de ses mots magnifiques et percutants, puisque ce seront eux qui vous guideront dans ce road trip pas comme les autres. Pour se procurer le recueil *Acadie Road*: Librairie La grande Ourse, Librairie acadienne, Librairie Pélagie, Librairie Matulu."

8. My translation; Wade's French original: "La poésie est un genre particulier en Acadie. Il n'y a que la musique qui la surpasse dans sa capacité à *marketer* l'Acadie, à *brander* quelque chose comme l'acadianité. Parmi les représentants littéraires actuels de la marque de commerce *Acadie™*, Gabriel Robichaud est en train de s'imposer comme une figure centrale. Il est l'archétype de la 'relève acadienne et francophone' et l'une des filiales les plus institutionnalisées de l'*Acadie™*. À l'aube de la trentaine, il a déjà à son actif trois recueils et une pièce de théâtre, plusieurs rôles en tant que comédien et il a su se tailler une place de choix dans l'écosystème de la francophonie canadienne officielle; il est littéralement le porte-drapeau de l'Acadie du Nouveau-Brunswick dans les circuits de la francophonie canadienne et mondiale."

WORKS CITED

Acadie Rock 2020. www.acadierock.ca/. Accessed 24 July 2020.

Belliveau, Joel. *Le "Moment 68" et la réinvention de l'Acadie*. Presses de l'Université d'Ottawa, 2014.

Bhabha, Homi K. "DissemiNation: Time, Narrative, and the Margins of the Modern Nation." *Nation and Narration*, edited by Homi K. Bhabha. Routledge, 1990, pp. 291–322.

Clarke, Patrick D. "L'Acadie du silence: Pour une anthropologie de l'identité acadienne." *Aspects de la nouvelle francophonie canadienne*, edited by Simon Langlois and Jocelyn Létourneau, Les Presses de l'Université Laval, 2003, pp. 19–57.

Cormier, Matthew. "Cultural Memory, National Identity: The Changing Paradigms of Acadian Literature." *National Literatures in Multinational States*, edited by Albert Braz and Paul D. Morris, University of Alberta Press, 2022, pp. 21–41.

Coser, Lewis A. "Publishers as Gatekeepers of Ideas." *Annals of the American Academy of Political and Social Science*, vol. 421, 1975, pp. 14–22.

Creelman, David. "Afterword: Congruence and Recurrence in the Literatures of New Brunswick." *New Brunswick at the Crossroads: Literary Ferment and Social Change in the East*, edited by Tony Tremblay, Wilfrid Laurier University Press, 2017, pp. 157–66.

Doyon-Gosselin, Benoit. "Je m'ennuie de Josée Yvon." *Astheure*, 19 October 2016, https://astheure.com/2016/10/19/je-mennuie-de-josee-yvon-benoit-doyon-gosselin/. Accessed 24 July 2020.

Doyon-Gosselin, Benoit. "Loin d'être un cul-de-sac!" *Astheure*, 23 August 2017, https://astheure.com/2017/08/23/loin-detre-un-cul-de-sac-benoit-doyon-gosselin/. Accessed 24 July 2020.

"Éditions Perce-Neige." Éditions Perce-Neige, www.editionsperceneige.ca. Accessed 24 July 2020.

Erll, Astrid. "Cultural Memory Studies: An Introduction." *A Companion to Cultural Memory Studies: An International and Interdisciplinary Handbook*, edited by Astrid Erll et al., De Gruyter, 2008, pp. 1–15.

Fragile. Galerie Sans Nom, www.galeriesansnom.org/fragile. Accessed 29 July 2020.

Lagacé, Clara. "Road Trip Identitaire." *Le mouton noir*, 13 May 2018, www.moutonnoir.com/2018/05/road-trip-identitaire. Accessed 24 July 2020.

Lonergan, David. *Acadie 1972: Naissance de la modernité acadienne*. Prise de parole, 2013.

Massicotte, Isabelle Kirouac. "L'*Acadie Road* rocke-t-elle?" *Astheure*, 8 May 2018, https://astheure.com/2018/05/08/lacadie-road-rocke-t-elle-isabelle-kirouac-massicotte/. Accessed 24 July 2020.

Rothberg, Michael. *Multidirectional Memory*. Stanford University Press, 2009.

Saunders, Max. "Life-Writing, Cultural Memory, and Literary Studies." *A Companion to Cultural Memory Studies: An International and Interdisciplinary Handbook*, edited by Astrid Erll et al., De Gruyter, 2008, pp. 321–31.

Tremblay, Tony. "Introduction: The Cultural Geography of New Brunswick." *New Brunswick at the Crossroads: Literary Ferment and Social Change in the East*, edited by Tony Tremblay, Wilfrid Laurier University Press, 2017, pp. 1–18.

Wade, Mathieu. "*Acadie Road*: Droit dans un cul-de-sac." *Astheure*, 22 March 2019, https://astheure.com/2019/03/22/acadie-road-droit-dans-un-cul-de-sac-mathieu-wade/. Accessed 24 July 2020.

CONTRIBUTORS

Jim Clifford is an associate professor in the Department of History at the University of Saskatchewan with an interest in British, environmental, digital and urban history. He is the author of *West Ham and the River Lea: A Social and Environmental History of London's Industrialized Marshland, 1839–1914* (UBC Press, 2017) and is one of the founding editors of ActiveHistory.ca.

Matthew Cormier is an assistant professor in the Département d'anglais at the Université de Moncton. His current research intersects the digital humanities, memory studies, affect theory, and contemporary apocalyptic writing in Canada. Cormier is the author of *Sieve Reading Beyond the Minor* (University of Ottawa Press, forthcoming), and his diverse work appears in several books as well as in a number of journals published across Canada, the United States, and Europe.

Erika Dyck is a professor and a Canada Research Chair in the History of Health & Social Justice at the University of Saskatchewan. She is the author or co-author of several books, including *Facing Eugenics* (University of Toronto Press, 2013); *Managing Madness* (University of Manitoba Press, 2017); *Challenging Choices* (McGill-Queens University Press, 2020), and *Psychedelics: A Visual Odyssey* (MIT Press, 2024). Erika is the co-editor of the *Canadian Bulletin for Medical History/ Bulletin canadien d'histoire de la medicine* and the co-editor of two McGill-Queen's University Press book series on the history of medicine and *Intoxicating Histories*. She is currently the president of the Alcohol and Drugs History Society.

Craig Harkema is the digital initiatives librarian and faculty lead of the Digital Research Centre. His current research focus is the development of metadata approaches for tracing the movement of objects in early modern collections of curiosities. He has led the development of Sask History Online among several other digital archives projects at the University of Saskatchewan.

Caroline Hodes is an associate professor, having joined the University of Lethbridge in 2015. She has published work on settler colonialism, gender, racism, and intersectional failure in Canadian law. She is the lead editor and contributor for the book *Racism in Southern Alberta and Anti-racist Activism for Change* from Athabasca University Press, and her current project, *Unsettling Law's Archive*, is under contract with University of Toronto Press and is partially funded through CREDO and SSHRC. A strong advocate for scholarly activism and epistemic pluralism, along with opposing invisible labour in the academy, she is a co-founder of the Support Network for Academics of Colour + Allies (SNAC+).

Russell J.A. Kilbourn is a professor of English and Film Studies at Wilfrid Laurier University. Dr. Kilbourn publishes on memory, critical posthumanism, Italian film, and postsecular cinema. His books include: *Feminist Posthumanism in Contemporary Science Fiction Film and Media: From Annihilation to High Life and Beyond* (co-edited with Julia Empey; Bloomsbury, 2023); *The Cinema of Paolo Sorrentino: Commitment to Style* (Wallflower/Columbia UP, 2020); and *W.G. Sebald's Postsecular Redemption: Catastrophe with Spectator* (NWU Press, 2018). Dr. Kilbourn is also one of the founders of the Brock/Wilfrid Laurier University Posthumanism Research Network and is an associate editor of *Interconnections: Journal of Posthumanism* and a member of the editorial board of the *Journal of Italian Cinema and Media Studies*.

Jordan B. Kinder is an assistant professor in the Department of Communication Studies at Wilfrid Laurier University. He previously held postdoctoral fellowships at McGill University and Harvard University.

Anna Kozak (she/her) is a PhD candidate at the University of Toronto in English with a collaborative graduate specialization in sexual diversity studies. She has research interests and publications in fields that include twentieth and twenty-first American literature, queer theory, affect theory, and autobiography.

Braidon Schaufert is a PhD candidate in the Department of English and Film Studies at the University of Alberta. His SSHRC-funded doctoral research focuses on performances of queer temporality that resist homonormative structures, and he has shared his research on gender, sexuality, technology, and popular culture in academic conferences across Canada. His work in the burgeoning field of queer game studies has been published as an article in the "Queerness and Video Games" special issue of the journal *Game Studies*. Outside of research, Braidon teaches English and communications at the Northern Alberta Institute of Technology.

Amanda Spallacci is currently a lecturer in the Department of English and Film Studies at the University of Alberta, where she received her PhD (2021) and was a SSHRC Doctoral Fellow as well as a Killam Laureate. Amanda's research and publications centre on survivor/victim representations of sexual assault across various media, including memoir, television, film, and social media, which she critically engages through frameworks including memory studies, affect theory, critical race theory, and feminist print culture studies, among others.

Matthew Tétreault (he/him) is a Métis and French Canadian from Ste. Anne, MB, and he is a citizen of the Manitoba Métis Federation. He is the author of *What Happened on the Bloodvein* (Pemmican Publications, 2016), a collection of short stories, and *Hold Your Tongue*

(NeWest Press, 2023), a novel that explores francophone Métis experiences in southeast Manitoba. He holds a PhD in English from the University of Alberta, where his dissertation on the literary history of the Red River Métis earned him a Governor General's Gold Medal. His research areas include Métis literature and literary history, as well as Indigenous literatures and creative writing. Matthew is an assistant professor in the Department of Indigenous Studies at the University of Manitoba.

Uchechukwu Peter Umezurike is an assistant professor in the Department of English, University of Calgary. Umezurike is the author of literary works such as *there's more* (University of Alberta Press, 2023), *Double Wahala, Double Trouble* (Griots Lounge Publishing, 2021), *Wish Maker* (Masobe Books, 2021), and a co-editor of *Wreaths for a Wayfarer* (Daraja Press, 2020). He is currently working on his monograph on Nigerian masculinities and a poetry collection on postwar masculinities and trauma.

Stephen Webb (he/him) is a PhD candidate in the Department of English and Film Studies, University of Alberta. He has served as a research assistant on the "Orlando Project: Feminist Literary History and Digital Humanities" and is an inaugural fellow of the University of Alberta Library's Digital Scholarship Centre Graduate Student Fellowship. He primarily researches book history, print culture, and authorship in the Romantic period, with a particular focus on the poet Lord Byron's library and reconstituting this as a database through digital methods.